THE
HEALTHY PERSONALITY
Readings

Edited by

HUNG-MIN CHIANG and ABRAHAM H. MASLOW

VAN NOSTRAND REINHOLD COMPANY
New York   Cincinnati   Toronto   London   Melbourne

Van Nostrand Reinhold Company Regional Offices:
Cincinnati, New York, Chicago, Millbrae, Dallas

Van Nostrand Reinhold Company Foreign Offices:
London, Toronto, Melbourne

Published by Van Nostrand Reinhold Company
450 West 33rd Street, New York, N.Y. 10001

Published simultaneously in Canada by
D. Van Nostrand Company (Canada), Ltd.

15   14   13   12   11   10   9   8   7   6   5   4   3   2   1

This book is dedicated to BERTHA and MEI-CHIH

Preface

One of the growing concerns of our age, one that is fast becoming a crucial, emerging problem, is the question of psychological health. Many of us have only just begun to ask seriously: "What constitutes psychological health, and what is meant by a healthy personality?" "What vision of the future do we have for our children?" "What would be the end goal of education? of religion? of the good society?"

Part of the question is undoubtedly as old as civilization. Many philosophers and social thinkers of the past grappled with it, but their answers were by no means unequivocal or final. In a world whose horizons are being rapidly widened in every dimension, we are today obliged to take a fresh perspective on the issue. We are perhaps better prepared to ask many significant questions such as: "What is the meaning of being fully human for our generation?" "What can science tell us about a healthy personality?" Although the questions are age-old, we see the possibility of a new kind of answer, the *empirical* one.

But a path to this new perspective is yet to be discovered. Neither orthodox Freudian psychoanalysis nor behaviorism has been definitively helpful in finding it. Of course, Freud has paved the way to our understanding of health with his studies of the psychodynamics and the psychopathology of the mind. Yet, as has often been pointed out, the Freudian view of man is anything but hopeful. Personality development is seen essentially as a never-ending conflict between the individual's craving for pleasure and the restrictions imposed upon him by society.

If the overriding tendency of orthodox psychoanalysis is to see human nature in the light of psychopathology, the other main school of thought, behaviorism, has committed itself to yet another form of reductionism. Because of their positivistic position, behaviorists tend to limit their attention to only those segments of behavior that can easily be manipulated and measured. They maintain that complex psychological processes should, and perhaps could, be explained through psychologically lower processes. Both man and animals are, in the last analysis, nothing but elaborate machines; man's nature can safely be deduced from our knowledge of animals.

What has been neglected by both is a study of man as man—man at his best, man who can measure up to his highest aspiration. This is urgently needed.

In this book we have selected significant papers by a number of well-known workers in psychology and related fields, who are known to be deeply concerned with the problem of psychological health. These people are, on the whole, more eclectic and problem-centered than many of their contemporaries. They are not at all afraid of raising questions which have been avoided by others—because these questions would seem to open up dizzyingly wide vistas. This new spirit of scientific inquiry, the courageous acceptance of humanness both in its height and depth, is perhaps best represented by (but not necessarily limited to) a movement now known as humanistic psychology.*

This book is meant to show the scope and the range of the problem concerned. It must be emphasized that the papers collected here are quite divergent in their nature and basic orientation. These divergent views can, however, each in its own way, shed additional light on the problem that is not only for *all* of us, but for *each* of us as well.

Some of the recurrent questions in the book are: What is normality? What do we know about man's potentialities, and how can they best be developed? What do we know about the phenomenology of joy, of happiness, of inner voices, of calls in life, or of the value of simply being a person? Does man have an intrinsic nature or is he completely malleable, like a lump of clay? If he does have an intrinsic nature, what is it? What appropriate methods are available to us in studying all these?

HUNG-MIN CHIANG
ABRAHAM H. MASLOW

* See A. H. Maslow, *Toward a Psychology of Being*, 2nd Edition, Van Nostrand, 1968; also J. F. T. Bugental (Ed.), *Challenges of Humanistic Psychology*, McGraw-Hill, 1967.

Acknowledgments

The compiling of a book of this nature would be impossible without the many pioneers who had done the groundwork. It required courage and foresight to tackle the problem at a time when so few people were actually aware of it. Our first acknowledgments as the editors of this book should, therefore, go to our contributors.

We also wish to express our appreciation to the faculty, staffs, and students at Brandeis University and Prince of Wales College. The book is a product of our warm and rewarding association with them. Especially fruitful has been our relationship with our students who are as keenly interested in the growing edge of humanistic science.

We are grateful to Professors Tiparat Schumrum, John Smith, David Aurandt, and Mrs. Dorothy Hicks of Prince of Wales College for their editorial assistance.

Our last, but not the least, appreciation is to our wives who, by their graceful presence, have helped the birth of the book. To them this book is dedicated.

Contents

1

Personality: Normal and Abnormal *

GORDON W. ALLPORT

The word *norm* means "an authoritative standard," and correspondingly *normal* means abiding by such a standard. It follows that a normal personality is one whose conduct conforms to an authoritative standard, and an abnormal personality is one whose conduct does not do so.

But having said this much we immediately discover that there are two entirely different kinds of standards that may be applied to divide the normal from the abnormal: the one statistical, the other ethical. The one pertains to the average or usual, and the other to the desirable or valuable.

These two standards are not only different, but in many ways they stand in flat contradiction to one another. It is, for example, *usual* for people to have some noxious trends in their natures, some pathology of tissues or organs, some evidences of nervousness and some self-defeating habits; but though usual or average such trends are not healthy. Or again, society's authoritative standard for a wholesome sex life is, if we are to accept the Kinsey Report, achieved by only a minority of American males. Here too the usual is not the desirable; what is normal in one sense is not normal in the other sense. And certainly no system of ethics in the civilized world holds up as a model for its children the ideal of becoming a merely average man. It is not the actualities, but rather the potentialities, of human nature that somehow provide us with a standard for a sound and healthy personality.

Fifty years ago this double meaning of *norm* and *normal* did not

* Address delivered at the Fifth Interamerican Congress of Psychology, Mexico City, December 1957; sponsored by the Interamerican Society of Psychology; reprinted by permission from the Congress Proceedings.

1

trouble psychology so much as it does today. In those days psychology was deeply involved in discovering average norms for every conceivable type of mental function. Means, modes and sigmas were in the saddle, and differential psychology was riding high. Intoxicated with the new-found beauty of the normal distribution curve, psychologists were content to declare its slender tails as the one and only sensible measure of "abnormality." Departures from the mean were abnormal and for this reason slightly unsavory.

In this era there grew up the concept of "mental adjustment," and this concept held sway well into the decade of the 20s. While not all psychologists equated adjustment with average behavior this implication was pretty generally present. It was, for example, frequently pointed out that an animal who does not adjust to the norm for his species usually dies. It was not yet pointed out that a human being who does so adjust is a bore and a mediocrity.

Now times have changed. Our concern for the improvement of average human behavior is deep, for we now seriously doubt that the merely mediocre man can survive. As social anomie spreads, as society itself becomes more and more sick, we doubt that the mediocre man will escape mental disease and delinquency, or that he will keep himself out of the clutch of dictators or succeed in preventing atomic warfare. The normal distribution curve, we see, holds out no hope of salvation. We need citizens who are in a more positive sense normal, healthy and sound. And the world needs them more urgently than it ever did before.

It is, for this reason, I think, that psychologists are now seeking a fresh definition of what is normal and what is abnormal. They are asking questions concerning the *valuable,* the *right,* and the *good* as they have never asked them before.

At the same time psychologists know that in seeking for a criterion of normality in this new sense they are trespassing on the traditional domain of moral philosophy. They also know that, by and large, philosophers have failed to establish authoritative standards for what constitutes the sound life—the life that educators, parents, and therapists should seek to mold. And so psychologists for the most part, wish to pursue the search in a fresh way and if they can, avoid the traditional traps of axiology. Let me briefly describe some recent empirical attempts to define normality and afterward attempt to evaluate the state of our efforts to date.

Naturalistic Derivations of "Normality"

During the past few months two proposals have been published that merit serious attention. Both are by social scientists, one a psychologist in the United States, the other a sociologist in England. Their aim is to derive a concept of normality (in the value sense) from the condition of man (in the naturalistic sense). Both seek their ethical imperatives from biology and psychology, not from value-theory directly. In short, they boldly seek the *ought* (the goal to which teachers, counsellors, therapists should strive) from the *is* of human nature. Many philosophers tell us that this is an impossible undertaking. But before we pass judgment let us see what success they have had.

E. J. Shoben asks, What are the principal psychological differences between man and lower animals? (*1*) While he does not claim that his answer is complete he centers upon two distinctively human qualities. And he makes the extra-psychological assumption that man *should* maximize those attributes that are distinctively human. The first quality is man's capacity for the use of propositional language (symbolization). From this particular superiority over animals Shoben derives several specific guidelines for normality. With the aid of symbolic language, for example, man can delay his gratifications, holding in mind a distant goal, a remote reward, an objective to be reached perhaps only at the end of one's life or perhaps never. With the aid of symbolic language, he can imagine a future for himself that is far better than the present. He can also develop an intricate system of social concepts that leads him to all manner of possible relations with other human beings, far exceeding the rigid symbiotic rituals of, say, the social insects.

A second distinctive human quality is related to the prolonged childhood in the human species. Dependence, basic trust, sympathy and altruism are absolutely essential to human survival, in a sense and to a degree not true for lower animals.

Bringing together these two distinctive qualities Shoben derives his conception of normality. He calls it "a model of integrative adjustment." It follows, he says, that a sense of *personal responsibility* marks the normal man for responsibility is a distinctive capacity derived from holding in mind a symbolic image of the future, delaying gratification, and being able to strive in accordance with one's conceptions of the best principles of conduct for oneself. Similarly *social responsibility* is normal; for all these symbolic capacities can interact with the unique factor of trust or altruism. Closely related is the criterion of *democratic social interest* which derives from both symbolization and trust. Similarly the *possession of ideals* and the necessity for *self control* follow from the same naturalistic analysis. Shoben rightly points out that a *sense of guilt* is an inevitable consequence of man's failure to live according to the distinctive human pattern, and so in our concept of normality we must include both guilt and devices for expiation.

Every psychologist who wishes to make minimum assumptions and who wishes to keep close to empirical evidence, and who inclines toward the naturalism of biological science, will appreciate and admire Shoben's efforts. Yet I imagine our philosopher friends will arise to confound us with some uncomfortable questions. Is it not a distinctively human capacity, they will ask, for a possessive mother to keep her child permanently tied to her apron strings? Does any lower animal engage in this destructive behavior? Likewise is it not distinctively human to develop fierce in-group loyalties that lead to prejudice, contempt, and war? Is it not possible that the burden of symbolization, social responsibility, and guilt may lead a person to depression and suicide? Suicide, along with all the other destructive patterns I have mentioned, is distinctively human. A philosopher who raises these questions would conclude, "No, you cannot derive the *ought* from the *is* of human nature. What is distinctively human is not necessarily distinctively good."

Let us look at a second attempt to achieve a naturalistic criterion of normality. In a recent book entitled *Towards a Measure of Man,* Paul Halmos prefers to start with the question, "What are the minimum conditions for survival?" (2) When we know these minimum conditions we can declare that any situations falling below this level will lead to abnormality, and tend toward death and destruction. He calls this criterion the *abnorm* and believes we can define it, even if we cannot define normality, because people in general agree more readily on what is bad for man than on what is good for him. They agree on the bad because all mortals are subject to the basic imperative of survival.

The need for survival he breaks down into the need for growth and the need for social cohesion. These two principles are the universal conditions of all life, not merely of human life. *Growth* means autonomy and the process of individuation. *Cohesion* is the basic fact of social interdependence, involving, at least for human beings initial trust, heteronomy, mating and the founding of family.

Now Halmos believes that by taking an inventory of conditions deleterious to growth and cohesion we may establish the "abnorm." As a start he mentions first and foremost disorders of child training. He says, "continued or repeated interruption of physical proximity between mother and child," or "emotional rejection" of the child by the mother are conditions that harm survival of the individual and the group. In his own terms this first criterion of abnormality lies in a "rupture in the transmutation of cohesion into love." Most of what is abnormal he traces to failures in the principle of cohesion, so that the child becomes excessively demanding and compulsive. Here we note the similarity to such contemporary thinkers as Bowlby, Erikson and Maslow.

The author continues his inventory of the "abnorm" by accepting syndromes that psychiatrists agree upon. For instance, it is abnormal (inimical to survival) if repetition of conduct occurs irrespective of the situation and unmodified by its consequences; also when one's accomplishments constantly fall short of one's potentialities; likewise when one's psychosexual frustrations prevent both growth and cohesion.

It is well to point out that the basic functions of growth and cohesion postulated by Halmos occur time and time again in psychological writing. Bergson, Jung and Angyal are among the writers who agree that normality requires a balance between individuation and socialization, between autonomy and heteronomy. There seems to be considerable consensus in this matter. Let me quote from one of the founders of this Society whose recent death has brought sorrow to us all. Werner Wolff writes:

> When an individual identifies himself to an extreme degree with a group, the effect is that he loses his value. On the other hand, a complete inability to identify has the effect that the environment loses its value for the individual. In both extreme cases the dynamic relationship between individual and environment is distorted. An individual behaving in such a way is called "neurotic." In a normal group each member preserves his individuality but accepts his role as participator also. (3)

While there is much agreement that the normal personality must strike a serviceable balance between growth as an individual and cohesion with society, we do not yet have a clear criterion for determining when these factors are in serviceable balance and when they are not. Philosophers, I fear, would shake their heads at Halmos. They would ask, "How do you know that survival is a good thing?" Further, "Why should all people enjoy equal rights to the benefits of growth and cohesion?" And, "How are we to define the optimum balance between cohesion and growth within the single personality?"

Imbalance and Creativity

Halmos himself worries especially about the relation between abnormality and creativity. It was Nietzsche who declared, "I say unto you: a man must have chaos yet within him to be able to give birth to a dancing star." Have not many meritorious works of music, literature, and even of science drawn their inspiration not from balance but from some kind of psychic chaos? Here, I think, Halmos gives the right answer. He says in effect that creativity and normality are not identical values. On the whole the normal person will be creative, but if valuable creations come likewise from people who are slipping away from the norm of survival, this fact can only be accepted and valued on the scale of creativity, but not properly on the scale of normality.

Imbalance and Growth

In this day of existentialism I sense that psychologists are becoming less and less content with the concept of adjustment, and correspondingly with the concepts of "tension reduction," "restoration of equilibrium," and "homeostasis." We wonder if a man who enjoys these beatific conditions is truly human. Growth we know is not due to homeostasis but to a kind of "transistasis." And cohesion is a matter of keeping our human relationships moving and not in mere stationary equilibrium. Stability cannot be a criterion of normality since stability brings evolution to a standstill, negating both growth and cohesion. Freud once wrote to Fliess that he finds "moderate misery necessary for intensive work."

A research inspired by Carl Rogers is interesting in this connection. One series of patients before treatment manifested a zero correlation between their self-image and their ideal self-image. Following treatment the correlation was $+ .34$, not high but approaching the coefficient of $+ .58$ that marked a healthy untreated group. Apparently this magnitude of correlation is a measure of the satisfaction or dissatisfaction that normal people have with their own personalities (4). In other words, a zero correlation between self and ideal self is too low for normality; it leads to such anguish that the sufferer seeks therapy. At the same time normal people are by no means perfectly adjusted to themselves. There is always a wholesome gap between self and ideal self, between present existence and aspiration. On the other hand, too high a satisfaction indicates pathology. The highest coefficient obtained, $+ .90$, was from an individual clearly pathological. Perfect correlations we might expect only from smug psychotics, particularly paranoid schizophrenics.

And so whatever our definition of normality turns out to be it must allow for serviceable imbalances within personality, and between person and society.

An Empirical Approach to Soundness

The work of Barron illustrates an approach dear to the psychologist's heart. He lets others establish the criterion of normality, or as he calls it, *soundness,* and then proceeds to find out what *"sound"* men are like. Teachers of graduate students in the University of California nominated a large number of men whom they considered sound, and some of the opposite trend. In testing and experimenting with these two groups, whose identities were unknown to the investigators, certain significant differences appeared (5). For one thing the sounder men had more realistic perceptions; they were not thrown off by distortions or by surrounding context in the sensory field. Further, on adjective check-lists they stood high on such traits as *integrated pursuit of goals, persistence, adaptability, good nature.* On the Minnesota Multiphasic Personality Inventory they were high in *equanimity, self-confidence, objectivity,* and *virility.* Their *self-insight* was superior, as was their *physical health.* Finally they came from homes where there was *little or no affective rupture*—a finding that confirms Halmos's predictions.

Inventory Approaches

Most authors do not have the benefit of professional concensus on soundness. They simply set forth in a didactic manner the attributes of normality, or health, or soundness, or maturity, or productivity, as they see them. Innumerable descriptive lists result. Perhaps the simplest of these is Freud's. He says the healthy person will be able to "love" and to "work." One of the most elaborate is Maslow's schedule of qualities that include among others: efficient perception of reality, philosophical humor, spontaneity, detachment, and an acceptance of self and others. Such lists are not altogether arbitrary since their authors base them on wide clinical experience, as did Freud, or on a deliberate analysis of case materials, as did Maslow (6).

There are so many lists of this type now available that a new kind of approach is possible,—namely, the combining of these insightful inventories. From time to time I have assigned this task to my students, and while all manner of groupings and re-groupings result, still there are recurrent themes that appear in nearly all inventories. If I were to attempt the assignment myself I should probably start with my own list of three criteria, published 20 years ago, but I would now expand it (7).

The three criteria I originally listed were:

    i. ego-extension—the capacity to take an interest in more than one's body and one's material possessions. The criterion covers, I think, the attributes that Fromm ascribes to the productive man.

    ii. self-objectification—which includes the ability to relate the feeling tone of the present experience to that of a past experience provided the latter does in fact determine the quality of the former; self-objectification also includes humor which tells us that our total horizon of life is too wide to be compressed into our present rigidities.

    iii. unifying philosophy of life—which may or may not be religious, but in any event has to be a frame of meaning and of responsibility into which life's major activities fit.

To this inventory I now would add:

    iv. the capacity for a warm, profound, relating of one's self to others—which may, if one likes, be called "extroversion of the libido" or "Gemeinschaftsgefühl."

    v. The possession of realistic skills, abilities, and perceptions with which to cope with the practical problems of life.

    vi. a compassionate regard for all living creatures—which includes respect for individual persons and a disposition to participate in common activities that will improve the human lot.

I am aware that psychoanalysts are partial to the criterion of "ego strength": a normal person has a strong ego, an abnormal person a weak ego. But I find this phrase ill defined, and would suggest that my six somewhat more detailed criteria succeed in specifying what we mean by the looser term, "ego strength."

The weakness of all inventories, including my own, is that the philosopher's persistent questions are still unanswered. How does the psychologist know that these qualities comprise normality, that they are good, and that all people should have them? Before I attempt to give a partial answer to our irritating philosopher friend, let me call attention to one additional psychological approach.

Continuity of Symptom and Discontinuity of Process

    I refer to a fresh analysis of the problem of continuity-discontinuity. Is abnormality merely an exaggerated normal condition? Is there unbroken continuity between health and disease? Certainly Freud thought so. He evolved his system primarily as a theory of neurosis. But he and his followers came to regard his formulations as a universally valid science of psychology. Whether one is normal or abnormal depends on the degree to which one can manage his relationships successfully. Furthermore, the earlier enthusiasm of psychologists for the normal distribution curve helped to entrench the theory of continuity. The strongest empirical evidence in favor of this view is the occurrence of borderline cases. Descriptively there is certainly a continuum. We encounter mild neurotics, borderline schizophrenics, hypomanics, and personalities that are paranoid, cycloid, epileptoid. And if scales and tests are employed there are no gaps; scores are continuously distributed.

But—and let me insist on this point—this continuum pertains only to symptoms, to appearances. The *processes* (*or "mechanisms"*) underlying these appearances are not continuous. There is, for example, a polar difference between confronting the world and its problems (which is an intrinsically wholesome thing to do) and escaping and withdrawing from the world (which is an intrinsically unwholesome thing to do). Extreme withdrawal and escape constitute psychosis. But you may ask, do not we all do some escaping? Yes, we do, and what is more, escapism may provide not only recreation but may sometimes have a certain constructive utility, as it has in mild day-dreaming. But still the process of escape can be harmless only if the *dominant* process is confrontation. Left to itself escapism spells disaster. In the psychotic this process has the upper hand; in the normal person, on the contrary, confrontation has the upper hand.

Following this line of reasoning we can list other processes that intrinsically generate abnormality, and those that generate normality. The first list deals with catabolic functions. I would mention:

Escape or withdrawal (including fantasy)
Repression or dissociation
Other "ego defences" including rationalization, reaction formation, projection, displacement
Impulsivity (uncontrolled)
Restriction of thinking to concrete level

Fixation of personality at a juvenile level

All forms of rigidification

The list is not complete, but the processes in question, I submit, are intrinsically catabolic. They are as much so as are the disease mechanisms responsible for diabetes, tuberculosis, hyperthyroidism, or cancer. A person suffering only a small dose of these mechanisms may appear to be normal, but only if the *anabolic* mechanisms predominate. Among the latter I would list:

Confrontation (or, if you prefer, "reality testing")

Availability of knowledge to consciousness

Self-insight, with its attendant humor

Integrative action of the nervous system

Ability to think abstractly

Continuous individuation (without arrested or fixated development)

Functional autonomy of motives

Frustration tolerance

I realize that what I have called processes, or mechanisms, are not in all cases logically parallel. But they serve to make my point, that normality depends on the dominance of one set of principles, abnormality upon the dominance of another. The fact that all normal people are occasionally afflicted with catabolic processes does not alter the point. The normal life is marked by a preponderance of the anabolic functions; the abnormal by a preponderance of the catabolic.

Conclusion

And now is it possible to gather together all these divergent threads, and to reach some position tenable for psychology today? Let us try to do so.

First, I think, we should make a deep obeisance in the direction of moral philosophy and gracefully concede that psychology by itself cannot solve the problem of normality. No psychologist has succeeded in telling us why man ought to seek good health rather than ill; nor why normality should be our goal for all men, and not just for some. Nor can psychologists account for the fact that meritorious creativity may be of value even if the creator himself is by all tests an abnormal person. These and a variety of other conundrums lie beyond the competence of psychology to solve. That moral philosophers have not agreed among themselves upon solutions is also true; but we gladly grant them freedom and encouragement to continue their efforts.

At the same time the lines of research and analysis that I have here reviewed are vitally related to the philosophers quest. After all it is the psychologists who deal directly with personalities in the clinic, in schools, industry, and in laboratories. It is they who gather the facts concerning normality and abnormality and who try to weave them into their own normative speculations. *A fact and a moral imperative are more closely interlocked than traditional writers on ethics may think.* Among the facts that psychology can offer are the following:

i. Investigations have told us much concerning the nature of human needs and motives, both conscious and unconscious. A grouping of these needs into the broad categories of growth and cohesion is helpful. Much is known concerning the pathologies that result from frustration and imbalance of these needs. It would be absurd for moral philosophers to write imperatives in total disregard of this evidence.

ii. We know much about childhood conditions that predispose toward delinquency, prejudice, and mental disorder. A moralist might do well to cast his imperatives in terms of standards for child training. I can suggest, for example, that the abstract imperative "respect for persons" should be tested and formulated from the point of view of child training.

iii. By virtue of comparative work on men and animals we know much about the motives common to both, but also, as Shoben has shown, about the qualities that are distinctively human. Let the philosophers give due weight to this work.

iv. While I have not yet mentioned the matter, psychology in cooperation with cultural anthropology has a fairly clear picture today of the role of culture in producing and in defining abnormality. We know the incidence of psychosis and neurosis in various populations; we know what conditions are labeled abnormal in some cultures but are regarded as normal in others. We also know, with some accuracy, those conditions that are considered abnormal in all cultures. Since our president, Professor Klineberg, is addressing the Congress on this subject I shall say no more about it; but shall simply point out that these facts are highly relevant to the deliberations of the moral philosopher.

v. Following the lead of Halmos, we may say that biologists, psychologists and sociologists know much about the conditions of individual and group survival. While these facts in themselves do not tell us why we should survive, still they provide specifications for the philosopher who thinks he can answer this riddle.

vi. Still more important, I think, is the empirical work on consensus that is now available. We have cited Barron's method of determining the attributes of men judged to be "sound" as distinguished from those of men judged to be "unsound." While the philosopher is not likely to accept the vote of university professors as an adequate definition of soundness, still he might do well to heed opinions other than his own.

vii. Another type of consensus is obtained from the inventories prepared by insightful writers. These authors have tried according to their best ability, to summarize as they see them the requirements of normality, health or maturity. They do so on the grounds of extensive experience. As we survey these inventories we are struck both by their verbal differences and by an underlying congruence of meaning that no one has yet succeeded fully in articulating. Here again the philosopher may balk at accepting consensus, and yet he would do well to check his own private reasoning against the conclusions of others no less competent, and probably more clinically experienced, than he.

viii. He would do well, I think, to explore the goals of psychotherapy as stated or implied in leading therapeutic systems. If he were to comb the writings of behavioristic therapists, for example, he might reasonably conclude that *efficiency* (the ability to cope with problems) is the principal goal; in Zen therapy, by contrast, the stress seems to be on restored *cohesion* with the group. Nondirective therapy clearly prizes the goal of *growth;* the desideratum for Goldstein, Maslow, and Jung is *self-actualization;* for Fromm *productivity;* for Frankl and the logotherapists *meaningfulness* and *responsibility.* Thus each therapist seems to have in mind a preponderant emphasis which, in terms of value theory, constitutes for him a definition of the good way of life and of health for the personality. While the emphasis differs and the labels vary, still there seems to be a confluence of these criteria. Taken together they remind us of the tributaries to a vast river system, none the less unified for all their differences of source and shape. This confluence is a factor that no moralist can afford to overlook.

ix. Finally the distinction between the anabolic and catabolic processes in the formation of personality represents a fact of importance. Instead of judging merely the end-product of action, perhaps the moralist would do well to focus his attention upon the processes by which various ends are achieved. Conceivably the moral law could be written in terms of strengthening anabolic functions in oneself and in others whilst fighting against catabolic functions.

It is true that the preferred method of moral philosophy is to work "from the top down." Apriorism and reason are the legitimate tools of philosophy. Up to now this method has yield a wide array of moral imperatives, including the following: *so act that the maxim of thy action can become a universal law; be a respecter of persons; seek to reduce your desires; harmonize your interests with the interests of other; thou are nothing, thy folk is everything; thou shalt love the Lord thy God with all thy heart, and with all thy soul, and with all thy mind . . . and thy neighbour as thyself.*

We have no wish to impede this approach from above, for we dare not block the intuitive and rational springs of ethical theory. But I would say—and this is my point of chief insistence—that each of these moral imperatives, and all others that have been or will be devised, can and should be tested and specified with reference to the various forms of psychological analysis that I have here reviewed. By submitting each imperative to psychological scrutiny we can tell whether men are likely to comprehend the principle offered; whether and in what sense it is within their capacity to follow it; what the long-run consequences are likely to be; and whether we find agreement among men in general and among therapists and other meliorists that the imperative is indeed good.

One final word. My discussion of the problem of normality and abnormality has in a sense yielded only a niggardly solution. I have said, in effect, that the criterion we seek has not yet been discovered; nor is it likely to be discovered by psychologists working alone, nor by philosophers working alone. The cooperation of both is needed. Fortunately today psychologists are beginning to ask philosophical questions, and philosophers are beginning to ask psychological questions. Working together they may ultimately formulate the problem aright and conceivably solve it.

In the meantime let me state it as my opinion that the work I have reviewed in this paper represents a high level of sophistication, far higher than that which prevailed a short generation ago. Psychologists who in their teaching and counselling follow the lines now laid down will not go far wrong in guiding personalities toward normality.

REFERENCES

1. E. J. SHOBEN, JR.: Toward a concept of the normal personality, *Amer. Psychologist, 12,* 183–189.
2. P. HALMOS: *Towards a Measure of Man: the Frontiers of Normal Adjustment,* London: Routledge & Kegan Paul, 1957.
3. W. WOLFF: *The Threshold of the Abnormal,* New York: Hermitage House, 1950, pp. 131 f.
4. Cited by C. HALL and G. LINDZEY: *Theories of Personality,* New York: John Wiley, 1957, pp. 492–496.
5. F. BARRON: *Personal Soundness in University Graduate Students.* (Publications of Personnel Assessment Research, No. 1.) Berkeley: California Univ. Press, 1954.
6. A. H. MASLOW: *Motivation and Personality,* New York: Harper, 1954, Chap. 12.
7. G. W. ALLPORT: *Personality: A Psychological Interpretation,* New York: Henry Holt, 1937, Chap. 8.

2

Psychological Vitality: An Attempt at Philosophical Definition*

FRANK BARRON

A quick glance at a good psychological library is sufficient to indicate that psychologists have traditionally been much more interested in psychological illness than in psychological health. Many and heavy are the books on mental illness but few and light are the books on mental health. In fact, when one looks closely at volumes whose titles suggest that they perhaps deal with mental health, they usually turn out to be much more concerned with mental illness.

Of course, this greater attention to disease and malfunction is not just an oddity of the psychological profession. Most of us pay little attention to our health when it is good, just as we pay little attention to our automobile as long as it is running well. It is when we are physically ill that our body comes to our notice, and it is usually when we are a bit upset and anxious that we become *self-conscious;* when we are just *being our natural self* we are in good health mentally. In brief, disease is more vivid and more noticeable than efficient functioning, and consequently has had more scientific attention paid to it.

This natural tendency to give more notice to the pathological resulted in a relative neglect in psychological theory of the conditions and characteristics that define psychological health. Just after World War II, however, a group of psychologists at the University of California, in reviewing what during the war they had learned at first hand of heroic human reactions to terrible stress, decided that it was high time that psychology should take a look at the positive side of human

* From Frank Barron, *Creativity and Personal Freedom.* Van Nostrand Insight Series, 1968.

nature and concern itself with unusual vitality in human beings rather than with disease. It appeared to them that psychological health had always been defined negatively, in terms of what is present when health is absent. So they decided to attempt a definition that would state *what is present when health is present.*

It was my pleasure to participate in this enterprise with what has turned out to be a very active research group at the University during the past dozen years. The first attempt we made at defining psychological health came during the first six months of our organizational life, shortly after we had begun work as the Institute of Personality Assessment and Research. Because we intended to employ the special research method known as the living-in assessment, in which the subjects live for several days at the Institute house (a former fraternity house, incidentally), we had at our disposal a well-furnished living room equipped with soft armchairs. One of our first decisions was to sit down in the armchairs and think about psychological health in positive terms.

With some half-dozen psychologists arrayed in a circle and comfortably seated, it was natural enough that a sort of informal symposium should quickly organize itself. We listened as a group as each of us in turn presented his own ideas of what the psychologically healthy person should be like. After a bit of listening, it became clear to me that I had fallen in with a group of rather noble souls, for the traits which they uniformly ascribed to the psychologically healthy person were the sort that would earn anyone a reward in the afterlife, if indeed he had not already been amply rewarded here below. As I listened further, however, I began to realize that the catalogue of named virtues would be somewhat more appropriate to an effectively functioning person in the temperate zone than in the tropical or arctic zones. Then it came to me that the effectively functioning person had had two other rather locally determined restrictions imposed upon him; namely, like each and every staff member of the Institute, he was a man rather than a woman, and rather closer to middle age than to adolescence. At the end of those first comfortable discussions, then, we had arrived at an excellent picture of an effectively functioning and notably virtuous man in his middle years in late summer at Berkeley, California.

Several of our staff members, however, have distinguished themselves by their penetrating psychological insights into ethnocentrism, and they could not long remain unconscious of a major if essentially rather gentle exhibition of it. A happy piece of data analysis finally made the diagnosis certain. In our first official contact with subjects selected for their general effectiveness as persons, we employed an adjective checklist by means of which each staff member described each subject whom we studied during three days of living-in assessment. Our intention was to derive from these checklists a composite staff description of each subject and then to correlate the composite description with external criterion ratings (i.e., real-life judgments by nonpsychologists) of the individual's so-called *Soundness as a Person*. This indeed we did, with interesting results; but we went further, and analyzed separately the individual checklists which went to make up the composite. Thus for staff member *A,* for example, we were able to discover with what adjectives he more often characterized subjects rated high on Soundness by external public opinion than subjects rated low. The results of this analysis were impressive. It turned out that individual staff members were using quite different adjectives to decribe the same person, but with great consistency they were describing highly effective people by exactly the adjectives with which in a private moment of good will toward themselves they would use to describe *themselves*. Moreover, they tended to describe clearly ineffective persons as possessing traits which in themselves they most strongly denied, i.e., possible human characteristics which they had repudiated with special vigor. Thus, one staff member noted for his simple and clear thought processes most frequently described an ineffective person as *confused;* another staff member who is especially well-behaved in matters of duty checked the adjectives *conscientious* and *responsible* most frequently in describing highly rated subjects. Our most notably nonethnocentric staff member found effective persons more *tolerant* than anything else; another staff member who has subsequently been interested professionally in independence of judgment saw effective subjects as *independent* and *fair-minded*. Each of us, in brief, saw his own image in what he judged to be good.

There is a rather strong ethical tone to some of these preconceptions, as I have suggested. But I would urge here that we must avoid any implication that the healthy person psychologically must necessarily be a good person morally. For the most part it is probably a healthy thing to be rather well behaved, and as a rule we are in better health when we are cool and collected than when we are agitated. But there are times when it is a mark of greater health to be unruly, and a sign of greater inner resources to be able to upset one's own balance and to seek a new order of selfhood.

The ability to permit oneself to become disorganized is in my judgment quite crucial to the development of a very high level of integration. Because we are capable of reflecting upon ourselves, we are committed, willy-nilly, to an artistic enterprise in the creation of our own personality. By our very nature as intelligent beings, we are compelled to make an image of ourselves which will be coherent and of enduring recognizability, to us and to others. One judges the degree of success of this inevitable reflective act by precisely the criteria with which one judges a work of art, or a scientific theory at that level of generality where science and art alike are concerned with problems of universal validities. We are accustomed to say of a mathematical explanation or of a scientific theory that it is most elegant when with a minimum of postulates it embraces a maximum of implications. In art the analogue to this is the art product that communicates the greatest richness and depth of experience in the simplest and clearest manner. I think that some such concept as that of elegance is needed if we are to talk meaningfully of psychological health. A person may be said to be most elegant, and most healthy, when his awareness includes the broadest possible aspects of human experience, and the deepest possible comprehension of them, while at the same time he is most simple and direct in his feelings, thoughts, and actions.

Certain facts concerning temporary upset and agitation in especially healthy or potentially healthy persons can thus be explained in terms of the creative act necessary in order to achieve integration at the most complex level. A certain amount of discord and disorder must be permitted into the perceptual system if a more complex synthesis is to result. Usually, of course, some discord is brought in by new experiences that are common to all of us. Weaning is one, toilet training is another, the discovery of pleasure in the genitals is a third. Many others might be mentioned, such as the first recognition that one is dependent for one's life upon the actions and feelings of others, and that regardless of anything else that occurs, one must finally die. At some time in life there arises also what might be called "the crisis in belief," in which it becomes necessary to re-examine the basis of one's religious or philosophical beliefs, and to come to some sort of explanation for oneself of what the universe is all about and what life itself signifies. The choice of a life work and the choice of a life mate are two other nearly universal crises.

The more energy a person has at his disposal, the more fully will he become committed to the most complex possible integration. In this connection I think it is important to remember that intelligence is a form of energy. Psychoanalysis has tended to represent the sexual drives as the most powerful and most basic source of energy in the organism, and indeed at times such drives are seen as most difficult to control, because they represent the forces of blind desire. But the capacity to symbolize, to create a valid image of reality, is the peculiarly human energy, the triumphant form of energy in the living world. In the world of living forms it is the most intelligent form, not the most instinct-dominated, which succeeds; within the human person we might expect a similar outcome. The fact is, of course, that intelligence in general does succeed in containing impulse, through the creation of an image of the self as differentiated from the surround, the interpersonal environment. The image of the self is a complicated pattern, an artistic endeavor, as I have suggested, to which we are committed whether we will or no. In psychological sickness our image of ourself blurs, the colors run, it is not integrated or beautiful. We become conscious of its existence momentarily, and hence awkwardness ensues. But in health there is no awkwardness, for the moment of health is the moment of unconscious creative synthesis, when without thinking about it at all we know that we make sense to ourselves and to others. In the most elegant of cases, this synthesis involves a tremendous interpenetration of symbols, drawn from our sexuality, our philosophy, and the meaning of our work, with complex overdetermination of actions and feelings which are themselves expressively simple.

When such simplicity amid complexity has been achieved, I think that two new and most important affects come into existence in the individual's experience. One of these is the feeling that one is free and that life and its outcome are in one's own hands. The other is a new experience of the passage of time, and a deeper sense of relaxed participation in the present moment. All of experience is consequently permanent at the very moment of its occurrence, and life ceases to be a course between birth and death and becomes instead a fully realized experience of change in which every single state is as valid and as necessary as every other.

For a detailed account of the above study, the reader is referred to Creativity and Personal Freedom *by Frank Barron (Van Nostrand, 1968). The above article is the introductory chapter to the book.*

3

Adult Growth and Emotional Maturity*

ROBERT W. WHITE

Growth implies both a process of change and a direction of change. It is easy to think about the direction if we confine ourselves to children and to obvious ways in which they develop. We expect them to get larger, stronger, smarter, better controlled, and more responsible. We expect them to grow up. By the time they are five or six they should have attained fairly complete locomotor control, being able to walk, run, hop, skip, jump, and climb. At about the same age they should have mastered the structure of language so that they can talk in relatively adult fashion. When they are ten they should be capable of applying themselves somewhat steadily to tasks and of managing a certain amount of social interaction without constant supervision. When they are sixteen or so they should be able to hold regular jobs and to drive a car safely and competently. When they are twenty-one they should be able to assume the further responsibilities of the ballot box and of financial self-management. But now they are "of age"—they have become legal adults—and while we do not suppose that personal development ceases at this point, it is now more difficult to define the directions of further growth. Being adult is hardly a sufficient description, especially when we reflect on the world at large and notice that its management by adults is something less than a howling success. Historically, directions of growth after the point at which biological development is complete have been defined in ethical terms. In recent years, with the rise of psychological and social science, attempts are being made to work later growth trends into a naturalistic system.

* From Chapter Nine from *Lives in Progress* (2nd Edition) by Robert W. White. Copyright 1952 by Robert W. White. Copyright © 1966 by Holt, Rinehart & Winston, Inc. Reprinted by permission of Holt, Rinehart & Winston, Inc.

Ideals derived largely from the study of behavior disorders have crystallized into three concepts: *mental health, adjustment,* and *emotional maturity.* These ideals have come to occupy a prominent and influential place in our thinking. In part their prominence comes from the prestige that is currently accorded to science and medicine. In part it comes from the decline of religion and ethics as guides to personal conduct. In part it comes from the confusion in secular values other than those derived from science. Mental health, adjustment, and emotional maturity are thus tending to fill an ideological vacuum. "The maturity concept," writes Overstreet, "is central to our whole enterprise of living. This is what our past wisdoms have been leading up to." [1] If these ideals are going to be considered as the culmination of past wisdoms, it is certainly essential to give them the closest scrutiny. For they are anything but inert ideas. They have a direct point of application in child training, guidance, and teaching, and they are being used every day to influence the development of personality.

The first two of these ideals do not stand up well under close scrutiny. It is worth while to examine them not only because they are currently influential but also because they bring up serious problems in thinking about personal growth. *Mental health* is strictly an extension of the medical concept of health, defined in the negative sense of not having anything wrong with you. Actually most writers go a little further and speak of positive or optimal mental health, but in doing so they overstep the bounds of the metaphor of health and use ideas that go better with the concept of emotional maturity.[2] *Adjustment* is generally used in a sense borrowed from biology, referring to the efforts made by a person to maintain himself in his physical and social environment. Like mental health, its use in this connection came from the study of disordered behavior in which the patient was clearly not adjusted to his environment. It is important

---

[1] H. A. Overstreet, *The Mature Mind,* New York: W. W. Norton & Co., 1949, p. 14.

[2] Ten criteria of optimum mental health, one of them being "adequate emotional maturity," are given in a representative statement by L. P. Thorpe, *The Psychology of Mental Health,* New York: The Ronald Press Co., 1950, pp. 116–117. The concept is thoughtfully extended by M. Jahoda, in *Current Concepts of Positive Mental Health,* New York: Basic Books, 1958.

to realize that both concepts spring from the mental hospital and psychiatric consulting room, from studies of the sick aspects of sick people. They have not been based primarily on the direct study of people conspicuous for their good adjustment and sound mental health. They do not come from the contemplation of successful life-patterns. For the most part, therefore, they are simply the logical opposites of the things that trouble sick people, things like dependence, inferiority, competitiveness, a harsh superego, failure to test the realities behind delusional and hallucinatory experience. When one adds up the qualities, derived from this process of extrapolation, that are supposed to characterize a mentally healthy or well-adjusted person, the resulting portrait bears little resemblance to any actual life. It takes no account of the conditions under which life is led, of the interaction between person and environment; and it can therefore shed no light at all on the process by which growth takes place.

When it is the fate of ideas to fill an ideological vacuum, taking the place of values that have crumbled, there is great danger that they will be misused. Mental health and adjustment were easy marks for distortion because their positive content was so thin and indeterminate. Instead of standing as first rough attempts to define directions of growth, they were seized upon as scientifically ratified guides to conduct and paths to perfection. Soon they had become distorted in two quite serious ways. Mental health was presented as a list of traits all of which one should possess, regardless of temperament, aptitude, and circumstances, while adjustment quickly degenerated into a doctrine of conformity. Both concepts were thus captured by those who had no respect for individuality. It is to be feared that in these forms they have done a good deal of harm.

Typical listings of the traits that signify mental health usually draw the portrait of a person who is flexible and adaptable, warm and sociable, with versatile skills, abundant interests, and boundless self-confidence. "The individual has faith in his ability to succeed," says one account; "he believes he will do reasonably well whatever he undertakes." This prescription is, of course, merely the opposite of the blockings, constrictions, and impaired self-confidence that are so common in disordered personalities. Bent on picturing freedom from a neurotic superego, it mentions nothing that sounds like conscience; urging the overcoming of inferiority feelings, it suggests nothing that resembles the ancient virtue of humility; opposing the withdrawal and social isolation of schizophrenics, it seems to advocate unceasing immersion in a social whirl, with expressions of warmth so widely diffused that one can hardly suppose them to be of very high temperature. The image is of a person diametrically unlike every patient that has ever been described.

Such lists of traits were never intended to carry implications about the nature of reality, but unavoidably they do. They imply that reality chiefly demands sudden changes, abrupt dislocations, and a boundless capacity to react to novel and unexpected situations. One might say that they depict the life of a traveling salesman who constantly meets new people in new territories and who shifts from company to company so that he has to keep learning the merits of new goods. Under some social and occupational circumstances there is much truth in this picture, but it certainly does not cover all the conditions of adult life. After adolescence a person starts to become a full partner in the social system. He begins to take on responsibilities that will last all his life. He cannot avoid concentrating his energies on a small number of ongoing interests, giving up many bright paths that all seemed possible while he was in school. He becomes committed, and he must make a go of his life with one wife, one home, one family of children, one line of work, and perhaps one chief circle of acquaintances. Sometimes there is very little demand for quick change in an adult's life. What is needed is a capacity for steady growth within a relatively constant framework of activities and relationships. Our images of adult reality must include not only that of the foot-loose traveling salesman but also that of the man who works in the same institution for forty-five years. They must include not only that of the versatile girl who can command the admiration of every partner at a dance but also that of the wife who can command the admiration of one husband all the way from wedding to golden wedding. Some features of life call for the broadening of experience; others require its deepening.

Furthermore, the scheme of listing traits does not make allowance for the extraordinary variety of actual life situations. Occupational role alone moves a person into a specialized path in which certain kinds of excellence are of crucial importance and others a matter of indifference. There is certainly no one pattern of traits that would be equally "healthy" in a surgeon, a composer of music, a personnel manager, a bookkeeper, and a shifter of scenery on a moving-picture lot. A research worker has to have unusual capacity for continuous study and thinking along a particular line. His work demands preoccupation and the accumulating of a rich store of specialized knowledge, and this is not easily compatible with the extraversion of interests that makes a person enthusiastically responsive to other people's enterprises, hence a good teacher. A trial lawyer, by way of contrast, must be able to concentrate fiercely on the case at hand, getting up quickly all kinds of relevant information; but once the case is tried he must be able to put it out of mind, apply himself to the next problem, and have no regret that the things he learns do not add up to a coherent picture of anything in particular. The idea of possessing all the virtues and being equal to everything is absurdly unreal when we think of the diverse ways in which people lead happy and useful lives.

The other type of distortion, which has been visited chiefly on the concept of adjustment, consists of assuming that it is a person's job to conform to the expectations of his social environment. This is an incorrect reading of the biological concept of adjustment or adaptation, which by no means excludes the possibility that an organism will change its surroundings in ways beneficial to its own requirements. Such interaction, however, is often lost in popular accounts of adjustment. "He establishes socially approved goals and makes reasonable progress toward attaining them"; no hint that he should ever criticize socially approved goals or try to formulate better ones. "He achieves a fundamental harmony with his environment"; no suggestion that he should ever take a stand against his environment or try to change it for the better. In all this thinking there is an implicit assumption that the physical and social environment is fixed and unchangeable, that the strong and the healthy can adjust themselves to it, that only the weak, the immature, the dependent, the egotistical, and the otherwise neurotically burdened people fail to take its demands in their stride. The doctrine that started as preventive medicine has become a slogan for social conformity. It has enshrined as its ideal the person who all-too-successfully adjusts to narrowing channels, monotonous routines, imposed restrictions, and the pressure to fulfill roles, a course of action that can succeed only at the cost of his power to object, to grow, to improve the roles, to enjoy, to invent, to act as a constructive force—in short, to have any creative front in his development.

A number of writers in recent years have described changes in the social system that put an increasing premium on conformity. The growth of large organizations in the worlds of business and public administration has lowered the importance of skill in workmanship and made a major virtue out of getting along well with the other people on the team. Success and advancement depend upon being a good "organization man," as W. H. Whyte expresses it, which implies a bland pattern of deference toward those in positions of power and amiable cooperation with everyone else, to the end that the organization will run smoothly.[3] Erich Fromm, describing similar economic trends, speaks of a "marketing orientation," in which the person feels himself to be a commodity that must be kept saleable. Self-esteem becomes dependent on conditions beyond his control; ego identity is but little founded on his sense of competence, being almost wholly defined by the judgments of others. "The marketing personality," Fromm observes, "must be free of all individuality."[4] These accounts may put the matter too strongly, but they point to forces in society that maintain a good deal of pressure in the direction of conformity. It is not surprising that the idea of adjustment has itself been adjusted by these pressures into a call to make oneself socially acceptable at whatever cost to individuality.

Everything we have learned in the earlier chapters of this book* testifies to the naturalness of individuality. Each person is at least a little different from every other person with respect to constitutional and temperamental endowment, aptitudes and potential skills,

---

[3] W. H. Whyte, Jr., *The Organization Man,* New York: Simon & Schuster, 1956.

[4] E. Fromm, *Man for Himself,* New York: Holt, Rinehart and Winston, 1947, pp. 67–82.

* This refers to the earlier discussions in *Lives in Progress* (Eds.).

a long history of learnings in the family and subsequent social systems, integration of these experiences to form a sense of identity, and actual life situation as defined by occupation, social position, marriage, and a host of other circumstances. Nobody is free to develop in every direction and maximize every quality that might appear on a mental health list. If conformity were the highest goal of development we would expect superior people to be very much alike. But if we pick out people who seem to have carried personal development to unusual heights, as Maslow has done in his studies of "self-actualizing people," we discover that, far from conforming to any fixed pattern, they are strikingly different and unusually individualized.[5] The study of growth trends in adulthood cannot be served by thinking about generalized patterns. It must aim to understand directions of growth and processes of change, always with the condition in mind that each life is bound to have a unique pattern.

It is likely that the concept of emotional maturity, which is also frequently tapped to fill the vacuum left by the weakening of traditional values, is liable to distortions of the same kind as have been worked upon mental health and adjustment. The idea is, however, more easily protected against this fate because it does not have to be expressed as the negative of mental disorder; it can be given a positive content of its own. It can be more readily founded on the study of lives in progress, on the examination of events and experiences that have enabled people to cope more successfully with problems, increase the effectiveness of strategies, deepen their appreciation of their surroundings, and expand their resources for happiness.

SUGGESTIONS FOR FURTHER READING

The concept of growth trends is widely used in developmental psychology, but research interest has been largely confined to the earlier and simpler manifestations of growth rather than its continuation in adult life. ANDRAS ANGYAL (*Foundations for a Science of Personality,* New York: The Commonwealth Fund, 1941) suggested two very general growth trends that extend throughout most of life, the trend toward increasing autonomy and the trend toward homonomy; see especially Chapters 2 and 6. The continuing of growth is the subject of two chapters in G. W. ALLPORT's *Pattern and Growth in Personality*

[5] A. Maslow, *Motivation and Personality,* New York: Harper & Row, 1954 Chap. 12.

(New York: Holt, Rinehart and Winston, 1961); the transformation of motives is discussed in Chapter 10 and the mature personality in Chapter 12. LEON J. SAUL's *Emotional Maturity: The Development and Dynamics of Personality* (Philadelphia: J. B. Lippincott Co., 2d ed., 1962) is organized on a principle very similar to that of growth trends. ABRAHAM MASLOW's study of self-actualizing people describes qualities that could easily be cast in the same form (*Motivation and Personality,* New York: Harper & Row, 1954, Chapter 12).

4

Growth and Crises of the Healthy Personality*

Erik H. Erikson

I will start out from Freud's far-reaching discovery that neurotic conflict is not very different in content from the conflicts which every child must live through in his childhood, and that every adult carries these conflicts with him in the recesses of his personality. I shall take account of this fact by stating for each childhood stage what these critical psychological conflicts are. For man, to remain psychologically alive, must resolve these conflicts unceasingly, even as his body must unceasingly combat the encroachment of physical decomposition. However, since I cannot accept the conclusion that just to be alive, or not to be sick, means to be healthy, I must have recourse to a few concepts which are not part of the official terminology of my field. Being interested also in cultural anthropology, I shall try to describe those elements of a really healthy personality which—so it seems to me—are most noticeably absent or defective in neurotic patients and which are most obviously present in the kind of man that educational and cultural systems seem to be striving, each in its own way, to create, to support, and to maintain.

I shall present human growth from the point of view of the conflicts, inner and outer, which the healthy personality weathers, emerging and re-emerging with an increased sense of inner unity, with an increase of good judgment, and an increase in the capacity to do well, according to the standards of those who are significant to him. The use of the words "to do well," of course, points up the whole question of cultural relativity. For example, those who are significant to a man may think he is doing well when he "does some good"; or

* From Erik H. Erikson, Identity and the Life Cycle. *Psychological Issues,* 1959, Vol. 1, No. 1. International Universities Press.

when he "does well" in the sense of acquiring possessions; or when he is doing well in the sense of learning new skills or new ways of understanding or mastering reality; or when he is not much more than just getting along.

Formulations of what constitutes a healthy personality in an adult are presented in other parts of the Fact-finding Committee's work. If I may take up only one, namely, Marie Jahoda's (1950) definition, according to which a healthy personality *actively masters his environment,* shows a certain *unity of personality,* and is able to *perceive the world and himself correctly,* it is clear that all of these criteria are relative to the child's cognitive and social development. In fact, we may say that childhood is defined by their initial absence and by their gradual development in many complicated steps. I consider it my task to approach this question from the genetic point of view: How does a healthy personality grow or, as it were, accrue from the successive stages of increasing capacity to master life's outer and inner dangers—with some vital enthusiasm to spare?

On Health and Growth

Whenever we try to understand growth, it is well to remember the *epigenetic principle* which is derived from the growth of organisms *in utero.* Somewhat generalized, this principle states that anything that grows has a *ground plan,* and that out of this ground plan the *parts* arise, each part having its *time* of special ascendancy, until all parts have arisen to form a *functioning whole.* At birth the baby leaves the chemical exchange of the womb for the social exchange system of his society, where his gradually increasing capacities meet the opportunities and limitations of his culture. How the maturing organism continues to unfold, not by developing new organs, but by a prescribed sequence of locomotor, sensory, and social capacities, is described in the child-development literature. Psychoanalysis has given us an understanding of the more idiosyncratic experiences and especially the inner conflicts, which constitute the manner in which an individual becomes a distinct personality. But here, too, it is important to realize that in the sequence of his most personal experiences the healthy child, given a reasonable amount of guidance, can be trusted to obey inner laws of development, laws which create a *succession of potentialities for significant interaction* with those who tend him. While such interaction varies from culture to culture, it must remain within the *proper rate and the proper sequence* which govern the *growth of a personality* as well as that of an organism. Personality can be said to develop according to steps predetermined in the human organism's readiness to be driven toward, to be aware of, and to interact with, a widening social radius, beginning with the dim image of a mother and ending with mankind, or at any rate that segment of mankind which "counts" in the particular individual's life.

It is for this reason that, in the presentation of stages in the development of the personality, we employ an *epigenetic diagram* analogous to one previously employed for an analysis of Freud's psychosexual stages.[1] It is, in fact, the purpose of this presentation to bridge the theory of infantile sexuality (without repeating it here in detail), and our knowledge of the child's physical and social growth within his family and the social structure. An epigenetic diagram looks like this (see Diagram A).

	Component 1	Component 2	Component 3
Stage I	I_1	I_2	I_3
Stage II	II_1	II_2	II_3
Stage III	III_1	III_2	III_3

DIAGRAM A

The double-lined squares signify both a sequence of stages (I to III) and a gradual development of component parts; in other words the diagram formalizes a *progression through time of a differentiation of parts*. This indicates (1) that each item of the healthy personality to be discussed is *systematically related to all others,* and that they all depend on the *proper development in the proper sequence of each item;* and

[1] See Part I of the author's *Childhood and Society* (1950a).

(2) that each item *exists in some form before "its" decisive and critical time* normally arrives.

If I say, for example, that a *sense of basic trust* is the first component of mental health to develop in life, a *sense of autonomous will* the second, and a *sense of initiative* the third, the purpose of the diagram may become clearer (see Diagram B).

First Stage (about first year)	BASIC TRUST	Earlier form of AUTONOMY	Earlier form of INITIATIVE
Second Stage (about second and third years)	Later form of BASIC TRUST	AUTONOMY	Earlier form of INITIATIVE
Third Stage (about fourth and fifth years)	Later form of BASIC TRUST	Later form of AUTONOMY	INITIATIVE

DIAGRAM B

This diagrammatic statement, in turn, is meant to express a number of fundamental relations that exist among the three components, as well as a few fundamental facts for each.

Each comes to its ascendance, meets its crisis, and finds its lasting solution (in ways to be described here) *toward the end of the stages* mentioned. All of them exist in the beginning in some form, although we do not make a point of this fact, and we shall not confuse things by calling these components different names at earlier or later stages. A baby may show something like "autonomy" from the beginning, for example, in the particular way in which he angrily tries to wriggle his hand free when tightly held. However, under normal conditions, it is not until the second year that he begins to experience the whole *critical alternative between being an autonomous creature and being a dependent one;* and it is not until then that he is ready for a *decisive encounter* with his environment, an environment which, in turn, feels called upon to convey to him its *particular ideas and concepts of autonomy and coercion* in ways decisively contributing to the character, the efficiency, and the health of his personality in his culture.

It is this *encounter,* together with the resulting crisis, which is to be described for each stage. Each stage becomes a *crisis* because incipient growth and awareness in a significant part function goes together with a shift in instinctual energy and yet causes specific vulnerability in that part. One of the most difficult questions to decide, therefore, is whether or not a child at a given stage is weak or strong. Perhaps it would be best to say that he is always vulnerable in some respects and completely oblivious and insensitive in others, but that at the same time he is unbelievably persistent in the same respects in which he is vulnerable. It must be added that the smallest baby's weakness gives him power; out of his very dependence and weakness he makes signs to which his environment (if it is guided well by a responsiveness based both on instinctive and traditional patterns) is peculiarly sensitive. A baby's presence exerts a consistent and persistent domination over the outer and inner lives of every member of a household. Because these members must reorient themselves to accommodate his presence, they must also grow as individuals and as a group. It is as true to say that babies control and bring up their families as it is to say the converse. A family can bring up a baby only by being brought up by him. His growth consists of a series of challenges to them to serve his newly developing potentialities for social interaction.

Each successive step, then, is a potential crisis because of a radical *change in perspective*. There is, at the beginning of life, the most radical change of all: from intrauterine to extrauterine life. But in postnatal existence, too, such radical adjustments of perspective as lying relaxed, sitting firmly, and running fast must all be accomplished in their own good time. With them, the interpersonal perspective, too, changes rapidly and often radically, as is testified by the proximity in time of such opposites as "not letting mother out of sight" and "wanting to be independent." Thus, *different capacities use different opportunities* to become full-grown components of the ever-new configuration that is the growing personality.

5

A Theory of Metamotivation: The Biological Rooting of the Value-Life[*] [1]

A. H. MASLOW

I

Self-actualizing individuals (more matured, more fully-human), by definition, already suitably gratified in their basic needs, are now motivated in other higher ways, to be called "metamotivations."

This is to say that they have a feeling of belongingness and rootedness, they are satisfied in their love needs, have friends and feel loved and loveworthy, they have status and place in life and respect from other people, and they have a reasonable feeling of worth and self-respect. If we phrase this negatively—in terms of the frustration of these basic needs and in terms of pathology—then this is to say that self-actualizing people do not (for any length of time) feel anxiety-ridden, rootless, or isolated, nor do they have crippling feelings of inferiority or worthlessness (Maslow, 1954, Chap. 12).

Of course this can be phrased in other ways and this I have done. For instance, since the basic needs had been assumed to be the only motivations for human beings, it was possible, and in certain contexts also useful, to say of self-actualizing people that they were "unmotivated" (Maslow, 1954, Chap. 15). This was to align these people with the Eastern philosophical view of health as the transcendence of striving or desiring.

It was also possible to describe self-actualizing people as expressing rather than coping, and to stress that they were spontaneous, and natural, that they were more easily themselves than other people.

[*] Abridged from *Journal of Humanistic Psychology*, 1967 (Fall), Vol. VII, No. 2.
[1] The twenty-eight italicized theses listed here are presented as testable propositions.

Each of these phrasings has its own operational usefulness in particular research contexts. But it is also true that for certain purposes it is best to ask the question, "What motivates the self-actualizing person?"

Clearly we must make an immediate distinction between the ordinary motives of people below the level of self-actualization—that is, people motivated by the basic needs—and the motivations of people who are sufficiently gratified in all their basic needs and therefore are no longer motivated by them primarily, but rather by "higher" motivations. It is therefore convenient to call these higher motives and needs of self-actualizing persons by the name "metaneeds" and also to differentiate the category of motivation from the category of "metamotivation."

(It is now more clear to me that gratification of the basic needs is not a sufficient condition for metamotivation, although it may be a necessary precondition. I have individual subjects in whom apparent basic-need-gratification is compatible with "existential neurosis," meaninglessness, valuelessness, or the like. Metamotivation now seems *not* to ensue automatically after basic-need-gratification. One must speak also of the additional variable of "defenses against metamotivation" [Maslow, 1967]. This implies that, for the strategy of communication and of theory-building, it may turn out to be useful to add to the definition of the self-actualizing person, not only [a] that he be sufficiently free of illess, [b] that he be sufficiently gratified in his basic needs, and [c] that he be positively using his capacities, but also [d] that he be motivated by some values which he strives for or gropes for and to which he is loyal.)

II

All such people are devoted to some task, call, vocation, beloved work ("outside themselves").

Generally the devotion and dedication is so marked that one can fairly use the old words vocation, calling, or mission to describe their passionate, selfless, and profound feeling for their "work." We could even use the words destiny or fate. I have sometimes gone so far as to speak of oblation in the religious sense, in the sense of offering oneself or dedicating oneself upon some altar for some particular task, some cause outside oneself and bigger than oneself, something not merely selfish, something impersonal.

I think it is possible to go pretty far with the notion of destiny or fate. This is a way of putting into inadequate words the feeling that one gets when one listens to self-actualizing people (and some others) talking about their work or task (Maslow, 1965a). One gets the feeling of a beloved job, and, furthermore, of something for which the person is a "natural," something that he is suited for, something that is right for him, even something that he was born for.

It should be said that the above seems to hold true for my female subjects even though in a different sense. I have at least one woman subject who devoted herself entirely to the task of being the mother, the wife, the housewife and the clan matriarch. Her vocation, one could very reasonably call it, was to bring up her children, to make her husband happy, and to hold together a large number of relatives in a network of personal relations. This she did very well and, as nearly as I could make out, this she enjoyed. She loved her lot completely and totally, never yearning for anything else so far as I could tell, and using all her capacities well in the process. Other women subjects have had various combinations of home life and professional work outside the home which could produce this same sense of dedication to something perceived simultaneously, both as beloved and also as important and worthwhile doing. In some women, I have also been tempted to think of "having a baby" as fullest self-actualization all by itself, at least for a time.

III

In the ideal instance, inner requiredness coincides with external requiredness, "I want to" with "I must."

I often get the feeling in this kind of situation that I can tease apart two kinds of determinants of this transaction. One can be spoken of as the responses within the person, e.g., "I love babies (or painting, or research, or political power) more than anything in the world. I am fascinated with it. . . . I am inexorably drawn to . . . I need to . . ." This we may call "inner requiredness" and it is felt as a kind of self-indulgence rather than as a duty It is different from and separable from "external requiredness," which is rather felt as a response to what the environment, the situation, requires of the person, as a fire "calls for" putting out, or as a helpless baby demands that one take care of it, or as some obvious injustice calls for righting (Maslow, 1963). Here one feels more the element of duty, or obligation, or responsibility, of being compelled helplessly to respond no matter what one was planning to do, or wished to do. It is more "I must, I have to, I am compelled" than "I want to."

In the ideal instance, which fortunately also happens in fact in many of my instances, "I want to" coincides with "I must."

I hesitate to call this simply "purposefulness" because that may imply that it happens only out of will, purpose, decision, or calculation, and doesn't give enough weight to the subjective feeling of being swept along, of willing and eager surrender, or yielding to fate and happily embracing it at the same time. Ideally, one also *discovers* one's fate; it is not only made or constructed or decided upon. It is recognized as if one had been unwittingly waiting for it. Perhaps the better phrase would be "Spinozistic" or "Taoistic" choice or decision or purpose— or even will.

The best way to communicate these feelings to someone who doesn't intuitively, directly understand them is to use as a model "falling in love." This is clearly different from doing one's duty, or doing what is sensible or logical. And clearly also "will," if mentioned at all, is used in a very special sense. And when two people love each other fully, then each one knows what it feels like to be magnet and what it feels like to be iron filings, and what it feels like to be both simultaneously.

IV

This ideal situation generates feelings of good fortune and also of ambivalence and unworthiness.

This model also helps to convey what is difficult to communicate in words, that is, their sense of good fortune, of luck, of gratuitous grace, of awe that this miracle should have occurred, of wonder that they should have been chosen, and of the peculiar mixture of pride fused with humility, of arrogance shot through with the pity-for-the-less-fortunate that one finds in lovers.

Of course the possibility of good fortune and success also can set into motion all sorts of neurotic fears, feelings of unworthiness, counter-values, Jonah-syndrome dynamics (Maslow, 1967), etc. These defenses against our highest possibilities must be overcome before the highest values can be wholeheartedly embraced.

V

At this level the dichotomizing of work and play is transcended; wages, hobbies, vacations, etc., must be defined at a higher level.

And then, of couse, it can be said of such a person with real meaningfulness that he is being his own kind of person, or being himself, or actualizing his real self. An abstract statement, an extrapolation out from this kind of observation toward the ultimate and perfect ideal would run something like this: This person is the best one in the whole world for this particular job, and this particular job is the best job in the world for this particular person and his talents, capacities, and tastes. He was meant for it, and it was meant for him.

Of course, as soon as we accept this and get the feel of it, then we move over into another realm of discourse, i.e., the realm of being (Maslow, 1962a; Maslow, 1962b), of transcendence. Now we can speak meaningfully only in the language of being ("The B-language," communication at the mystical level, etc.). For instance, it is quite obvious with such people that the ordinary or conventional dichotomy between work and play is transcended totally (Marcuse, 1955; Maslow, 1965a). That is, there is certainly no distinction between work and play in such a person in such a situation. His work is his play and his play is his work. If a person loves his work and enjoys it more than any other activity in the whole world and is eager to get to it, to get back to it after any intrruption, then how can we speak about "labor" in the sense of something one is forced to do against one's wishes?

VI

Such vocation-loving individuals tend to identify (introject, incorporate) with their "work" and to make it into a defining-characteristic of the self. It becomes part of the self.

If one asks such a person, i.e., self-actualizing, work-loving, "Who are you?" or "What are you?" he often tends to answer in terms of his "call," e.g., "I am a lawyer." "I am a mother." "I am a psychiatrist." "I am an artist," etc.

Or, if one asks him, "Supposing you were not a scientist (or a teacher, or a pilot), then what would you be?" Or, "Supposing you were not a psychologist, then what?" It is my impression that his response is apt to be one of puzzlement, thoughtfulness, being taken aback, i.e., not having a ready answer. Or the response can be one of amusement, i.e., it is funny. In effect, the answer is, "If I were not a mother (anthropologist, industrialist), then I wouldn't be *me*. I would be someone else. And I can't imagine being someone else."

This kind of response parallels the confused response to the question, "Supposing you were a woman rather than a man?"

A tentative conclusion is then that in self-actualizing subjects, their beloved calling tends to be perceived as a defining characteristic of the self, to be identified with, incorporated, introjected. It becomes an inextricable aspect of one's being.

VII

The tasks to which they are dedicated seem to be interpretable as embodiments or incarnations of intrinsic values (rather than as a means to ends outside the work itself, and rather than as functionally autonomous). The tasks are loved (and introjected) BECAUSE they embody these values. That is, ultimately it is the values that are loved rather than the job as such.

For these people the profession seems to be *not* functionally autonomous, but rather to be a carrier of, an instrument of, or an incarnation of ultimate values. For them the profession of, e.g., law is a means to the end of justice, and not an end in itself. Perhaps I can communicate my feeling for the subtle difference in this way: for one man the law is loved because it *is* justice, while another man, the pure value-free technologist, might love the law simply as an intrinsically lovable set of rules, precedents, procedures without regard to the ends or products of their use.

VIII

These intrinsic values overlap greatly with the B-values, and perhaps are identical with them.

I feel it desirable to use my description of the B-values, not only because it would be theoretically pretty if I could, but also because they are operationally definable in so many different ways (Maslow, 1962b; 1964a, Appendix G). That is to say, they are found at the end of so many different investigative roads, that the suspicion arises that there is something in common between these different paths, e.g., education, art, religion, psychotherapy, peak-experiences, science, mathematics, etc. If this turns out to be so, we may perhaps add as another road to final values, the "cause," the mission, the vocation, that is to say, the "work" of self-actualizing people.

IX

This introjection means that the self has enlarged to include aspects of the world and that therefore the distinction between self and not-self (outside, other) has been transcended.

These B-values or metamotives are no longer *only* intrapsychic or organismic. They are equally inner and outer. The metaneeds, insofar as they are inner, and the requiredness of all that is outside the person move toward becoming indistinguishable, that is, toward fusion.

Certainly simple selfishness is transcended here and has to be defined at higher levels. For instance, we know that it is possible for a person to get more pleasure (selfish? unselfish?) out of food through having his child eat it than through eating it with his own mouth. His self has enlarged enough to include his child. Hurt his child and you hurt him. Clearly the self can no longer be identified with the biological entity which is applied with blood from his heart along his blood vessels. The psychological self can obviously be bigger than its own body.

There are other important consequences of this incorporation of values into the self. For instance, you can love justice and truth in the world or in a person out there. You can be made happier as your friends move toward truth and justice, and sadder as they move away from it. This is easy to understand. But supposing you see yourself moving successfully toward truth, justice, beauty, and virtue? Then of course you may find that, in a peculiar kind of detachment and objectivity toward oneself, for which our culture has no place, you will be loving and admiring yourself, in the kind of healthy self-love that Fromm (1947) has described. You can respect yourself, admire yourself, take tender care of yourself, reward yourself, feel virtuous, love-worthy, respect-worthy. You may then treat yourself with the responsibility and otherness that, for instance, a pregnant woman does, whose self now has to be defined to include not-self. So also may a person with a great talent protect it and himself as if he were a carrier of something which is simultaneously himself and not himself. He may become his own guardian, so to speak.

X

Less evolved persons seem to use their work more often for achieving gratification of lower basic needs, of neurotic needs, as a means to an end, out of habit, or as a response to cultural expectations, etc. However, it is probable that these are differences of degree. Perhaps all human beings are (potentially) metamotivated to a degree.

The conventional categories of career, profession, or work may serve as channels of many other kinds of motivations, not to mention sheer habit or convention or functional autonomy. They may satisfy or seek vainly to satisfy any or all of the basic needs as well as various neurotic needs. They may be a channel for "acting out" or for "defensive" activities as well as for real gratifications.

All these various habits, determinants, motives, and metamotives are acting simultaneously in a very complex pattern which is centered more toward one kind of motivation or determinedness than the others. This is to say that the most highly developed persons we know are metamotivated to a much higher degree, and are basic-need-motivated to a lesser degree than average or diminished people are.

XI

The full definition of the person or of human nature must then include intrinsic values, as part of human nature.

If we then try to define the deepest, most authentic, most constitutionally based aspects of the real self, of the identity, or of the authentic person, we find that in order to be comprehensive we must include not only the person's constitution and temperament, not only anatomy, physiology, neurology, and endocrinology, not only his capacities, his biological style, not only his basic instinctoid needs, but also the B-values, which are also *his* B-values.

XII

These intrinsic values are instinctoid in nature, i.e., they are needed (a) to avoid illness and (b) to achieve fullest humanness or growth. The "illnesses" resulting from deprivation of intrinsic values (metaneeds) we may call metapathologies. The "highest" values, the spiritual life, the highest aspirations of mankind are therefore proper subjects for scientific study and research. They are in the world of nature.

These "illnesses" (which come from deprivation of the B-values or metaneeds or B-facts) are new and have not yet been described as such, i.e., as pathologies, except unwittingly, or by implication, or, as by Frankl (1966), in a very general and inclusive way, not yet teased apart into researchable form. In general, they have been discussed through the centuries by religionists, historians, and philosophers under the rubric of spiritual or religious shortcomings, rather than by physicians, scientists, or psychologists under the rubric of psychiatric or psychological or biological "illnesses" or stuntings or diminutions. To some extent also there is some overlap with sociological and political disturbances, "social pathologies," and the like.

I will call these "illnesses" (or, better, diminutions of humanness) "metapathologies" and define them as the consequences of deprivation of the B-values either in general or of specific B-values.

XIII

The metapathologies of the affluent and indulged young come partly from deprivation of intrinsic values, frustrated "idealism," from disillusionment with a society they see (mistakenly) motivated only by lower or animal or material needs.

My hypothesis is that this behavior can be a fusion of continued search for something to believe in, combined with anger at being disappointed. (I sometimes see in a particular young man total despair or hopelessness about even the *existence* of such values.)

Of course, this frustrated idealism and occasional hopelessness is partially due to the influence and ubiquity of stupidly limited theories of motivation all over the world. Leaving aside behavioristic and positivistic theories—or rather non-theories—as simple refusals even to see the problem, i.e., a kind of psychoanalytic denial, then what is available to the idealistic young man and woman?

Not only does the whole of official nineteenth-century science and orthodox academic psychology offer him nothing, but also the major motivation theories by which most men live can lead him only to depression or cynicism. The Freudians, at least in their official writings (though not in good therapeutic practice), are still reductionistic about all higher human values. The deepest and most real motivations are seen to be dangerous and nasty, while the highest human values and virtues are essentially fake, being not what they seem to be, but camouflaged versions of the "deep, dark, and dirty." Our social scientists are just as disappointing in the main. A total cultural determinism is still the official, orthodox doctrine of many or most of the sociologists and anthropologists. This doctrine not only denies intrinsic higher motivations, but comes perilously close sometimes to denying "human nature" itself. The economists, not only in the West but also in the East, are essentially materialistic. We must say harshly of the "science" of economics that it is generally the skilled, exact, technological application of a totally false theory of human needs and values, a theory which recognizes only the existence of lower needs or material needs (Schumacher, 1967; Weisskopf, 1963; Wootton, 1967).

How could young people not be disappointed and disillusioned? What else could be the result of *getting* all the material and animal gratifications and then *not being happy,* as they were led to expect, not only by the theorists, but also by the conventional wisdom of parents and teachers, and the insistent gray lies of the advertisers?

What happens then to the "eternal verities"? to the ultimate truths? Most sections of the society agree in handing them over to the churches and to dogmatic, institutionalized, conventionalized religious organizations. But this is also a denial of high human nature! It says in effect that the youngster who is looking for something will definitely *not* find it in human nature itself. He must look for ultimates to a non-human, non-natural source, a source which is definitely mistrusted or rejected altogether by many intelligent young people today.

XIV

This value-starvation and value-hunger come both from external deprivation and from our inner ambivalence and counter-values.

Not only are we passively value-deprived into metapathology by the environment. We also fear the highest values, both within ourselves and outside ourselves. Not only are we attracted; we are also awed, stunned, chilled, frightened. That is to say, we tend to be ambivalent and conflicted. We defend ourselves against the B-values. Repression, denial, reaction-formation, and probably all the Freudian defense-mechanisms are available and are used against the highest within ourselves just as they are mobilized against the lowest within ourselves. Humility and a sense of unworthiness can lead to evasion of the highest values. So also can the fear of being overwhelmed by the tremendousness of these values. (In another paper [1967] I have called this the Jonah-syndrome and described it more fully.)

XV

The hierarchy of basic needs is prepotent to the metaneeds.

Basic needs and metaneeds are in the same hierarchical-integration, i.e., on the same continuum, in the same realm of discourse. They have the same basic characteristic of being "needed" (necessary, good for the person) in the sense that their deprivation produces "illness" and diminution, and that their "ingestion" fosters growth toward full-humanness, toward greater happiness and joy, toward psychological "success," toward more peak-experiences, and in general toward living more often at the level of being. That is, they are *all* biologically desirable, and *all* foster biological success. And yet, they are also different in definable ways.

First of all, it is clear that the whole hierarchy of the basic needs is prepotent to the metaneeds, or, to say it in another way, the metaneeds are postpotent (less urgent or demanding, weaker) to the basic needs. I intend this as a generalized statistical statement because I find some single individuals in whom a special-talent or a unique sensitivity makes truth or beauty or goodness, for that single person, more important and more pressing than some basic need.

Secondly, the basic needs can be called deficiency-needs, having the various characteristics already described for deficiency-needs, while the metaneeds seem rather to have the special characteristics described for "growth-motivations" (Maslow, 1962a, Chap. 3).

XVI

The metaneeds are equally potent among themselves, on the average —i.e., I cannot detect a generalized hierarchy of prepotency. But in any given individual, they may be and often are hierarchically arranged according to idiosyncratic talents and constitutional differences.

The metaneeds (or B-values, or B-facts) so far as I can make out are not arranged in a hierarchy of prepotency, but seem, all of them, to be equally potent on the *average*. Another way of saying this, a phrasing that is useful for other purposes, is that each individual seems to have his own priorities or hierarchy or prepotency, in accordance with his own talents, temperament, skills, capacities, etc. Beauty is more important than truth to one person, but for his brother it may be the other way about with equal statistical likelihood.

XVII

It looks as if any intrinsic or B-value is fully defined by most or all of the other B-values. Perhaps they form a unity of some sort, with each specific B-value being simply the whole seen from another angle.

That is, truth, to be fully and completely defined, must be beautiful, good, perfect, just, simple, orderly, lawful, alive, comprehensive, unitary, dichotomy-transcending, effortless, and amusing (Maslow, 1962b). (The formula, "The truth, the whole truth, and nothing but the truth," is certainly quite inadequate.) Beauty, fully defined, must be true, good, perfect, alive, simple, etc.

XVIII

The value-life (spiritual, religious, philosophical, axiological, etc.) is an aspect of human biology and is on the same continuum with the "lower" animal life (rather than being in separated, dichotomized, or mutually exclusive realms). It is probably therefore species-wide, supracultural even though it must be actualized by culture in order to exist.

The spiritual life is part of the human essence. It is a defining-characteristic of human nature, without which human nature is not full human nature. It is part of the Real Self, of one's identity, of one's specieshood, of full-humanness. To the extent that pure expressing of oneself, or pure spontaneity, is possible, to that extent will the metaneeds also be expressed. "Uncovering" or Taoistic or existential therapeutic or logotherapeutic (Frankl, 1966), or "ontogogic" techniques (Bugental, 1965), should uncover and strengthen the metaneeds as well as the basic needs.

Depth-diagnostic and therapeutic techniques should ultimately also uncover these same metaneeds because, paradoxically, our "highest nature" is also our "deepest nature." The value life and the animal life are not in two separate realms as most religions and philosophies have assumed, and as classical, impersonal science has also assumed. The spiritual life (the contemplative, "religious," philosophical, or value-life) is within the jurisdiction of human thought and is attainable in principle by man's own efforts. Even though it has been cast out of the realm of reality by the classical, value-free science which models itself upon physics, it can be reclaimed as an object of study and technology by humanistic science.

Let me also make quite explicit the implication that metamotivation is species-wide, and is, therefore, supracultural, common-human, not created arbitrarily by culture. Since this is a point at which misunderstandings are fated to occur, let me say it so: the metaneeds seem to me to be instinctoid, that is, to have an appreciable hereditary, species-wide determination. But they are potentialities, rather than actualities. Culture is definitely and absolutely needed for their actualization; but also culture can fail to actualize them, and indeed this is just what most known cultures actually seem to do and to have done throughout history. Therefore, there is implied here a supracultural factor which can criticize any culture from outside and above that culture, namely, in terms of the degree to which it fosters or suppresses self-actualization, full-humanness, and metamotivation (Maslow, 1964b).

The so-called spiritual (or transcendent, or axiological) life is clearly rooted in the biological nature of the species. It is a kind of "higher" animality whose precondition is a healthy "lower" animality, i.e., they are hierarchically-integrated (rather than mutually exclusive). But this higher, spiritual "animality" is so timid and weak, and so easily lost, is so easily crushed by stronger cultural forces, that it can become widely actualized *only* in a culture which approves of human nature, and therefore actively fosters its fullest growth.

XIX

Pleasures and gratifications can be arranged in hierarchy of levels from lower to higher. So also can hedonistic theories be seen as ranging from lower to higher, i.e., metahedonism.

The B-values, seen as gratifications of metaneeds, are then also the highest pleasures or happinesses that we know of.

I have suggested elsewhere (1966) the need for and usefulness of being conscious that there is a hierarchy of pleasures, ranging from, e.g., relief from pain, through the contentment of a hot tub, the happiness of being with good friends, the joy of great music, the bliss of having a child, the ecstasy of the highest love-experiences, on up to the fusion with the B-values.

Such a hierarchy suggests a solution of the problem of hedonism, selfishness, duty, etc. If one includes the highest pleasures among the pleasures in general, then it becomes true in a very real sense that fully-human people also seek only for pleasure, i.e., metapleasure. Perhaps we can call this "metahedonism" and then point out that at this level there is then no contradiction between pleasure and duty since the highest obligations of human beings are certainly to truth, justice, beauty, etc., which however are also the highest pleasures that the species can experience. And of course at this level of discourse the mutual exclusiveness between selfishness and unselfishness has also disappeared. What is good for us is good for everyone else, what is gratifying is praiseworthy, our appetites are now trustworthy, rational, and wise, what we enjoy is good for us, seeking our own (highest) good is also seeking the general good, etc.

XX

Since the spiritual life is instinctoid, all the techniques of "subjective biology" apply to its education.

The spiritual life (B-values, B-facts, metaneeds, etc.) can in principle be introspected. It has "impulse voices" or "inner signals" which, though weaker than basic needs, can yet be "heard," and which therefore comes under the rubric of the "subjective biology" I have described (Maslow, 1965b, 1967).

In principle, therefore, all the principles and exercises which help to develop (or teach) our sensory awarenesses, our body awarenesses, our sensitivities to the inner signals (given off by our needs, capacities, constitution, temperament, body, etc.)—all these apply also, though less strongly, to our inner metaneeds, i.e., to the education of our yearnings for beauty, law, truth, perfection, etc. I have used the term "experientially empty" to describe those persons whose inner signals are either absent or remain unperceived. Perhaps we can also invent some such term as "experientially rich" to describe those who are so sensitive to the inner voices of the self that even the metaneeds can be consciously introspected and enjoyed.

It is this experiential richness which in principle should be "teachable" or recoverable, I feel confident, at least in degree, perhaps with the proper use of psychedelic chemicals, with Esalen-type, non-verbal methods,[2] with meditation and contemplation techniques, with further study of the peak-experiences, or of B-cognition, etc.

XXI

But B-values seem to be the same as B-facts. Reality then is ultimately fact-values or value-facts.

The traditional dichotomizing of *is* and *ought* turns out to be characteristic of lower levels of living, and is transcended at the highest level of living, where fact and value fuse. For obvious reasons, those words which are simultaneously descriptive and normative can be called "fusion words" (Maslow, 1967).

At this fusion level "love for the intrinsic values" is the same as "love of ultimate reality." Devotion *to* the facts here implies love *for* the facts. The sternest effort at objectivity or perception, i.e., to reduce as much as possible the contaminating effect of the observer, and of his fears and wishes and selfish calculations, yields an emotional, esthetic,

---

[2] The Esalen Institute at Big Sur, California, specializes in such methods. The tacit assumption underlying this new kind of education is that both the body and the "spirit" can be loved, and that they are synergic and hierarchically-integrated rather than mutually exclusive, i.e., one can have both.

and axiological result, a result pointed toward and approximated by our greatest and most perspicuous philosophers, scientists, artists, and spiritual inventors and leaders.

Contemplation of ultimate values becomes the same as contemplation of the nature of the world. Seeking the truth (fully defined) may be the same as seeking beauty, order, oneness, perfection, rightness (fully defined) and truth may then be sought *via* any other B-value. Does science then become indistinguishable from art? love? religion? philosophy? Is a basic scientific discovery about the nature of reality also a spiritual or axiological affirmation?

XXII

Not only is man PART *of nature, and it part of him, but also he must be at least minimumly isomorphic with nature (similar to it) in order to be viable in it. It has evolved him. His communion with what transcends him therefore need not be defined as non-natural or supernatural. It may be seen as a "biological" experience.*

Perhaps man's thrilling to nature (perceiving it as true, good, beautiful, etc.) will one day be understood as a kind of self-recognition or self-experience, a way of being oneself and full functional, a way of being at home, a kind of biological authenticity, of "biological mysticism," etc. Perhaps we can see mystical or peak-fusion not only as communion with that which is most worthy of love, but also as fusion with that which *is,* because he belongs there, being truly part of what is, and being, so to speak, a member of the family:

> . . . one direction in which we find increasing confidence is the conception that we are basically one with the cosmos instead of strangers to it (Gardner Murphy).

This *biological* or evolutionary version of the mystic experience or the peak-experience—here perhaps no different from the spiritual or religious experience—reminds us again that we must ultimately outgrow the obsolescent usage of "highest" as the opposite of "lowest" or "deepest." Here the "highest" experience ever described, the joyful fusion with the ultimate that man can conceive, can be seen simultaneously as the deepest experience of our ultimate personal animality and specieshood, as the acceptance of our profound biological nature as isomorphic with nature in general.

XXIII

The B-values are not the same as our personal attitudes toward these values, nor our emotional reactions to them. The B-values induce in us a kind of "requiredness feeling" and also a feeling of unworthiness.

The B-values had better be differentiated from our human attitudes toward these B-values, at least to the extent that is possible for so difficult a task. A listing of such attitudes toward ultimate values (or reality) included: love, awe, adoration, humility, reverence, unworthiness, wonder, amazement, marveling, exaltation, gratitude, fear, joy, etc. (Maslow, 1964a, p. 94). These are clearly emotional-cognitive reactions within a person witnessing something not the same as himself, or at least verbally separable. Of course, the more the person fuses with the world in great peak or mystic experiences, the less of these intra-self reactions there would be and the more the self would be lost as a separable entity.

XXIV

The vocabulary to describe motivations must be hierarchical, especially since metamotivations (growth-motivations) must be characterized differently from basic needs (deficiency-needs).

This difference between intrinsic values and our attitudes toward these values also generates a hierarchical vocabulary for motives (using this word most generally and inclusively). In another place I have called attention to the levels of gratification, pleasures, or happiness corresponding to the hierarchy of needs to metaneeds (Maslow, 1966). In addition to this, we must keep in mind that the concept of "gratification" itself is transcended at the level of metamotives or growth-motives, where satisfactions can be endless. So also for the concept of happiness which can also be altogether transcended at the highest levels. It may then easily become a kind of cosmic sadness or soberness or non-emotional contemplation. At the lowest basic need levels we can certainly talk of being driven and of desperately craving, striving, or needing, when, e.g., cut off from oxygen or experiencing great pain. As we go on up the hierarchy of basic needs, words like desiring, wishing, or preferring, choosing, wanting become more appropriate. But at the highest levels, i.e., of metamotivation, all these words become subjectively inadequate, and such words as yearning for, devoted to, aspiring to, loving, adoring, admiring, worshipping, being drawn to or fascinated by, describe the metamotivated feelings more accurately.

XXV

The B-values call for behavioral expression or "celebration" as well as inducing subjective states.

We must agree with Heschel's (1965, p. 117) stress on "celebration" which he describes as "an act of expressing respect or reverence for that which one needs or honors. . . . Its essence is to call attention to the sublime or solemn aspects of living. . . . To celebrate is to share in a greater joy, to participate in an eternal drama."

It is well to notice that the highest values are not only receptively enjoyed and contemplated, but that they often also lead to expressive and behavioral responses, which of course would be easier to investigate than subjective states.

XXVI

There are certain educational and therapeutic advantages in differentiating the realm (or level) of being from the realm (or level) of deficiencies, and in recognizing language differences at these levels.

I have found it most useful for myself to differentiate between the realm of being (B-realm) and the realm of deficiencies (D-realm), that is, between the eternal and the "practical." Simply as a matter of the strategy and tactics of living well and fully and of choosing one's life instead of having it determined for us, this is a help.

I have found this vocabulary useful also in teaching people to be more aware of values of being, of a language of being, of the ultimate facts of being, of the life of being, of unitive consciousness, etc. The vocabulary is certainly clumsy and sometimes grates on the sensibilities, but it does serve the purpose (Maslow, 1964a, Appendix I: An example of B-analysis).

XXVII

"Intrinsic conscience" and "intrinsic guilt" are ultimately biologically rooted.

Stimulated by Fromm's discussion of "humanistic conscience" (1941) and Horney's (1939) reconsideration of Freud's "superego," other humanistic writers have agreed that there is an "intrinsic conscience" beyond the superego, as well as "intrinsic guilt" which is a deserved self-punishment for betrayal of the intrinsic self.

I believe that the biological rooting of metamotivation theory can clarify and solidify these concepts further.

One's personal biology is beyond question a *sine qua non* component of the "Real Self." Being oneself, being natural or spontaneous, being authentic, expressing one's identity, all these are also biological statements since they imply the acceptance of one's constitutional, temperamental, anatomical, neurological, hormonal, and instinctoid-motivational nature. Such a statement is in both the Freudian line and in the Neo-Freudian line (not to mention Rogerian, Jungian, Sheldonian, Goldsteinian, *et al.*). It is a cleansing and a correction of what Freud was groping toward and of necessity glimpsed only vaguely. I therefore consider it to be in the *echt*-Freudian or *"epi*-Freudian" tradition. I think Freud was trying to say something like this with his various instinct theories. I believe also that this statement is an acceptance of, plus an improvement upon, what Horney was trying to say with her concept of a Real Self.

If my more biological interpretation of an intrinsic self is corroborated, then it would also support the differentiation of neurotic guilt from the intrinsic guilt which comes from defying one's own nature and from trying to be what one is not.

XXVIII

Many of the ultimate religious functions are fulfilled by this theoretical structure.

From the point of view of the eternal and absolute that mankind has always sought, it may be that the B-values could also, to some extent, serve this purpose. They are *per se,* in their own right, not dependent upon human vagaries for their existence. They are perceived, not invented. They are trans-human and trans-individual. They exist beyond the life of the individual. They can be conceived to be a kind of perfection. They could conceivably satisfy the human longing for certainty.

And yet they are also human in a specifiable sense. They are not only his, but him as well. They command adoration, reverence, celebration, sacrifice. They are worth living for and dying for. Contemplating them or fusing with them gives the greatest joy that a human being is capable of.

And so for other functions that the organized religions have tried to fulfill. Apparently all, or almost all, the characteristically religious experiences that have ever been described in any of the traditional religions, in their own local phrasings, whether theist or non-theist, Eastern or Western, can be assimilated to this theoretical structure and can be expressed in an empirically meaningful way, i.e., phrased in a testable way.

REFERENCES

BUGENTAL, J. *The Search for Authenticity.* New York: Holt, Rinehart & Winston, 1965.

FRANKL, V. Self-transcendence as a human phenomenon. *J. humanistic Psychol.,* 1966, 6, 97–106.

FROMM, E. *Escape from Freedom.* New York: Farrar & Rinehart, 1941.

FROMM, E. *Man for Himself.* New York: Rinehart, 1947.

HESCHEL, A. *Who Is Man?* Stanford, Calif.: Stanford Univer. Press, 1965.

HORNEY, K. *New Ways in Psychoanalysis.* New York: Norton, 1939.

MARCUSE, H. *Eros and Civilization.* Boston: Beacon Press, 1955.

MASLOW, A. H. *Motivation and Personality.* New York: Harper & Row, 1954.

MASLOW, A. H. *Toward a Psychology of Being.* New York: Van Nostrand, 1962a.

MASLOW, A. H. Notes on being-psychology. *J. humanistic Psychol.,* 1962b, 2, 47–71.

MASLOW, A. H. *Religions, Values, and Peak-Experiences.* Columbus, Ohio: Ohio State Univer. Press, 1964a.

MASLOW, A. H. & GROSS, L. Synergy in society and in the individual. *J. indiv. Psychol.,* 1964b, 20, 153–164.

MASLOW, A. H. *Eupsychian Management: A Journal.* Homewood, Illinois: Irwin-Dorsey, 1965a.

MASLOW, A. H. Criteria for judging needs to be instinctoid. In M. R. Jones (Ed.), *Human Motivation: A Symposium.* Lincoln, Nebr.: Univer. Nebr. Press, 1965b.

MASLOW, A. H. *The Psychology of Science: A Reconnaissance.* New York: Harper & Row, 1966.

MASLOW, A. H. Comments on Dr. Frankl's paper. *J. humanistic Psychol.,* 1966, 6, 107–112.

MASLOW, A. H. Neurosis as a failure of personal growth. *Humanitas,* 1967, 3, 153–169.

SCHUMACHER, E. F. Economic development and poverty. *Manas,* Feb. 15, 1967, 20, 1–8.

WEISSKOPF, W. Economic growth and human well-being. *Manas,* Aug. 21, 1963.

WOOTTON, G. *Workers, Unions and the State.* New York: Schocken, 1967.

For a more extensive bibliography, see *Toward a Psychology of Being,* by A. H. Maslow. Van Nostrand, 1968, second edition.

6

To Be and Not To Be: Contributions of
Existential Psychotherapy*

Rollo May

The fundamental contribution of existential therapy is its understanding of man as *being*. It does not deny the validity of dynamisms
and the study of specific behavior patterns in their rightful places. But
it holds that drives of dynamisms, by whatever name one calls them,
can be understood only in the context of the structure of the existence
of the person we are dealing with. The distinctive character of existential analysis is, thus, that it is concerned with *ontology,* the science of
being, and with *Dasein,* the existence of this particular being sitting
opposite the psychotherapist.

Before struggling with definitions of *being* and related terms, let us
begin existentially by reminding ourselves that what we are talking
about is an experience every sensitive therapist must have countless
times a day. It is the experience of the instantaneous encounter with
another person who comes alive to us on a very different level from
what we know *about* him. "Instantaneous" refers, of course, not to the
actual time involved but to the quality of the experience. We may
know a great deal about a patient from his case record, let us say, and
may have a fairly good idea of how other interviewers have described
him. But when the patient himself steps in, we often have a sudden,
sometimes powerful, experience of here-is-a-new-person, an experience
that normally carries with it an element of surprise, not in the sense of
perplexity or bewilderment, but in its etymological sense of being
"taken from above." This is of course in no sense a criticism of one's
colleagues' reports; for we have this experience of encounter even with

* Pp. 37–50 from EXISTENCE edited by Rollo May, Ernest Angel and Henri F. Ellen-
berger, © 1958 by Basic Books, Inc., Publishers, New York.

persons we have known or worked with for a long time.[1] The data we learned *about* the patient may have been accurate and well worth learning. But the point rather is that *the grasping of the being of the other person occurs on a quite different level from our knowledge of specific things about him.* Obviously a knowledge of the drives and mechanisms which are in operation in the other person's behavior is useful; a familiarity with his patterns of interpersonal relationships is highly relevant; information about his social conditioning, the meaning of particular gestures and symbolic actions is of course to the point, and so on *ad infinitum.* But all these fall on to a quite different level when we confront the overarching, most real fact of all—namely, the immediate, living person himself. When we find that all our voluminous knowledge about the person suddenly forms itself into a new pattern in this confrontation, the implication is not that the knowledge was wrong; it is rather that it takes its meaning, form, and significance from the reality of the person of whom these specific things are expressions. Nothing we are saying here in the slightest deprecates the importance of gathering and studying seriously all the specific data one can get about the given person. This is only common sense. But neither can one close his eyes to the experiential fact that this data forms itself into a configuration given in the encounter with the person himself. This also is illustrated by the common experience we all have had in interviewing persons; we may say we do not get a "feeling" of the other person and need to prolong the interview until the data "breaks" into its own form in our minds. We particularly do not get this "feeling" when we ourselves are hostile or resenting the relationship—that is, keeping the other person out—no matter how intellectually bright we may be at the time. This is the classical distinction between *knowing* and *knowing about.* When we seek to know a person, the knowledge *about* him must be subordinated to the overarching fact of his actual existence.

In the ancient Greek and Hebrew languages the verb "to know" is the same word as that which means "to have sexual intercourse." This is illustrated time and again in the King James translation of the

---

[1] We may have it with friends and loved ones. It is not a once-and-for-all experience; indeed, in any developing, growing relationship it may—probably should, if the relationship is vital—occur continually.

Bible—"Abraham knew his wife and she conceived . . ." and so on. Thus the etymological relation between knowing and loving is exceedingly close. Though we cannot go into this complex topic, we can at least say that knowing another human being, like loving him, involves a kind of union, a dialectical participation with the other. This Binswanger calls the "dual mode." One must have at least a readiness to love the other person, broadly speaking, if one is to be able to understand him.

The encounter with the being of another person has the power to shake one profoundly and may potentially be very anxiety-arousing. It may also be joy-creating. In either case, it has the power to grasp and move one deeply. The therapist understandably may be tempted for his own comfort to abstract himself from the encounter by thinking of the other as just a "patient" or by focusing only on certain mechanisms of behavior. But if the technical view is used dominantly in the relating to the other person, obviously one has defended himself from anxiety at the price not only of the isolation of himself from the other but also of radical distortion of reality. For one does not then really *see* the other person. It does not disparage the importance of technique to point out that technique, like data, must be subordinated to the fact of the reality of two persons in the room.

This point has been admirably made in a slightly different way by Sartre. If we "consider man," he writes, "as capable of being analyzed and reduced to original data, to determined drives (or 'desires'), supported by the subject as properties of an object," we may indeed end up with an imposing system of substances which we may then call mechanisms or dynamisms or patterns. But we find ourselves up against a dilemma. Our human being has become "a sort of indeterminate clay which would have to receive [the desires] passively— or he would be reduced to a simple bundle of these irreducible drives or tendencies. In either case the *man* disappears; we can no longer find 'the one' to whom this or that experience has happened." [2]

[2] Jean-Paul Sartre, *Being and Nothingness*, trans. by Hazel Barnes (1956), p. 561. Sartre goes on, ". . . either in looking for the *person* we encounter a useless, contradictory metaphysical substance—or else the being whom we seek vanishes in a dust of phenomena bound together by external connections. But what each of us requires in this very effort to comprehend another is that he should never resort to this idea of substance, which is inhuman because it is well this side of the human" (p. 52). Also, "If we admit

To Be and Not To Be

It is difficult enough to give definitions of "being" and *Dasein*, but our task is made doubly difficult by the fact that these terms and their connotations encounter much resistance. Some readers may feel that these words are only a new form of "mysticism" (used in its disparaging and quite inaccurate sense of "misty") and have nothing to do with science. But this attitude obviously dodges the whole issue by disparaging it. It is interesting that the term "mystic" is used in this derogatory sense to mean anything we cannot segmentize and count. The odd belief prevails in our culture that a thing or experience is not real if we cannot make it mathematical, and somehow it must be real if we can reduce it to numbers. But this means making an abstraction out of it—mathematics is the abstraction par excellence, which is indeed its glory and the reason for its great usefulness. Modern Western man thus finds himself in the strange situation, after reducing something to an abstraction, of having then to persuade himself it is real. This has much to do with the sense of isolation and loneliness which is endemic in the modern Western world; for the only experience we let ourselves believe in as real is that which precisely is not. Thus we deny the reality of our own experience. The term "mystic," in this disparaging sense, is generally used in the service of obscurantism; certainly avoiding an issue by derogation is only to obscure it. Is not the scientific attitude rather, to try to see clearly what it is we are talking about and then to find whatever terms or symbols can best, with least distortion, describe this reality? It should not so greatly surprise us to find that "being" belongs to that class of realities, like "love" and "consciousness" (for two other examples), which we cannot segmentize or abstract without losing precisely what we set out to

---

that the person is a totality, we can not hope to reconstruct him by an addition or by an organization of the diverse tendencies which we have empirically discovered in him. . . ." Every attitude of the person contains some reflection of this totality, holds Sartre. "A jealousy of a particular date in which a subject posits himself in history in relation to a certain woman, signifies for the one who knows how to interpret it, the total relation to the world by which the subject constitutes himself as a self. In other words this *empirical attitude* is by itself the expression of the 'choice of an intelligible character.' There is no mystery about this" (p. 58).

study. This does not, however, relieve us from the task of trying to understand and describe them.

A more serious source of resistance is one that runs through the whole of modern Western society—namely, the psychological need to avoid and, in some ways, repress, the whole concern with "being." In contrast to other cultures which may be very concerned with being— particularly Indian and Oriental—and other historical periods which have been so concerned, the characteristic of our period in the West, as Marcel rightly phrases it, is precisely that the awareness of "the sense of the ontological—the sense of being—is lacking. Generally speaking, modern man is in this condition; if ontological demands worry him at all, it is only dully, as an obscure impulse." [3] Marcel points out what many students have emphasized, that this loss of the sense of being is related on one hand to our tendency to subordinate existence to function: a man knows himself not as a man or self but as a ticket-seller in the subway, a grocer, a professor, a vice president of A. T. & T., or by whatever his economic function may be. And on the other hand, this loss of the sense of being is related to the mass collectivist trends and widespread conformist tendencies in our culture. Marcel then makes this trenchant challenge: *"Indeed I wonder if a psychoanalytic method, deeper and more discerning than any that has been evolved until now, would not reveal the morbid effects of the repression of this sense and of the ignoring of this need."* [4]

"As for defining the word 'being,' " Marcel goes on, "let us admit that it is extremely difficult; I would merely suggest this method of approach: being is what withstands—or what would withstand—an exhaustive analysis bearing on the data of experience and aiming to reduce them step by step to elements increasingly devoid of intrinsic or significant value. (An analysis of this kind is attempted in the theoretical works of Freud.)" [5] This last sentence I take to mean that when Freud's analysis is pushed to the ultimate extreme, and we know, let us say, everything about drives, instincts, and mechanisms,

[3] Gabriel Marcel, *The Philosophy of Existence* (1949), p. 1.

[4] *Ibid.* Italics mine. For data concerning the "morbid effects of the repression" of the sense of being, cf. Fromm, *Escape from Freedom,* and David Riesman, *The Lonely Crowd.*

[5] *Ibid.*, p. 5.

we have everything *except* being. Being is that which remains. It is that which constitutes this infinitely complex set of deterministic factors into a person *to whom* the experiences happen and who possesses some element, no matter how minute, of freedom to become aware that these forces are acting upon him. This is the sphere where he has the potential capacity to pause before reacting and thus to cast some weight on whether his reaction will go this way or that. And this, therefore, is the sphere where he, the human being, is never merely a collection of drives and determined forms of behavior.

The term the existential therapists use for the distinctive character of human existence is *Dasein*. Binswanger, Kuhn, and others designate their school as *Daseinsanalyse*. Composed of *sein* (being) plus *da* (there), *Dasein* indicates that man is the being who *is there* and implies also that he *has* a "there" in the sense that he can know he is there and can take a stand with reference to that fact. The "there" is moreover not just any place, but the particular "there" that is mine, the particular point *in time* as well as space of my existence at this given moment. Man is the being who can be conscious of, and therefore responsible for, his existence. It is this capacity to become aware of his own being which distinguishes the human being from other beings. The existential therapists think of man not only as "being-in-itself," as all beings are, but also as "being-for-itself." Binswanger and other authors in the chapters that follow speak of "*Dasein* choosing" this or that, meaning "the person-who-is-responsible-for-his-existence choosing. . . ."

The full meaning of the term "human being" will be clearer if the reader will keep in mind that "being" is a participle, a verb form implying that someone is in the process of *being something*. It is unfortunate that, when used as a general noun in English, the term "being" connotes a static substance, and when used as a particular noun such as *a* being, it is usually assumed to refer to an entity, say, such as a soldier to be counted as a unit. Rather, "being" should be understood, when used as a general noun, to mean *potentia,* the source of potentiality; "being" is the potentiality by which the acorn becomes the oak or each of us becomes what he truly is. And when used in a particular sense, such as *a* human being, it always has the dynamic connotation of someone in process, the person being something. Perhaps, therefore, *becoming* connotes more accurately the meaning of the term in this country. We can understand another human being only as we see what he is moving toward, what he is becoming; and we can know ourselves only as we "project our *potentia* in action." The significant tense for human beings is thus the *future*—that is to say, the critical question is what I am pointing toward, becoming, what I will be in the immediate future.

Thus, being in the human sense is not given once and for all. It does not unfold automatically as the oak tree does from the acorn. For an intrinsic and inseparable element in being human is self-consciousness. Man (or *Dasein*) is the particular being who has to be aware of himself, be responsible for himself, if he is to become himself. He also is that particular being who knows that at some future moment he will not be; he is the being who is always in a dialectical relation with non-being, death. And he not only knows he will sometime not be, but he can, in his own choices, slough off and forfeit his being. "To be and not to be"—the "and" in our subtitle to this section is not a typographical error—is not a choice one makes once and for all at the point of considering suicide; it reflects to some degree a choice made at every instant. The profound dialectic in the human being's awareness of his own being is pictured with incomparable beauty by Pascal:

> Man is only a reed, the feeblest reed in nature, but he is a thinking reed. There is no need for the entire universe to arm itself in order to annihilate him: a vapour, a drop of water, suffices to kill him. But were the universe to crush him, man would yet be more noble than that which slays him, because he knows that he dies, and the advantage that the universe has over him; of this the universe knows nothing.[6]

In the hope of making clearer what it means for a person to experience his own being, we shall present an illustration from a case history. This patient, an intelligent woman of twenty-eight, was especially gifted in expressing what was occurring within her. She had come for

---

[6] Pascal's *Penseés,* Gertrude B. Burfurd Rawlings, trans. and ed. (Peter Pauper Press), p. 35. Pascal goes on, "Thus all our dignity lies in thought. By thought we must raise ourselves, not by space and time, which we cannot fill. Let us strive, then, to think well, —therein is the principle of morality." It is perhaps well to remark that of course by "thought" he means not intellectualism nor technical reason but self-consciousness, the reason which also knows the reasons of the heart.

psychotherapy because of serious anxiety spells in closed places, severe self-doubts, and eruptions of rage which were sometimes uncontrollable.[7] An illegitimate child, she had been brought up by relatives in a small village in the southwestern part of the country. Her mother, in periods of anger, often reminded her as a child of her origin, recounted how she had tried to abort her, and in times of trouble had shouted at the little girl, "If you hadn't been born, we wouldn't have to go through this!" Other relatives had cried at the child, in family quarrels, "Why didn't you kill yourself?" and "You should have been choked the day you were born!" Later, as a young woman, the patient had become well-educated on her own initiative.

In the fourth month of therapy she had the following dream: "I was in a crowd of people. They had no faces; they were like shadows. It seemed like a wilderness of people. Then I saw there was someone in the crowd who had compassion for me." The next session she reported that she had had, in the intervening day, an exceedingly important experience. It is reported here as she wrote it down from memory and notes two years later.

> I remember walking that day under the elevated tracks in a slum area, feeling the thought, "I am an illegitimate child." I recall the sweat pouring forth in my anguish in trying to accept that fact. Then I understood what it must feel like to accept, "I am a Negro in the midst of privileged whites," or "I am blind in the midst of people who see." Later on that night I woke up and it came to me this way, "I accept the fact that I am an illegitimate child." *But* "I am not a child anymore." So it is, "I am illegitimate." That is not so either: "I was born illegitimate." Then what is left? What is left is this, *"I Am."* This *act* of contact and acceptance with "I am," once gotten hold of, gave me (what I think was for me the first time) the experience "Since I am, I have the right to be."
>
> What is this experience like? It is a primary feeling—it feels like receiving the deed to my house. It is the experience of my own aliveness not caring whether it turns out to be an ion or just a wave. It is like when a very young child I once reached the core of a peach and cracked the pit, not knowing what I would find and then feeling the wonder of finding the inner seed, good to eat in its bitter sweetness. . . . It is like a sailboat in the harbor being

---

[7] Since our purpose is merely to illustrate one phenomenon, namely, the experience of the sense of being, we shall not report the diagnostic or other details of the case.

given an anchor so that, being made out of earthly things, it can by means of its anchor get in touch again with the earth, the ground from which its wood grew; it can lift its anchor to sail but always at times it can cast its anchor to weather the storm or rest a little. . . . It is my saying to Descartes, *"I Am, therefore* I think, I feel, I do."

It is like an axiom in geometry—never experiencing it would be like going through a geometry course not knowing the first axiom. It is like going into my very own Garden of Eden where I am beyond good and evil and all other human concepts. It is like the experience of the poets of the intuitive world, the mystics, except that instead of the pure feeling of and union with God it is the finding of and the union with my own being. It is like owning Cinderella's shoe and looking all over the world for the foot it will fit and realizing all of a sudden that one's own foot is the only one it will fit. It is a "Matter of Fact" in the etymological sense of the expression. It is like a globe before the mountains and oceans and continents have been drawn on it. It is like a child in grammar finding the *subject* of the verb in a sentence—in this case the subject being one's own life span. It is ceasing to feel like a theory toward one's self. . . .

We shall call this the "I-am" experience.[8] This one phase of a complex case, powerfully and beautifully described above, illustrates the emergence and strengthening of the sense of being in one person. The experience is etched the more sharply in this person because of the more patent threat to her being that she had suffered as an illegitimate child and her poetic articulateness as she looked back on her experience from the vantage point of two years later. I do not believe either of these facts, however, makes her experience different in fundamental quality from what human beings in general, normal or neurotic, go through.

---

[8] Some readers will be reminded of the passage in Exodus 3:14 in which Moses, after Yahweh had appeared to him in the burning bush and charged him to free the Israelites from Egypt, demands that the God tell his name. Yahweh gives the famous answer, "I am that I am." This classical, existential sentence (the patient, incidentally, did not consciously know this sentence) carries great symbolic power because, coming from an archaic period, it has God state that *the quintessence of divinity is the power to be.* We are unable to go into the many rich meanings of this answer, nor the equally intricate translation problems, beyond pointing out that the Hebrew of the sentence can be translated as well, "I shall be what I shall be." This bears out our statement above that being is in the future tense and inseparable from becoming; God is creative *potentia,* the esssence of the power to become.

We shall make four final comments on the experience exemplified in this case. First, the "I-am" experience is not in itself the solution to a person's problems; it is rather the *precondition* for their solution. This patient spent some two years thereafter working through specific psychological problems, which she was able to do on the basis of this emerged experience of her own existence. In the broadest sense, of course, the achieving of the sense of being is a goal of all therapy, but in the more precise sense it is a relation to one's self and one's world, an experience of one's own existence (including one's own identity), which is a prerequisite for the working through of specific problems. It is, as the patient wrote, the "primary fact," a *ur* experience. It is not to be identified with any patient's discovery of his or her specific powers—when he learns, let us say, that he can paint or write or work successfully or have successful sexual intercourse. Viewed from the outside, the discovery of specific powers and the experience of one's own being may seem to go hand in hand, but the latter is the underpinning, the foundation, the psychological precondition of the former. We may well be suspicious that solutions to a person's specific problems in psychotherapy which do not presuppose this "I-am" experience in greater or lesser degree will have a pseudo quality. The new "powers" the patient discovers may well be experienced by him as merely compensatory—that is, as proofs that he is of significance despite the fact that he is certain on a deeper level that he is not, since he still lacks a basic conviction of "*I Am,* therefore I think, I act." And we could well wonder whether such compensatory solutions would not represent rather the patient's simply exchanging one defense system for another, one set of terms for another, without ever experiencing himself as existing. In the second state the patient, instead of blowing up in anger, "sublimates" or "introverts" or "relates," but still without the act being rooted in his own existence.

Our second comment is that this patient's "I-am" experience is not to be explained by the transference relationship. That the positive transference, whether directed to therapist or husband,[9] is obviously

---

[9] We omit for purposes of the above discussion the question whether this rightly should be called "transference" or simply human trust at this particular point in this case. We do not deny the validity of the concept of transference rightly defined, but it never makes sense to speak of something as "just transference," as though it were all carried over simply from the past.

present in the above case is shown in the eloquent dream the night before in which there was one person in the barren, depersonalized wilderness of the crowd who had compassion for her. True, she is showing in the dream that she could have the "I-am" experience only if she could trust some other human being. But this does not account for the experience itself. It may well be true that for any human being the possibility of acceptance by and trust for another human being is a necessary condition for the "I-am" experience. But the awareness of one's own being occurs basically on the level of the grasping of one's self; it is an experience of *Dasein,* realized in the realm of self-awareness. It is not to be explained *essentially* in social categories. The acceptance by another person, such as the therapist, shows the patient that he no longer needs to fight his main battle on the front of whether anyone else, or the world, can accept him; the acceptance *frees* him to experience his own being. This point must be emphasized because of the common error in many circles of assuming that the experience of one's own being will take place automatically if only one is accepted by somebody else. This is the basic error of some forms of "relationship therapy." The attitude of "If-I-love-and-accept-you, this-is-all-you-need," is in life and in therapy an attitude which may well minister to increased passivity. The crucial question is what the individual himself, in his own awareness of and responsibility for his existence, does with the fact that he can be accepted.

The third comment follows directly from the above, that *being* is a category which cannot be reduced to introjection of social and ethical norms. It is, to use Nietzsche's phrase, "beyond good and evil." To the extent that my sense of existence is authentic, is is precisely *not* what others have told me I should be, but is the one Archimedes point I have to stand on from which to judge what parents and other authorities demand. Indeed, *compulsive and rigid moralism arises in given persons precisely as the result of a lack of a sense of being.* Rigid moralism is a compensatory mechanism by which the individual persuades himself to take over the external sanctions because he has no fundamental assurance that his own choices have any sanction of their own. This is not to deny the vast social influences in anyone's morality, but it is to say that the ontological sense cannot be wholly reduced to such influences. The ontological sense *is not a superego* phenomenon.

By the same token the sense of being gives the person a basis for a self-esteem which is not merely the reflection of others' views about him. For if your self-esteem must rest in the long run on social validation, you have, not self-esteem, but a more sophisticated form of social conformity. It cannot be said too strongly that the sense of one's own existence, though interwoven with all kinds of social relatedness, is in basis not the product of social forces; it always presupposes *Eigenwelt,* the "own world" (a term which will be discussed below).

Our fourth comment deals with the most important consideration of all, namely that the "I-am" experience must not be identified with what is called in various circles the "functioning of the ego." That is to say, it is an error to define the emergence of awareness of one's own being as one phase of the "development of the ego." We need only reflect on what the concept of "ego" has meant in classical psychoanalytic tradition to see why this is so. The ego was traditionally conceived as a relatively weak, shadowy, passive, and derived agent, largely an epiphenomenon of other more powerful processes. It is "derived from the Id by modifications imposed on it from the external world" and is "representative of the external world." [10] "What we call the ego is essentially passive," says Groddeck, a statement which Freud cites with approval.[11] The developments in the middle period of psychoanalytic theory brought increased emphasis on the ego, to be sure, but chiefly as an aspect of the study of defense mechanisms; the ego enlarged its originally buffeted and frail realm chiefly by its negative, defensive functions. It "owes service to three masters and is consequently menaced by three dangers: the external world, the libido of the Id, the severity of the Super-ego." [12] Freud often remarked that the ego does very well indeed if it can preserve some semblance of harmony in its unruly house.

A moment's thought will show how great is the difference between this ego and the "I-am" experience, the sense of being which we have been discussing. The latter occurs on a more fundamental level and

[10] Healy, Bronner and Bowers, *The Meaning and Structure of Psychoanalysis* (1930), p. 38. We give these quotations from a standard summary from the classical middle period of psychoanalysis, not because we are not aware of refinements made to ego theory later, but because we wish to show the essence of the concept of the ego, an essence which has been elaborated but not basically changed.

[11] *Ibid.,* p. 41.   [12] *Ibid.,* p. 38.

is a precondition for ego development. The ego is a *part* of the personality, and traditionally a relatively weak part, whereas the sense of being refers to one's whole experience, unconscious as well as conscious, and is by no means merely the agent of awareness. The ego is a reflection of the outside world; the sense of being is rooted in one's own experience of existence, and if it is a mirroring of, a reflection of, the outside world alone, it is then precisely not one's own sense of existence. My sense of being is *not* my capacity to see the outside world, to size it up, to assess reality; it is rather my capacity to see myself as a being in the world, *to know myself as the being who can do these things*. It is in this sense a precondition for what is called "ego development." The ego is the *subject* in the subject-object relationship; the sense of being occurs on a level prior to this dichotomy. Being means not "I am the subject," but "I am the being who can, among other things, know himself as the subject of what is occurring." The sense of being is not in origin set against the outside world but it must include this capacity to set one's self against the external world if necessary, just as it must include the capacity to confront non-being, as we shall indicate later. To be sure, both what is called the ego and the sense of being presuppose the emergence of self-awareness in the child somewhere between the first couple of months of infancy and the age of two years, a developmental process often called the "emergence of the ego." But this does not mean these two should be identified. The ego is said normally to be especially weak in childhood, weak in proportion to the child's relatively weak assessment of and relation to reality; whereas the sense of being may be especially strong, only later to diminish as the child learns to give himself over to conformist tendencies, to experience his existence as a reflection of others' evaluation of him, to lose some of his originality and primary sense of being. Actually, the sense of being—that is, the ontological sense—is presupposed for ego development, just as it is presupposed for the solution of other problems.[13]

[13] If the objection is entered that the concept of the "ego" at least is more precise and therefore more satisfactory scientifically than this sense of being, we can only repeat what we have said above, that precision can be gained easily enough on paper. But the question always is the bridge between the concept and the reality of the person, and the scientific challenge is to find a concept, a way of understanding, which does not do violence to reality, even though it may be less precise.

We are of course aware that additions and elaborations are occurring in ego theory of late decades in the orthodox psychoanalytic tradition. But one cannot strengthen such a weak monarch by decking him with additional robes, no matter how well-woven or intricately tailored the robes may be. The real and fundamental trouble with the doctrine of the ego is that it represents, par excellence, the subject-object dichotomy in modern thought. Indeed, it is necessary to emphasize that *the very fact that the ego is conceived of as weak, passive, and derived is itself an evidence and a symptom of the loss of the sense of being in our day, a symptom of the repression of the ontological concern.* This view of the ego is a symbol of the pervasive tendency to see the human being primarily as a passive recipient of forces acting upon him, whether the forces be identified as the Id or the vast industrial juggernaut in Marxian terms or the submersion of the individual as "one among many" in the sea of conformity, in Heidegger's terms. The view of the ego as relatively weak and buffeted about by the Id was in Freud a profound symbol of the fragmentation of man in the Victorian period and also a strong corrective to the superficial voluntarism of that day. But the error arises when this ego is elaborated as the basic norm. The sense of being, the ontological awareness, must be assumed below ego theory if that theory is to refer with self-consistency to man as man.

We now come to the important problem of *non-being* or, as phrased in existential literature, *nothingness*. The "and" in the title of this section, "To Be *and* Not To Be," expresses the fact that non-being is an inseparable part of being. To grasp what it means to exist, one needs to grasp the fact that he might not exist, that he treads at every moment on the sharp edge of possible annihilation and can never escape the fact that death will arrive at some unknown moment in the future. Existence, never automatic, not only can be sloughed off and forfeited but is indeed at every instant threatened by non-being. Without this awareness of non-being—that is, awareness of the threats to one's being in death, anxiety, and the less dramatic but persistent threats of loss of potentialities in conformism—existence is vapid, unreal, and characterized by lack of concrete self-awareness. But with the confronting of non-being, existence takes on vitality and immediacy, and the individual experiences a heightened consciousness of himself, his world, and others around him.

Death is of course the most obvious form of the threat of non-being. Freud grasped this truth on one level in his symbol of the death instinct. Life forces (being) are arrayed at every moment, he held, against the forces of death (non-being), and in every individual life the latter will ultimately triumph. But Freud's concept of the death instinct is an ontological truth and should not be taken as a deteriorated psychological theory. The concept of the death instinct is an excellent example of our earlier point that Freud went beyond technical reason and tried to keep open the tragic dimension of life. His emphasis on the inevitability of hostility, aggression, and self-destructiveness in existence also, from one standpoint, has this meaning. True, he phrased these concepts wrongly, as when he interpreted the "death instinct" in chemical terms. The use of the word "thanatos" in psychoanalytic circles as parallel to libido is an example of this deteriorated phraseology. These are errors which arise from trying to put ontological truths, which death and tragedy are, into the frame of technical reason and reduce them to specific psychological mechanisms. On that basis Horney and others could logically argue that Freud was too "pessimistic" and that he merely rationalized war and aggression. I think that is a sound argument against the usual oversimplified psychoanalytic interpretations, which are in the form of technical reason; but it is not a sound argument against Freud himself, who tried to preserve a real concept of tragedy, ambivalent though his frame of reference was. He had indeed a sense of non-being, despite the fact that he always tried to subordinate it and his concept of being to technical reason.

It is also an error to see the "death instinct" only in biological terms, which would leave us hobbled with a fatalism. The unique and crucial fact, rather, is that the human being is the one who *knows* he is going to die, who anticipates his own death. The critical question thus is how he relates to the fact of death: whether he spends his existence running away from death or making a cult of repressing the recognition of death under the rationalizations of beliefs in automatic progress or providence, as is the habit of our Western society, or obscuring it by saying "one dies" and turning it into a matter of public statistics which serve to cover over the one ultimately important fact, that he himself at some unknown future moment will die.

The existential analysts, on the other hand, hold that the confronting of death gives the most positive reality to life itself. It makes the individual existence real, absolute, and concrete. For "death as an irrelative potentiality singles man out and, as it were, individualizes him to make him understand the potentiality of being in others [as well as in himself], when he realizes the inescapable nature of his own death." [14] Death is, in other words, the one fact of my life which is not relative but absolute, and my awareness of this gives my existence and what I do each hour an absolute quality.

Nor do we need to go as far as the extreme example of death to see the problem of non-being. Perhaps the most ubiquitous and ever-present form of the failure to confront non-being in our day is in *conformism,* the tendency of the individual to let himself be absorbed in the sea of collective responses and attitudes, to become swallowed up in *das Man,* with the corresponding loss of his own awareness, potentialities, and whatever characterizes him as a unique and original being. The individual temporarily escapes the anxiety of non-being by this means, but at the price of forfeiting his own powers and sense of existence.

On the positive side, the capacity to confront non-being is illustrated in the ability to accept anxiety, hostility, and aggression. By "accept" we mean here to tolerate without repression and so far as possible to utilize constructively. Severe anxiety, hostility, and aggression are

---

[14] This is an interpretation of Heidegger, given by Werner Brock in the introduction to *Existence and Being* (Regnery, 1949), p. 77. For those who are interested in the logical aspects of the problem of being vs. non-being, it may be added that the dialectic of "yes vs. no," as Tillich points out in *The Courage to Be,* is present in various forms throughout the history of thought. Hegel held that non-being was an integral part of being, specifically in the "antithesis" stage of his dialectic of "thesis, antithesis, and synthesis." The emphasis on "will" in Schilling, Schopenhauer, Nietzsche, and others as a basic ontological category is a way of showing that being has the power of "negating itself without losing itself." Tillich, giving his own conclusion, holds that the question of how being and non-being are related can be answered only metaphorically: "Being embraces both itself and non-being." In everyday terms, being embraces non-being in the sense that we can be aware of death, can accept it, can even invite it in suicide, in short, can by self-awareness encompass death.

states and ways of relating to one's self and others which would curtail or destroy being. But to preserve one's existence by running away from situations which would produce anxiety or situations of potential hostility and aggression leaves one with the vapid, weak, unreal sense of being—what Nietzsche meant in his brilliant description we quoted in the previous chapter of the "impotent people" who evade their aggression by repressing it and thereupon experience "drugged tranquillity" and free-floating resentment. Our point does not at all imply the sloughing over of the distinction between the *neurotic* and *normal* forms of anxiety, hostility, and aggression. Obviously the one constructive way to confront neurotic anxiety, hostility, and aggression is to clarify them psychotherapeutically and so far as possible to wipe them out. But that task has been made doubly difficult, and the whole problem confused, by our failure to see the normal forms of these states—"normal" in the sense that they inhere in the threat of nonbeing with which any being always has to cope. Indeed, is it not clear that *neurotic* forms of anxiety, hostility, and aggression develop precisely because the individual has been unable to accept and deal with the *normal* forms of these states and ways of behaving? Paul Tillich has suggested far-reaching implications for the therapeutic process in his powerful sentence, which we shall quote without attempting to elucidate, "The self-affirmation of a being is the stronger the more nonbeing it can take into itself."

7

The Absolute and the Relative:
Two Aspects of Dynamic Experience*

JAMES B. KLEE

I

By the absolute aspect of dynamic experience I mean the "thing-in-itself" quality which is accepted in the naive realism of everyday living. By dynamic experience I am trying to indicate that motivation, or value generally, is part of the experience itself, is intrinsic to the experience and is not superimposed by some drive or force external to the experience. Experience itself is forceful and self-driven. The emphasis, however, in this description of naive experience is not on either the objective reality of the alleged referent of experience or the subjective reality of the experiencer. This dichotomization of experience into organism and environment is legitimate only from the point of view of an external observer during the experience or before and/or after the experience relative to the experiencer. The absoluteness of experience concerns the immediacy of the dynamic experience. The experience is absolute as long as the object is not identified as such and the perceiver is not conscious of his relationship to the object as perceiver; or it is absolute as long as the relation of the simultaneousness of object and perceiver itself has become the absolute of experience. The absolute is that which Northrop calls "the immediately apprehended differentiated aesthetic continuum" with both "terms," the object and the subject, reduced to one, experience. Whatever you may

* "The Absolute and the Relative" by James B. Klee. *Darshana International,* Moradabad (India), 1964, Vol. IV, Nos. 1 & 2.

wish to call this absoluteness of dynamic experience, this statement of immediate relationship, is irrelevant. James Joyce has suggested the use of the term "epiphany" in the brief discussion of aesthetics in *Stephan Hero* and this may well be accepted because of the seemingly miraculous element in all experience. The point remains that recognition must be given to this existential consciousness. Of all that which from a relativistic aspect could have been the particular relationships of organism and environment, only the only experience did in fact occur and that is the given, that is the condition of existence and for good or bad you're stuck with it. Perhaps the thinker could have had other thoughts and perhaps other contents were available yet the particular thought as the combination of specific thinker and content was absolute and irrevocable. The particular experience experienced, the experiencer goes on from there.

This absoluteness of immediate apprehension, or the epiphany of aesthetic reality, this dynamic experience in itself is easy to recognize in one's response to inventions, scientific discoveries, moral statements (categorical imperatives), political or economic principles, historical events, the act of love, and to works of art, for these have a discreteness, a "standing alone" quality which frequently tends to prevent comparisons or other types of relational activity with other areas of experience. In a sense no continuum or choice scale is immediately recognized. These events have the arresting and numbing quality of a thorough seduction. For the moment, the individual is captivated and encapsulated from all the rest of the world. He becomes selfless and seems to exist neither in time or space for indeed such questions about subject or object, time or space, are not likely to arise. He is the experience and vice versa, and seems to move in a relatively effortless way towards—satiation. This is most frequently called the aesthetic experience. And yet it is but an aspect of the whole of experience and as such can be treated as noncorrelative. It is but one factor in the matrix of experience, a factor which enables the uniqueness of each experience, a moment of the exact time and space which makes the past past and the object always that object, the subject always that subject, and no other. Such is the dimension in which all experience is discrete, unique, and limited in time and space. By such is meant the absolute.

II

If art helps us to define the absolute, so madness brings us to a closer understanding of the relative. For whereas we sometimes can accept the aesthetic, the immediacy of the work of art, we fight acceptance of the products of the deluded and call it madness. We say no to the possessions, the compulsions, the hallucinations. We deny their uniqueness, their absoluteness and immediacy, and place them in relation to something that can be accepted. We say these are the products of diseased minds, of sick brains and glands, of distorting heat waves, of propaganda and suggestion, or drugs and poisons, of the experience of frustration, conflict, and trauma. For these other categories are acceptable. The unacceptable is thus related to the sick organism, to the false culture, to the disproportionate environment: we feel safe once again. And we may be at that, sometimes. For in the relational dimension there is mobility, change, and the chance to choose. One is not captivated entirely; one can compare, discriminate, and select. It is possible to move from or toward, increase or decrease one over the other. Then there is the chance to get out of trouble or into still more. There is freedom to the $n - 1$ absolutes available within the perspective allowed. One has gone from the principle of pleasure to the principle of reality; but when no choice continuum is offered, when there are no degrees of freedom, then one is frustrated in that dimension. We may try to fight as long as there is some dimly sensed hope, but when that too disappears that dimension is dead for us and we are left just a little less alive.

Of course for him who is "adjusted" to his madness, who accepts his mission, who no longer questions his lot, the same epiphanous structure of experience is evident as in the case of the experience called aesthetic. There is no need to distinguish between abnormality in the absolute dimension of experience. The madman like the priest accepts his calling. In fact it is not unusual for the inventive genius to claim the voice of God as the only authority. For the new absolute is not derivative, has no ultimate sanction beyond its being, its epiphany. Each individual, including the reader, must refer to his own insight for an ostensive definition.

To some extent experience in madness and aesthetic experience differ only as a matter of taste. There is no difference that cannot be questioned. Each may be accepted for itself and that is the point. It is only in so far as we see that each leads to consequences of different value to us that any distinction between the two may be noticed. Madness too frequently is self-limiting, and as such defeats its protective function by ultimately removing or devaluating that which it would protect. The question which madness does not answer or answers but poorly is: "Madness, then what?" In fact any inability to answer the question: "Then what?" is revealing of madness; to the degree that the answer evades this question, to that degree there is madness.

That is the only test of the abnormal. The normal epiphany of experience is, like most science and art, open ended. Growth may still occur, selection take place, change be accepted with grace and interest. Life can expand in depth and scope, in richness of action and experience. The completion of one leads to the opening of the next, not to boredom, self-destruction, or fear. Theoretically, if the paths chosen were completely normal, there should be no termination to life. Even at present there is usually continuity of life on into the future somewhere of some species. And that life can be called normal, the healthy life. No, it is not in the absolute dimension that the difference between normal and abnormal lies. It is only in the relative dimension that such a consideration gains significance. Then why do we continue to make the mistake of judging the absolute as good and bad, healthy and diseased, normal and abnormal? I do not know entirely the probable answer to this but the fact is that we do confuse these and I would like to point to a few crucial areas where this confusion causes no end of needless suffering to those so misinformed. This includes all of us.

III

Actually a good part of the difficulty starts in the confusions relating to the nature and scope of one's own experience and particularly as it is extended to the interpretation of one's relation to others. This is especially obvious when one is in an authoritative relation to another as expert, leader, or parent. True, good and evil exists for us in our pain and misery, joy and exaltation. Yet the thing-in-itself is not good or bad but only in its relationships. Any one thing is sometimes good and sometimes evil and only the extremely misexperienced can ultimately fail to see this. Very recently some things like love were good, others like sex were bad. Yet how can this be if one is of the other? We admired the highly motivated but despised the over emotional yet the intense disregard of emotion is nothing but the negative aspect of high motivation. To do any one thing intensively is for that time to neglect and obviate all other values. Too often we developed pairs of names to designate the good and bad aspects of a thing separately, yet failed to realize we were but naming the same thing twice instead of the different relationships which were the actual basis of the differentiations. The epiphanous experience in and of itself is always ambivalent. Only the context enables the discrimination of its relative values. The psychoanalyst has long been aware of this ambivalence and of course it has been long recognized as the "golden mean," "tao," or "way."

From birth, and possibly from even before, such choices are apparent and are usually mishandled by those in the dominant political (power) relationship to the developing individual. For the authority in attempting to choose for someone else sets up rules or lists by which to ease this task for himself. No longer can he permit others the exercise of taste for obviously his tastes are his own and not the others'. An authority then, if *he* is to control the actions of others, must resort to standards and external sanctions. Only in this way can he maintain *his* special privilege. And yet if dynamic experience or taste is the basis of choice how mad he must be to think he can in any way choose for another. Because of his often superhuman sense of power and its complement of obligation he feels it his responsibility, which, of course it would be if he were omniscient. Yet does not the parent think he knows better in relation to the child, the child to the dog, the teacher to the student, the lawyer to his client, the doctor to his patient, the governor to his people, the priest to his parish? The superior, the expert, because it is what he knows is his own absolute experience is misled to believe it is all that is to be known and so offers a rule, a list of sanctions and values. And because the recipient is likely to be unaware of such origins in the absolutes and relationships in the experience of the authority, he can only apply the rules to the thing and so probably is doubly mistaken and confused.

The last statement is somewhat misleading for the submitter does not experience the list or rule of things entirely without relationships. In fact, the matter is far worse than one might suspect. The additional trouble lies in that there is always and very definitely a relationship but it is to the authority and not to the situation that the relationship is established. To borrow from Norbert Wiener (out of Heisenberg) the concept of the "evil eye," the authority by trying to establish an experience of relationships to some situation succeeds only in establishing it to himself. But when asked for what he has done this he will usually deny that was his intent and answer instead that he was trying for the development of independent and responsible experience in the existence of the other. As such, all authority is truly mad. At best the expert, the individual, who, because of more experience has some advantage, can only lead by example and guidance and not by command and instruction if both of these dilemmas are to be circumvented.

Specific examples of this type of difficulty are extremely easy to find for they are most of our life. The mother who is anxious for the welfare of her newly born child prevents it from putting strange objects in its mouth for fear of contaminative results to the infant. She has just established that habit when the time for weaning arrives and she must now cope with a child which rejects what is for it, the "bad" strange objects, its new solid food. Simultaneously this rejection of what was learned to be avoided incurs the loss of his mother's affections for which the avoidance relationship has been established in the first place. He soon ceases to trust the evidence of his senses and in his turn seeks signs of eternal truth instead of reliable knowledge. Again strictures regarding sexuality, especially for females, cause them to abhor the act for the first third of their existence but then they discover after receiving the ring that it takes the next third of existence to overcome this former set of values so what formerly was bad is now good. No wonder that so many reach the menopause thoroughly confused. The student in submitting to "basic disciplines" soon abandons thinking about the subject matter of the discipline and instead thinks primarily of how to please his superior, the teacher. And since his own original work is likely to be highly unbasic or individual and not in strict conformity with the "basic discipline" he too ceases to trust in his own experience and seeks sanctions in a white coat, collar, or skin color. Yet when out of school he discovers that he must learn to choose for himself. We can only pray he hasn't learned the original lesson too well. Of course one could continue to develop food aversions, frigidity, or slavish professionalism instead of fighting through the handicap. Such individuals are frequently comfortable in their selves even though to others they are dull and a threat to the freedom of everyone. It is possible to let the ambivalent remain bad always or good always. One *can* place the blame or praise elsewhere and so not have to choose now one way now another according to the relative circumstances. I just suggest that since choice is *possible,* and if we wish to have a democratic society with a self-choosing and responsible people, we can do much to make such choosing *probable.* We do not *have to* give in to totalitarian measures. They are not necessary.

IV

On the more intimate level of the belief in one's own experiences the same sorts of consideration apply. Actually of course one need not apply principles to experience since, as experience is unique—"solid," discrete, or absolute—principle or form can be found to be intrinsic to it in the first place. It is this of which I speak.

The individual accepts or rejects his own immediate experience to the degree that he is able to reject or accept the declarations of authority. This is particularly noticeable in the case where the two may be found to conflict. Perhaps such conflict does not exist in the vast majority of cases. This may even be the case for most of us a good part of the time. After all, we all eat much the same food (if given the chance), we all sleep, drink, etc. It may even seem at first that to give up total totalitarian control of our more dependable experiences, just to make room for the vagaries of a few individuals or our own rare contradictory experiences, may be too great a price for the immediate security which the totalistic system apparently would offer. The anxiety which at first glance seems to be the alternative may easily spur the defeated individual to re-establish a security system far worse than the one so hesitantly left behind. And the despair following defeat certainly seems horrible at first. Such anxiety, the "dizziness of freedom" as Kierkegaard put it, should never be underestimated. Anxiety is always the first payment towards the price of freedom. Yet the longer the first step is postponed the more difficult it may appear to be to take it. And the main point is overlooked, anyway. If such motives or dynamic experiences (anger, eating, love) are so dependable in the first place, would it not be wiser to recognize that it is not necessary to insist upon them? Can we not see that they will so likely insure themselves that any systematic organization can be developed democratically and need not be imposed from above? The stupidity and madness of totalitarian discipline lie in the fact that in the hysterical haste to regulate and constantify life one loses sight of the truth that life contains in itself sufficient limitation and self-discipline as to obviate the need for regulation if given half a chance. Life itself is its own discipline, contains its own order, is self-regulating. More order in and of itself within the life structure is unnecessary.

Perhaps the story is apocryphal, but an acquaintance once said he came across Mondrian in the Metropolitan Museum of Art, seated before a Breughel making sketches for one of his "compositions." In the Breughel could be seen the order he was abstracting. But it could not have been the other way. What is necessary is to expand and enrich living, to bring more into the scope of living. This will not occur if we deliberately cut off the paths to the future by distracting attention to the internal disorder which is disordered only by our misunderstandings and fear and by the unconsidered vagaries of existence which have induced or elicited it. Actually the cues to further internal order are outside the system and these can only be found by continual expansion, not by involution and contraction. Creativity and invention, although they restructure the experience at hand, do so only because of the additional experience of other sorts which create new contexts and dimensions of experience. They do not come from more of the same for all that provides are the permutations and combinations of what one already has. In the latter case the need for *creativity* is obviated. If what one had at hand solved one's problems entirely one would have no problems to begin with. The staticity, the balance, the homeostasis, the ordered discipline sought under authoritarian ideals is found only in the unperpetuating machine. As such it is regular and trustworthy provided it is well maintained. But it is insufficient in the long run, leading only to the boredom of self-imposed impoverishment and to the destruction caused by one's own excess of timidity.

V

As a matter of fact it would seem that wherever ambivalence or conflict arises within a problem it can only be solved by reference to at least a third point of reference. Just as a plane needs to be fixed in space by at least one more point than the two necessary to a line, so any complementary schism needs an additional referent in order to avert mutual destruction. This has usually been popularly recognized in any situation where civil warfare threatens in either the individual or social dimension. It frequently takes an external enemy to bring the individual together with himself, to reunite the quarreling family, to bring the nation together, to restructure the idea. However, it is not necessary that the "third force" be negative and threatening; a common goal can unite the split group or individual. And in fact that is the essential aspect even under negative pressure. For in the latter case, unless there were a place to which or a way in which they could go together, pressure in and of itself need only have a purely chance result. It would even seem that only by a third external factor can any problem, insolvable within the stated limits, be solved. Every trick puzzle bears this out as do all the psychological experimentations on "direction" in thinking. Once a split has occurred into mutual or complementary oppositions, reconciliation must always be through re-organization via the mediation of at least a third factor. Besides, if this were not so, there could be no division or differentiation in the first place. For as indicated above it is the contexts that enable discrimination and for a context to exist there must be at least one more absolute than the thing contexted to provide the relationship.

But what is more, the neglect of the self-regulation of living structures is not dissipated entirely unless the authoritarian control is ab-

solute and perfect. Usually the ignored capacities find enough nourish-
ment on their own to continue independently. The remaining viability
is amazingly tough and is likely to fight back as Toynbee's internal
proletariat or Freud's unconscious "id" well suggest. As such psychoanalysts as Wilhelm Reich and Carl Jung and the other scientists who
have a sense of the continuity of things and their expansive evolution
and development have pointed out, the chaos and lack of discipline
of which we are most afraid and confronting which we are most
anxious and insecure we have ourselves created. For it is but complementary to the restrictive discipline we have attempted to impose. In
a sense, whenever one makes a thing disproportionately some one definite thing, one also creates its opposite through neglect or repression.
One creates one's own nemesis in dialectical fashion. Only by a grasp of
the thing in its entirety can one go on from there. Otherwise one remains in a state of internecine warfare, which will bring either the
group or the individual to its own destruction long before its time. In
our fear of burning the candle at both ends we burn it in the middle
and thus fall apart the sooner.

I do not intend that this has to be of *necessity* in some mystical
fashion for that would be as dogmatically limiting as the tendencies
to which this argument is offered in opposition. The "failure of nerve,"
the neurotic hesitancy, the search for perfection of experience before
action is equally as destructive and for the same reasons. Rather the
whole evidence of evolution is suggestive of the fact that the complementary, that which is left out in the plans of the present, usually
finds reinforcement somewhere or it would not be extant in the first
place. One would not have neurosis if the things fought against were
not sufficiently nourished by one's environment to enable their viability.
There would not be the anguish of frustration and the conflict within
the individual, the misery of civil warfare between the peoples of a
state or states, or the waste of warfare of mankind against the other
creatures of his environment, if the opposition were not in some
measure in and of itself successful and valuable.

If we were perfect, if we had the exclusive solution, there would be
no anxiety, no doubt, no disease. But in fact there has always been
something else left to be desired and in an expanding universe one

would have to have colossal conceit, superhuman knowledge and experience, to ever not feel that something remains unexplored in this universe. Every art, every science, every system has at one time or another found itself unnecessarily limited by its own conceit and has admitted its humility or has perished. This is as much a fact of experience as any "hard fact" in any field of endeavor. There is little reason to believe that this state of affairs will ever change.

And the recognition of this is in experience itself. Sometimes we deny those murmurings of things to come which are before, nay in and of our eyes. Yet these are in our experience as absolute as that which we do accept, that which we do affirm. As we throw off the totalistic and authoritarian aspects of our experience these new items emerge, not because they are newly created but because they were there all along and have for reasons relating to their evolution only now reached sufficient proportions to be taken cognizance of. Or perhaps we have lost fear of the earlier contents of experience by acceptance of their implicit organization, we have been liberated for what we had potential in us all along. Within the potentially expanding experience of the individual is all that he *can* use, all that he could use to regulate *his* life and set an example in the experience of others. That all that he may need is not *in* his own experience at a particular absolute moment is the tragedy of existence, is the source of his forlornness, his loneliness, his anguish and despair. Yet, to believe that another's experience can do it for him is to deny his own experience, is only to lead to an acceleration of his own destruction and that of the others, too.

REFERENCES

Klee, J. B. *Problems of Selective Behavior.* University of Nebraska, 1951.

Klee, J. B. Religion as facing forward in-time. *Existential Inquiries,* 1960, Vol. 1, No. 2, pp. 19–32.

Klee, J. B., and H. G. Schrickel. Prolegomena to a psychology of signs: I. The symbolistic revolution. *Psychologia,* 1963, 6, 193–206.

8

*A Theoretical Model for Personality Studies**

Andras Angyal

In this paper I shall present a particular model which I have advocated previously for the formulation of a theory of personality, reformulating certain aspects of this theoretical orientation and illustrating my points with pertinent examples taken mainly from the field of psychotherapeutic theory and practice.

Personality may be described most adequately when looked upon as a unified dynamic organization—dynamic, because the most significant fact about a human being is not so much his static aspect as his constituting a specific *process:* the life of the individual. This process, the life of the person, is an organized, patterned process, a Gestalt, an organization. A true organization presupposes an organizing principle, a unifying pattern. All part processes obtain their specific meaning or specific function from this unifying over-all pattern. Therefore it seems plausible that a tentative phrasing of the nature of this total pattern—the broad pattern of human life—may serve as an adequate model for the formulation of the problems pertaining to the study of personality.

The over-all pattern of personality function can be described from two different vantage points. Viewed from one of these vantage points, the human being seems to be striving basically to assert and to expand his self-determination. He is an autonomous being, a self-governing entity that asserts itself actively instead of reacting passively like a physical body to the impacts of the surrounding world. This fundamental tendency expresses itself in a striving of the person

* From Andras Angyal, A theoretical model for personality studies, *Journal of Personality,* Vol. 20, September 1951, pp. 131–135. Reprinted with permission of Duke University Press.

to consolidate and increase his self-government, in other words to exercise his freedom and to organize the relevant items of his world out of the autonomous center of government that is his self. This tendency—which I have termed "the trend toward increased autonomy"—expresses itself in spontaneity, self-assertiveness, striving for freedom and for mastery. In an objective fashion this tendency can be described as follows: the human being is an autonomous unity that, acting upon the surrounding world, molds and modifies it. His life is a resultant of self-determination on the one hand and the impacts of the surrounding world, the situation, on the other. This basic tendency, the trend toward increased autonomy, expresses the person's striving from a state of lesser self-determination (and greater situational influence) to a state of greater self-determination (and lesser situational influence).

Seen from another vantage point, human life reveals a very different basic pattern from the one described above. From this point of view the person appears to seek a place for himself in a larger unit of which he strives to become a part. In the first tendency we see him struggling for centrality in his world, trying to mold, to organize, the objects and the events of his world, to bring them under his own jurisdiction and government. In the second tendency he seems rather to strive to surrender himself willingly to seek a home for himself in and *to become an organic part of something that he conceives as greater than himself*. The superindividual unit of which one feels oneself a part, or wishes to become a part, may be variously formulated according to one's cultural background and personal understanding. The superordinate whole may be represented for a person by a social unit—family, clan, nation—by a cause, by an ideology, or by a meaningfully ordered universe. In the realm of aesthetic, social, and moral attitudes this basic human tendency has a central significance. Its clearest manifestation, however, is in the religious attitude and religious experience.

I wish to state with emphasis that I am not speaking here about a tendency which is an exclusive prerogative of some people only, e.g., of those with a particular religious bent or aesthetic sensitivity, but of a tendency that I conceive as a universal and basic characteristic in all human beings.

These two tendencies of the human being, the tendency to increase his self-determination in his expanding personal world, and the tendency to surrender himself willingly to a superordinate whole, can be summed up by saying that the human being comports himself *as if he were a whole of an intermediate order.* By this I mean a "part-Gestalt" like, for example, the cardiovascular system, or the central nervous system, each of which is a *whole,* an organization of many parts, but at the same time a *part* with regard to its superordinate whole, the body. The human being is both a *unifier,* an organizer of his immediate personal world, and a *participant* in what he conceives as the superordinate whole to which he belongs.

The basic human attitude that makes man behave as a part of a larger whole reflects itself also in his "horizontal relationships," that is in his relationship to the other "parts," to other persons. Were man's behavior determined exclusively by his urge for mastery, his attitude toward others could be only as toward means to his ends. Experiencing others as coparticipants in a larger whole brings, however, another facet of his nature into manifestation. To avoid the coining of some outlandish term, we call this basic relation "love." In common usage this word has been badly misused to denote not only cheap sentimentality but even relationships that are actually founded on exploitation, possessiveness, helplessness, and similar destructive attitudes. The basic nature of love consists in a recognition of the *value* and acceptance of the *otherness* of the loved "object" while at the same time one experiences an essential *sameness* that exists between oneself and what one loves.

To recognize and to accept the otherness of a person means to respect him as a valuable being in his own right, in his independence. This attitude is incongruous with any idea of possessiveness or any tendency to use him as means to an end, be this in the form of exploitation, domination, possessiveness, or some other attitude. In other words, it is incongruous with the nature of love to try to reduce the loved person to "an item in one's personal world," or to try to make him comply with one's demands, or to try to exert power over him in whatever way. Love has to be recognized as a basic human attitude which is quite distinct from and irreducible to man's self-assertive tendencies.

The recognition and acceptance of the otherness of the person implies, furthermore, an *understanding* of him. There can be no real love without understanding of the other person, only some sort of deceptive feeling based on an illusion. One does not recognize the otherness of a person as a reality by projecting into him one's fantasies, however flattering they may be. And when one sees in a person one's mother or father or anyone else, one ignores the person as he really is. In the last analysis this is a fundamental disregard for and destructive attitude toward the other person. The understanding of the other person—as we are now using this expression—is not some sort of shrewd "practical psychology" which has a keen eye for the weakness of people, but a deep perception of the core, of the essential nature of the other person. In love this essential nature of the other person is experienced as a value, as something that is very dear to one. Love is not "blind" but visionary: it sees into the very heart of its object, and sees the "real self" behind and in the midst of the frailties and shortcomings of the person.

Love has a second basic component which is complementary to respect for the otherness of its object: the experience of a certain fundamental belongingness and *sameness* between lover and the loved. Experientially, this is not "identification," that is, an identity that is more or less artificially created, but an existing identity that is *acknowledged*. Man behaves in certain fundamental respects *as if* he were a part, a shareholder in some kind of superordinate unit, in some kind of commonwealth. When two persons love one another they clearly or dimly have the feeling that something greater is involved therein than their limited individualities, that they are one in something greater than themselves or, as the religious person says, they are "one in God." [1]

Without such an implicit orientation all interests of a person would be centered in himself alone as an individual. He, as an isolated entity, would be facing an alien world and his reaching beyond himself would be only to possess, master, and govern the surrounding world. He

---

[1] This statement does not have to be understood in a theological sense. In this context it is not our concern, e.g., whether or not the "superordinate whole" is reality or not; we state only that man appears to function *as if* he were or would experience himself as a part of a superordinate whole.

would compete with other people or he would calculatingly cooperate with them, but he would not love them. In order to love, it is essential that a man come out of his shell, that he transcend his individuality, that he "lose himself." Somehow this self-abandonment is the precondition to a broadened existence in loving. One rejoices in the characteristic ways, in the real being, beyond the surface of pretense, of the other; one suffers in the other's misfortunes and in his misdeeds: therein one gains a whole new life with its joys and sorrows. One is enriched through a vital participation in another life without wanting, however, to possess the other person. The significant truth is expressed in the paradox that the one "who loses his life [of isolation], will gain it [in a broadened existence]." The paradox is resolved by recognizing that man functions as a part of a large whole. He has a life as a part—and that is all he has, as long as he remains in his self-enclosure. But it is possible for him to have a greater life, the life of the whole, as it is manifested in himself, in the other "parts," and in the totality.

I have described the over-all pattern of personality functioning as a two-directional orientation: *self-determination* on the one hand and *self-surrender* on the other. The first is the adequate attitude toward the items within one's individual world, the second, toward the greater whole toward which one behaves as a part. A particularly important aspect of this second orientation is the "horizontal" relatedness of the parts to other parts within the whole. I spoke in some detail of love because I believe—largely in agreement with current clinical views—that this is the crux of the entire problem of personality and of interpersonal relationships.

Actual samples of behavior, however, cannot be ascribed exclusively to one or the other orientation. It is only in the counterfeit, the unhealthy, behavior that one or the other of these basic orientations is partially obliterated; in a well-integrated person the behavioral items always manifest both orientations in varying degrees. Instead of conflicting, the two orientations complement each other. As in the tendency toward increased autonomy, one strives to master and govern the environment, one discovers that one cannot do this effectively by direct application of force, by sheer violence, but can do it by obedience, understanding, and respect for the laws of the environment—

attitudes that in some way are similar to those of loving relationships. Similarly, bringing one's best to a loving relationship requires not only capacity for self-surrender but also a degree of proficient mastery of one's world, resourcefulness, and self-reliance, without which the relationship is in danger of deteriorating into helpless dependency, exploitation, possessiveness, etc.

REFERENCES

ANGYAL, A. *Foundations for a Science of Personality*. Commonwealth Fund, 1941.

ANGYAL, A. *Neurosis and Treatment: A Holistic Theory*. Wiley, 1965.

9

The Psychology of the Scientist*

ANNE ROE

Science is the creation of scientists, and every scientific advance bears somehow the mark of the man who made it. The artist exposes himself in his work; the scientist seems rather to hide in his, but he is there. Surely the historian of science must understand the man if he is fully to understand the progress of science, and he must have some comprehension of the science if he is to understand the men who make it.

The general *public* image of the scientist has not been and indeed is not now a flattering one, and at best it certainly is not an endearing one. Characterizations of scientists almost always emphasize the objectivity of their work and describe their cold, detached, impassive, unconcerned observation of phenomena which have no emotional meaning for them. This could hardly be further from the truth. The scientist as a person is a nonparticipating observer in only a very limited sense. He does not *interact* with what he is observing, but he does participate as a person. It is, perhaps, this fact—that the scientist does not expect, indeed does not want, the things that he is concerned with to be equally concerned with him—that has given others this impression of coldness, remoteness, and objectivity. (The social scientist is in a remarkably difficult position since the "objects with which he is concerned" are people, and both they and he may be more than a little ambivalent about this matter of interaction. But this is a special problem which I will by-pass here, noting only that in many ways the social scientist differs from the natural scientist in terms of personality and motivations.)

* Anne Roe, The psychology of the scientist. *Science,* Vol. 134, pp. 456–459. 18 August 1961. Copyright 1961 by the American Association for the Advancement of Science.

The truth of the matter is that the creative scientist, whatever his field, is very deeply involved emotionally and personally in his work, and that he himself is his own most essential tool. We must consider both the subjectivity of science and what kinds of people scientists are.

The Personal Factor

But first we must consider the processes of science. Suppose we take the scientist at the time when he has asked a question, or has set up a hypothesis which he wants to test. *He* must decide what observations to make. It is simply not possible to observe everything that goes on under a given set of conditions: he must choose what to observe, what measurements to make, how fine these measurements are to be, now to record them. These choices are never dictated entirely by the question or hypothesis (and anyway, that too bears his own particular stamp). One has only to consider how differently several of his colleagues would go about testing the same hypothesis to see that personal choice enters in here.

But this is just the beginning. Having decided what is to be observed, and having set up the techniques for observing, the scientist comes to the point of making the actual observations, and of recording these observations. All the complex apparatus of modern science is only a means of extending the range of man's sensory and perceptual capacities, and all the information derived through such extensions must eventually be reduced to some form in which man, with his biological limitations, can receive it. Here, too, in spite of all precautions and in spite of complete honesty, the personal factor enters in. The records of two observers will not dovetail exactly, even when they read figures from a dial. Errors may creep in, and the direction of the error is more likely than not to be associated with the observer's interest in how the findings come out. Perhaps the clearest evidence on this point comes from research on extrasensory perception. A scientist who is deeply committed to a hypothesis is well advised to have a neutral observer if the import of an observation is immediately apparent. Often, of course, such errors are minor, but they can be important, not only to the immediate problem but to society. I have wondered to what extent the disparity in figures on radioactive fallout may reflect such factors. Very few scientists, including psychologists, who have demonstrated selective perception as a laboratory exercise, take account of the phenomenon in their own work.

Once the observations are recorded, other questions are asked: When is the evidence sufficient to be conclusive, one way or the other? How important are discrepancies? What degree of generalization is permissible? Here, again, we may expect personally slanted answers. Taxonomy offers a very clear illustration of the effect of personality: One biologist may classify a given set of specimens into a few species, and another may classify them into many species. Whether the specimens are seen as representing a few or many groups depends largely on whether one looks for similarities or for differences, on whether one looks at the forest or the trees. A "lumper" may honestly find it impossible to understand how a "splitter" arrives at such an obviously incorrect solution, and vice versa. Such differences cannot be resolved by appeal to the "facts"—there are no facts which cannot be perceived in different ways. This is not to say that the facts are necessarily distorted. The problem of the criterion exists in all science, although some scientists are more aware of it than others.

The matter of personal commitment to a hypothesis is one that deserves more consideration than it usually receives. Any man who has gone through the emotional process of developing a new idea, of constructing a new hypothesis, is to some extent, and usually to a large extent, committed to that hypothesis in a very real sense. It is his baby. It is as much his creation as a painting is the personal creation of the painter. True, in the long run it stands or falls, is accepted or rejected, on its own merits, but its creator has a personal stake in it. The scientist has more at stake than the artist, for data which may support or invalidate his hypothesis are in the public domain in a sense in which art criticism never is. It may even be because of this that scientists customarily check their hypotheses as far as they can before they state them publicly. And, indeed, the experienced scientist continues to check, hoping that if errors are to be found, it will be he who finds them, so that he will have a chance to make revisions, or even to discard the hypothesis, should that prove necessary. He finds it less difficult to discard his hypothesis if, in his efforts at checking, he has been able to come up with another one.

The extent of personal commitment to a hypothesis is a prominent factor in the historical interplay between scientists. The degree of this commitment varies in an individual with different hypotheses, and varies between individuals. One very important factor here is the scientist's productivity. If he has many new ideas he will be less disturbed (and less defensive) if one fails to pan out. If he has very few ideas, an error is much harder to take, and there are many historical instances of errors which the author of the idea has never been able to see himself. I think many scientists are genuinely unaware of the extent, or even of the fact, of this personal involvement, and themselves accept the myth of impersonal objectivity. This is really very unfortunate. It is true that only a man who is passionately involved in his work is likely to make important contributions, but the committed man who knows he is committed and can come to terms with this fact has a good chance of getting beyond his commitment and of learning how to disassociate himself from his idea when this is necessary. There is little in the traditional education of scientists to prepare them for this necessity, and there are many who are still unaware of it. The extent of a scientist's personal involvement in a theory can now be a matter of grave public concern. Scientists who become advisers on political or other policy have an extraordinarily heavy responsibility for achieving some detachment from their own theories. How many of them realize this?

But once one hypothesis is found acceptable, this is not the end of it. One hypothesis inevitably leads to another; answering one question makes it possible to ask other, hopefully more precise ones. And so a new hypothesis or a new theory is offered. How is this new theory arrived at? This is one expression of the creative process, and it is a completely personal process. It is personal regardless of whether one or more individuals is involved, for in every advance made by a group, the person contributing at the moment has had to assimilate the contributions of the others and order them in his own personal way.

The Creative Process

There have been many millions of words written about the creative process, few of them very illuminating. The reason is not hard to find. The process is intimate and personal and characteristically takes place not at the level of full consciousness but at subconscious or preconscious levels. It has been inaccessible to study largely because we have not yet found any means for controlling it. Many effective scientists and artists have learned a few techniques which may reduce interference with it, but no one to my knowledge has discovered any means by which he can set it in motion at will.

It is probable that the fundamentals of the creative process are the same in all fields, but in those fields in which an advance in knowledge is sought, there is an additional requirement—or rather, one requirement receives particular emphasis. This is the need for a large store of knowledge and experience. The broader the scientist's experience and the more extensive his stock of knowledge, the greater the possibility of a real breakthrough.

The creative process involves a scanning or searching through stocks of stored memories. There seems to be a rather sharp limit to the possibility of very significant advance through voluntary, logical scanning of these stores. For one thing, they vary enormously in their accessibility to conscious recall and in the specificity of their connections, so that reliance upon conscious, orderly, logical thinking is not likely to produce many results at this stage, however essential such procedures become later in vertification. This scanning is typically for patterns and complex associations rather than for isolated units. It may be, however, that a small unit acts as a sort of key to a pattern. What seems to happen, in creative efforts in science as well in every other field, is that the individual enters a state in which logical thinking is submerged and in which thought is prelogical. Such thought is described as random largely because it typically tries seemingly illogical and distantly related materials, and it often makes major advances in just this way. It is not fully random, however, because it is goal-directed and because even in this preconscious work there is appropriate selection and rejection of available connections. This stage of the creative process is accompanied by generally confused or vague states of preoccupation of varying degrees of depth; it is well described as "stewing." It is this stage which apparently cannot be hurried or controlled.

Although termination of this stage (finding a solution, or "getting insight," as it is often called) quite frequently occurs in a moment of dispersed attention, it apparently does not help to induce a state of dispersed attention in the hope of provoking a quicker end to the process. It should be added that, while insights do frequently occur "in a flash," they need not do so, and that the process is the same whether or not the insight turns out to have validity.

To acquire the necessary store of knowledge requires long and difficult application, and as science advances, the amount of information to be assimilated becomes greater and greater, despite increasing generalization in the organizing of the data. Obviously, as more experience is stored and as the interconnections become better established and more numerous, the scanning becomes more effective. Such interconnections develop more and more readily as the process of acquiring experience takes on significance in the light of theory. This process requires not only the basic capacity to assimilate experiences but very strong motivation to persist in the effort. Strong motivation is also required if one is to continue with a search which may for a long time be unproductive. Motivation of this kind and strength derives from the needs and structure of the personality. Its sources are rarely obvious, although they can sometimes be traced. They do not necessarily derive from "neurotic problems," although they frequently do. It is no cause for dismay when they do. The ability of the human being to find in a personal problem motivation for a search for truth is one of the major accomplishments of the species.

If past experiences have brought about a compartmentalization of the storage areas, so that some portions are partially or wholly inaccessible, obviously the scientist is limited in his search. Compartmentalization of particular areas may result from personal experiences of a sort that lead to neurotic structures generally, or it may result from specific cultural restrictions, such as political or religious indoctrination. The extent to which such indoctrination will inhibit creative effort, however, depends upon how close the inaccessible areas are in content to the problems at issue. We have fairly conclusive evidence that political indoctrination need not interfere with inquiry into mathematical and physical science. Religious indoctrination can interfere strongly at any point, as history has documented very fully for us. The conclusion is no different from the basic principle of therapy: the more areas of experience there are accessible to conscious and preconscious thought, the better are the prospects for creativity.

Once an apparent answer to the scientist's question has been found, there is still a long process of pursuing and checking to be gone through. Not every man who can produce new ideas is also good at the business of checking them, and of course the reverse is also true. It is in the utilization of such personal differences as these that a "team approach" can make sense.

The Creative Scientist

This, then, is a brief review of what little we know of the process of creation. What do we know of the characteristics of scientists who can use this process effectively? Many lines of inquiry have demonstrated that the range of characteristics that are associated with creative productivity in a human being is very wide. These characteristics fall into almost all categories into which personal traits have been divided for purpose of study—abilities, interests, drives, temperament, and so on.

To limit our discussion to scientific productivity, it is clear to start with that there are great variations in the amount of curiosity possessed by different people. Curiosity appears to be a basic drive. I suspect it may vary consistently with sex, on either a biological or a cultural basis, but we have as yet no idea how to measure such drives. No one becomes a scientist without a better-than-average amount of curiosity, regardless of whether he was born with it, was brought up in a stimulating environment, or just did not have it severely inhibited.

Intelligence and creativity are not identical, but intelligence does play a role in scientific creativity—rather more than it may play in some other forms of creativity. In general, one may summarize by saying that the minimum intelligence required for creative production in science is considerably better than average, but that, given this, other variables contribute more to variance in performance. It must also be noted that special abilities (numerical, spatial, verbal, and so on) play somewhat different roles in different scientific fields, but that ability must in no case be below average. A cultural anthropologist, for example, has little need for great facility with numbers. An experimental physicist, on the other hand, does require facility with numbers, although he need not have great facility with words.

Personality Patterns

A number of studies have contributed to the picture of the personality patterns of productive scientists, and it is rather striking that quite different kinds of investigations have produced closely similar results. These can be briefly summarized in six different groups, as follows:

1. Truly creative scientists seek experience and action and are independent and self-sufficient with regard to perception, cognition, and behavior. These findings have been expressed in various studies in such terms as the following: they are more observant than others and value this quality; they are more independent with respect to cognition and value judgments; they have high dominance; they have high autonomy; they are Bohemian or radical; they are not subject to group standards and control; they are highly egocentric.

2. They have a preference for apparent but resolvable disorder and for an esthetic ordering of forms of experience. They have high tolerance for ambiguity, but they also like to put an end to it in their own way—and in their own time.

3. They have strong egos (whether this derives from or is responsible for their independence and their tolerance for ambiguity is a moot question). This ego strength permits them to regress to preconscious states with certainty that they will return from these states. They have less compulsive superegos than others. They are capable of disciplined management of means leading to significant experience. They have no feeling of guilt about the independence of thought and action mentioned above. They have strong control of their impulses.

4. Their interpersonal relations are generally of low intensity. They are reported to be ungregarious, not talkative (this does not apply to social scientists), and rather asocial. There is an apparent tendency to femininity in highly original men, and to masculinity in highly original women, but this may be a cultural interpretation of the generally increased sensitivity of the men and the intellectual capacity and interests of the women. They dislike interpersonal controversy in any form and are especially sensitive to interpersonal aggression.

5. They show much stronger preoccupation with things and ideas than with people. They dislike introversive and affect-associated pre-occupations, except in connection with their own research.

6. They like to take the calculated risk, but it must involve nature, not people, and must not depend on simple luck.

Conclusions

How do these personality characteristics relate to the creative process in science as I have discussed it? An open attitude toward experience makes possible accumulation of experience with relatively little com-partmentalization; independence of perception, cognition, and behavior permit greater than average reordering of this accumulated experience (the behavioral eccentricities so often noted are consistent with this). The strong liking for turning disorder into order carries such in-dividuals through the searching period which their tolerance for am-biguity permits them to enter. The strong egos, as noted, permit re-gression to prelogical forms of thought without serious fear of failure to get back to logical ones. Preoccupation with things and ideas rather than with people is obviously characteristic of natural scientists, and even of some social scientists. This characteristic is not directly related to creativity, I think, but rather to the content of it.

I need not add that such statements as these are generalizations and that any individual case may be an exception. We may go farther, however, and generalize differences among men who follow different branches of science. That a man chooses to become a scientist and succeeds means that he has the temperament and personality as well as the ability and opportunity to do so. The branch of science he chooses, even the specific problems he chooses and the way he works on them, are intimately related to what he is and to his deepest needs. The more deeply engaged he is, the more profoundly is this true. To understand what he does, one must try to know what his work means to him. The chances are that he does not know or care to know. Indeed, he does not need to know. We do.

The conclusion reached by Dr. Roe in this essay is mainly based upon her studies of physical scientists. She has reminded us here and elsewhere (Roe, 1953) that "in many ways the social scientist differs from the natural scientist in terms of personality and motivation." It has been found, for example, that social scientists are more interested in interpersonal relationships while physical scientists are less so.

The apparent "coldness, remoteness and objectivity" of the physical scientists, however, might be related to the commonly accepted notion of science as a purely impersonal thing. If so, it would be interesting to speculate what possible effects a "humanization of science" (Maslow, 1966) might have upon the personality dynamics of future scientists.

REFERENCES

KUBIE, LAWRENCE. Some unsolved problems of the scientific career, *The American Scientist,* Vol. XLI, No. 4 (1956) and Vol. XLII, No. 1, pp. 3–32.

McCLELLAND, DAVID. The psychodynamics of creative physical scientists, in *The Roots of Consciousness,* by David McClelland. Van Nostrand, 1964.

MASLOW, ABRAHAM H. *The Psychology of Science,* Harper, 1966.

ROE, ANNE. A psychological study of eminent psychologists and anthropologists, and a comparison with biological and physical scientists. *Psychol. Monogr.,* 1953, *67,* No. 2.

ROE, ANNE. *The Making of a Scientist.* Dodd, Mead, 1953.

10

The Psychology of Natural Childbirth*

Deborah Tanzer

Introduction

Psychological aspects of childbirth have been insufficiently investi-
gated, given the importance of childbirth to both the individual and
the species. This is especially true for natural childbirth, despite its
rapidly growing use. Natural childbirth has at its core the elimination
or reduction of analgesic and anesthetic agents in labor and delivery,
the resulting consciousness and participation of the mother during the
entire birth process, and various kinds of preparatory education and
activity during pregnancy; it also frequently includes active husband
participation.

Past investigations of natural childbirth, motivated by considerations
of possible dangers from drugs, have concentrated on obstetrical
aspects, despite general acknowledgment by investigators that its
greatest value seemed in the psychological sphere.

Further motivation for the present investigation was a belief that
it could illuminate some broader areas. Psychological topics included
self concepts and self-actualization, growth and fulfillment, marital
interaction, mother-child relations, female psychology and male-female
differences, and peak experiences. Psychophysiological topics included
psychosomatic interrelations, particularly the relationship of fear and
anxiety to pain, the diminution of pain by psychological procedures,
and cortico-visceral interaction.

The basic method was to compare two groups of women (41 altogether), one using the Psychoprophylactic Method of natural child-

---

* Abridged from Deborah Tanzer, *The Psychology of Pregnancy and Childbirth: An
Investigation of Natural Childbirth*. Ph.D. dissertation, Brandeis University, 1967.

birth training and procedures and the other not using natural child-birth. Each subject was given extensive batteries of psychological and psychophysiological tests, twice during pregnancy and once post-partum; a narrative description of the entire labor and delivery experience was also obtained. Both quantitative and qualitative analyses were performed on the data.

The Experience of Childbirth

The overwhelming conclusion that emerges from examination of the descriptions of childbirth given by our subjects is that as a subjective experience, and in certain objective ways as well, childbirth is vastly different for women having natural childbirth and women not having it. With few exceptions, it was a very positive event for the former group, and a very negative one for the latter.

From our narrative material we shall see how, in their own words, the women described the various events of childbirth.

We will examine first some of the descriptions of the birth given by the natural childbirth subjects. How did they experience the "delivery" of their children into the world, and their first contacts with them?

> I was pushing all the way into the delivery room, and it was really the most wonderful thing in the world to watch the baby being born. It was just fantastic. And to push with all my might to get him out, and to see him, his little body.[1]

* * *

> After that point I think the baby was born. There were a couple of more pushes, and there was a point where Dr. V. said "Don't push now." Right after the episiotomy, the baby's head was born, then the forearm and the shoulders, and it was marvelous. Everything else came so quickly. It was such a wonderful feeling, I can't tell you. Dr. V. said "Look, you have a son!" He was just as enthused as we were.

* * *

[1] Asterisks appear between statements of different subjects. To preserve confidentiality fictitious names and initials have been substituted in references to subjects, their husbands, their babies, and their doctors.

Everything happened very rapidly. I couldn't say how many pushes it was. All of a sudden he said "This is your baby's arm." I think I pushed another time, and he said "stop," and he said "You have a baby girl." It was that fast. And then I said "Don't I have to push out the placenta?" and they said "It's out." And I said "Well I didn't *feel* anything, did you give me anesthesia?" And they all laughed and said no.

We turn now to the statements given by the controls. How did they describe the events at the time of birth, or as close to it as they came? What were their recollections?

The next thing was about 8:20 A.M., and the doctor had my husband leave, and I remember being wheeled into the delivery room. The doctor just gave me a shot, and the next thing, he held up the baby, and put her on my stomach. And I remember yelling "Take her away!"

*   *   *

All I know is they gave me something that knocked me out, and I woke up, and I thought I was still in the labor room, but I was in the recovery room. And the same nurse who had been so mean was very nice. And I couldn't believe it. I didn't even feel my stomach the way they say you do, or say "is he healthy," or "isn't that nice." I just couldn't believe it.

The first difference that emerges, perhaps, is a difference of tone. The statements of natural childbirth women are largely positive, descriptions of feelings of happiness, excitement, joy. The statements of the control group do not describe a happy experience. They describe screaming, yelling, pain, moaning, fear and hostility.

The second difference that emerges is a tremendous sense of the *gap* in the experience of the controls, and the continuous, whole nature of the experience for the natural childbirth women.

A third important difference, and one which may well contribute to the ultimate difference in the meaning and tone of the experience, is the fact that the control group women were anesthetized. That is, the experience of receiving and succumbing to anesthesia may be sufficiently unpleasant and frightening to contribute significantly, by conscious or unconscious association, to a negative memory of childbirth.

The nature of the experience of being anesthetized is described graphically by some of our subjects:

> Then he said "we're going to put you to sleep," and they immediately put the thing over my face. I don't know if you've ever had it, but I've talked to a lot of people, and it's a very scary feeling. You can hear them, but you feel you're going asleep. I felt like I was dying. Like I was between worlds. That this was permanent. That this was death.

The Role of the Husband

Our findings have shown strikingly the effects of a husband's presence at the birth of his child. In every case where the woman experienced rapturous or peak-experience feelings in childbirth, her husband had been present in the delivery room. The husband's presence would seem necessary for, almost an integral part of, the peak experience in childbirth.

The outstanding thing that emerges at once is that there *are* vast differences in the way the husbands were perceived by the different groups of women.

The greatest general difference is in the overall tone of the statements about the husband, the direction of the "sign" given him. From the feelings and perceptions of the "natural childbirth" women, the husband emerges as a highly positive figure; from those of the "non-natural childbirth" women he emerges as negative or neutral. That is, almost all of the *statements* made by the natural childbirth group are positive, while most from the other group have a negative or neutral character. Let us now examine this in detail. We will consider first the statements of the "natural childbirth" women.

The husband is often described as a strong figure, to be praised explicitly, and whose presence and contribution were almost a necessity:

> There were moments, from the first phase of labor through delivery, that I could relive, that I wouldn't mind reliving again and again. Because people were so marvelous, and I can repeat this again and again, my husband and Dr. J.

*   *   *

> Roy was there, holding up my back. He was marvelous. He said a nurse was also doing it, but to me it was all Roy.

We see, then, that for the woman having natural childbirth, the husbands were viewed quite uniformly in highly positive terms. They were seen as important or indispensable in their presence, as strong and competent, as helpful in a variety of ways including active participation at the time of birth. They were described overall by very positive words. What, then, about the husbands of the controls, of the women not having natural childbirth? How did they see their husbands? How did they describe them, and how did they feel toward them?

The general tone that emerges from the statements by this group of women about their husbands is a negative or neutral one. The husband is seen with substantial uniformity as an impotent or weak figure, one who is in the way, or one who needs to be worried about and taken care of.

Thus, one woman did not even want to tell her husband she was in labor, for the following reason:

> I didn't want to tell my husband right away, because he's very nervous, he'd be hysterical all day.

Another woman stated:

> My husband was kind of tense. More so than I was at that point, and throughout.

THE EFFECTS ON THE HUSBAND

Unfortunately, the study of the effects on a man of participating in his wife's childbirth, like the questions of its other effects, has been virtually ignored. This despite what would seem to be its obvious importance for theoretical questions in psychology, as well as its importance because the incidence of men "participating" in childbirth is constantly increasing.

Our own examination did not study the husbands directly, and hence we cannot categorically answer the questions posed above. We can, however, learn something about the husbands' behavior and feelings indirectly, from the statements of their wives, as well as from certain other sources we shall examine.

And his apparent reactions were in some cases a positive surprise both to him and to his wife:

> I think till then I was worrying about the technique, all the drips, demerol, etc. . . . And about John, who was having to do so much. And I was worried he'd not be able to stand up to it all.
> Dr. N. came in and told me to push. I pushed for a half hour in the labor room. I remember John saying things like "Funny, I'm not at all squeamish." Because he's very fastidious. He was very helpful, including he kept lifting me up to get into position to push. And it was not very pretty at that point. Pushing was terrifically hard work, but it was okay.

The husband was described by one wife as feeling like a participant, to whom information was useful, *just as it was to her:*

> He explained all along everything that was going on, which was very good. It made me feel even more like a participant, and it was good for Ken too.

> * * *

> After everyone left, the nurse was cleaning up in there, and only John and I were there. And I felt terrifically proud of myself. Very replete. John was so vocal, more than usual. He kept running around like a maniac, really *manic.*

> * * *

> Bill was sitting on one side of me, and the baby was on the other . . . We sat there, the three of us, about forty minutes . . . and we sat there, and decided what to call him.

Many of the women spoke of how they and their husbands were *both,* or together, thrilled at the joint experience:

> Then they took the baby and me up to my room, and Ted was there. It was after one by this time. We were both absolutely exhausted, but exhilarated. So neither of us slept that night. Oh that night after you give birth is an endless, endless night. You can't wait for morning.

Contrary to many popular and academic notions about masculinity and femininity, the husbands of our study expressed interest in this area, wanted to and did *participate,* and had positive feelings about having done so.

This greater male "involvement" in childbirth by no means represents a de-masculinization of men. The husband who was involved in childbirth was not "feminized" or "sissified," as common thinking might expect, and which expectation may well lead many men *away* from involvement in childbirth. On the contrary, the "natural childbirth" husband emerged as strong, competent, important, and someone on whom in most cases his wife leaned and depended. These are attributes of traditional "maleness" or masculinity. In contrast, it was the uninvolved father, the "non-natural childbirth" one, who emerged as weak, impotent, childlike, someone to be worried about rather than depended on at this time. And the corollary of this is that the non-natural childbirth woman may become more dominant, controlling, contemptuous or, if one wishes, "castrating" toward her husband—the very charges that are frequently made against women having natural childbirth! It would seem then, that not having natural childbirth might result in greater polarization of the sexes, but hardly in a healthy direction!

Another major topic borne on by our findings about husband participation in childbirth is the question of growth, development, actualization in a woman. To these, it seems, a husband may contribute. Her conscious perceptions and attitudes may mature, even very rapidly, as we saw with one of our subjects, from her husband's presence with her in childbirth. By "non-conscious" mechanisms of operation, his presence may contribute to her experience of rapturous feelings and healthier perceptions of her self and the world. Thus in terms of growth and therapeutic development in a woman, a husband's presence at childbirth may be a significant contributing factor.

And most important of all, it may be that the husband-at-delivery is himself included in, *an integral part of the peak or rapturous experience* in the wife—not just necessary for its appearance, but an inextricable part of it. In support of this, one of the most graphic descriptions we obtained of childbirth contained a vivid depiction of the emotions and perceptions involved, and indeed, included the husband as part of the description:

Rob . . . they had him all done up in the O.R. mask and shoes. And he was a sweetheart, a *sweetheart*. I think it was harder for him than for me, because at the end I was in so much pain I didn't care. But he said he felt so helpless. . . . And people said he kept going to the hall, asking couldn't someone do something for her.

About forty minutes of pushing, then it was just all joy. It seems I was pushing for years. The joy at the end was such a knockout. I felt maybe there was a submarine in me, and the back pain was unbearable. And I thought maybe I would break my spine and it would be the first time in recorded history. And all of a sudden he said "Stop, don't push." And it was the first time I felt the urge to push. Edna directed my breathing to direct it.

And then the head was born and he said "It's a boy!" It was one of the real wild experiences of my life. It became a baby for the first time . . . Then finally I felt the rest of the baby slide out, and that was heaven, just pure heaven. Then I heard the baby cry, and the feeling was a new one. It was real joy. Then he held him up, and I felt a big rush of fluid, and the backache was gone. And I felt every little bit of the baby. It was really something. . . . It was somewhat of an orgasm of a sort. . . . Oh my, that was really something.

Like an orgasm . . . a different kind . . . the wonderful free feeling . . . the In-Space marvelous feeling. Joy, a wild joy. I had known it, but it was very special . . . seeing a real honest-to-goodness baby. He looked like a porcelain eskimo, and all kinds of colors—blue, green, red, and shiny. And having Rob there . . . great.

Finally, it may well be that participation in childbirth can lead to a peak experience for a man as well. We present now a document, not gathered as a part of our study directly, but presented to us as a personal communication from someone who knew of the research in progress.[2] It was written by a man who is a writer by profession, shortly after the birth of his son.

I want especially to report on my own recent experience, becoming a father. You say that you have no knowledge of a father having a peak-experience associated with the birth of his child. I

[2] Personal communication by William Mathes to Dr. Abraham H. Maslow. Presented here with permission of the author and the recipient.

think this is probably because most fathers are not present nor intimately participating in the birth.

I was lucky enough to be present (my wife Pat and I attended a series of classes, exercise and preparation, before the delivery; I was totally ready for the experience; it was amazing to me to realize how many "old wives' tales" I carried around inside my head, about birth, about fact and function of reproduction!) during the labor and delivery of our first child, Christopher, who is now twelve weeks and thriving.

The first stage of my wife's labor was long (about fifteen hours) during which she used a variety of breathing-techniques and I coached her, rubbed her back, brought her magazines and tea, and generally made her as comfortable as possible. She was beginning to get too tired, so our doctor gave her a para-cervical block (novicane—my spelling is bad) and this was the only medication she had. She had some minor discomfort to this point, nothing she wasn't on top of. Then we went into the delivery room, where she pushed the baby out in fifteen minutes. We were both tired, but the experience in the delivery room was for me (and her too, but I am here talking about a father's reaction) a full fifteen minutes + of intense peak-experiences.

I administered oxgen to her between contractions and coached her on pushing, holding her around the shoulders as support during each push. She was magnificent. Slowly I began to feel a kind of holiness about all of us there, performing an ageless human drama, a grand ritual of life. The trigger was probably the emergence of the baby's head—coughing, twisting, covered with blood, as purple as ever, so eager for life—that set me into such intensities of joy and excitement that I cannot possibly adequately describe them. It was all so powerful I felt as though my head might come off, that I might simply explode with joy and a sense of profound participation in a profound mystery. I did explode, was literally re-born myself, saw how my birth, all births, the idea of birth is profoundly right, good, joyous.

Christopher was placed in my wife's arms even before the umbilicus was cut; shortly after it was cut he was wrapped (still dripping and wonderfully new like a chick out of an egg) and given to me to hold while my wife got her strength back.

He was very alert, apparently able to focus his attention on me and on other objects in the room; as I held him he blossomed into pink, the various parts of his body turning from deep purple and almost blue, to pink, to rose. I was fascinated by the colors, time stopped; I thought my friends hooked on LSD should simply take a wife, have a baby, and watch it born!

Shortly, my wife sat up and nursed Christopher on the delivery table; our doctor and nurse left us alone; the three new people got acquainted.

The method of delivery (a modified Lamaze, Dick-Read method) in which the fathers participate and in which the medications are only a local, if that—it brings the child into the world quickly and almost easily, alert, able to feel alive and in the world as it is born. The mother has emotional and physical support from her husband; she experiences the birth as a grand effort; the couple are closer than ever at the supreme moment of their creation.

As you know, peak-experiences are difficult to describe; about all you can say is that when you have one, you know it. My first look at my son—and the days after his birth—are further experiences of the "peak" in my life. Even now as I write I am again caught up in the feeling, seem to expand and overflow as I recall.

The birth experience was so intense that my only regret—if you can call it that—was in not being able to adequately express the feeling. It called for a dance, or a physical-emotional expression of some kind. The irony in so much of being human is that one can feel (good and bad feelings) much more than one can "do anything about," express. There are probably a whole set of affective expressions potentially available to us that we were either not taught, or that have atrophied in the species. . . . I know I wished I had a more refined nervous system in which to more completely experience and express what I felt. The peak experience is fulfilling, but it often does not seem to apply to an expression; one is almost stuck with it like a pot boiling with a tight lid.

REFERENCES

For the reader who is interested in gaining general knowledge of the natural childbirth method, the following list can be useful.

KARMEL, MARJORIE. *Thank You, Dr. Lamaze: A Mother's Experiences in Painless Childbirth.* Philadelphia: J. B. Lippincott Co., 1959.

DICK-READ, GRANTLY. *Childbirth Without Fear: The Principles and Practice of Natural Childbirth.* 2nd edition revised. New York: Harper and Brothers, 1959.

CHABON, IRWIN. *Awake and Aware: Participating in Childbirth Through Psychoprophylaxis.* New York: Delacorte Press, 1966.

CHERTOK, L. *Psychosomatic Methods in Painless Childbirth: History, Theory and Practice.* Translated by Denis Leigh. New York: Pergamon Press, 1959.

LAMAZE, FERNAND. *Painless Childbirth: Psychoprophylactic Method.* Translated by L. R. Celestin. London: Burke Publishing Co., Ltd., 1958.

BUXTON, C. Lee. *A Study of Psychophysical Methods for the Relief of Childbirth Pain.* Philadelphia: W. B. Saunders Co., 1962.

Dr. Tanzer's work is one of the few research reports dealing with the psychological aspects of the natural childbirth. A condensed version of it has appeared in *Psychology Today,* October 1968.

Another excellent research report, dealing with the same psychoprophylactic (Lamaze) method, is the following; it deals primarily with obstetrical aspects, but with significant psychological implications and observations:

YAHIA, CLEMENT, and ULIN, PRISCILLA R. Preliminary experience with a psychophysical program of preparation for childbirth, *American Journal of Obstetrics and Gynecology,* Vol. XCIII, No. 7 (Dec. 1, 1965), pp. 942–949.

11

*The Ecology of Imagination in Childhood**

Edith Cobb

The present essay is an abridgment of a longer work in process, which attempts the difficult task first of defining what we mean by the genius of childhood as a common human possession; and second of showing that a major clue to mental health lies in the spontaneously creative imagination of childhood both as a form of learning and as a function of the organizing powers of the nervous system. Of necessity, the exploration includes tracing the relationship of this early psychophysical force in human development to those uncommon forms of genius which constitute the high point of achievement in human growth potential, with roots, as I believe, in the child's perceptual relations with the natural world. . . .

My position is based upon the fact that the study of the child in nature, culture, and society (the evolution of social attitudes toward childhood into present realization of its importance in everyone's life history) reveals that there is a special period, the little-understood, prepubertal, halcyon, middle age of childhood, approximately from five or six to eleven or twelve—between the strivings of animal infancy and the storms of adolescence—when the natural world is experienced in some highly evocative way, producing in the child a sense of some profound continuity with natural processes and presenting overt evidence of a biological basis of intuition *(1)*.

These concepts have evolved from four principal sources: first, biographical and autobiographical memories of gifted people; second, the Freudian concept of childhood as the core of human development, particularly as this is treated in social casework *(2)*, which furthers adap-

* Reprinted by permission of DAEDALUS, *Journal of the American Academy of Arts and Sciences*, Boston, Mass. Summer 1959, "Current Work and Controversies."

tation of the unique individual to his total environment; third, a study of the plastic, dynamic nature of imagery in contrast to the more static condensed simultaneity of the symbol; last, and as a tool for the implementation of these sources, an investigation of studies of the changing imagery in the language of natural description, which disclosed this special trend in perception, a trend in the cultural evolution of attitudes toward nature which has produced the concept of ecology, the study of mutual relations, the give-and-take between organisms and their complete and total environment. The science of ecology provides us with a plastic image of behaving organisms in a behaving world, and a tool for synthesis as well as analysis of the system of meaning and verbal imagery which we use to describe nature.

In my collection (3) of some three hundred volumes of autobiographical recollections of their own childhood by creative thinkers from many cultures and eras, ranging from a fragment from the sixteenth century to the present, it is principally to this middle-age range in their early life that these writers say they return in memory in order to renew the power and impulse to create at its very source, a source which they describe as the experience of emerging not only into the light of consciousness but into a living sense of a dynamic relationship with the outer world. In these memories the child appears to experience both a sense of discontinuity, an awareness of his own unique separateness and identity, and also a continuity, a renewal of relationship with nature as process. This apprehension is certainly not intellectual; I believe it is rational at least in a limited sense, a preverbal experience of an "aesthetic logic" both in nature's formative processes and in the gestalt-making powers of the child's own developing nervous system, aesthetic powers that overlap meaningfully in these moments of form-creating expansion and self-consciousness. . . .

Instead of working backward from the adult's position to the child's, I found it necessary in my exploration of the genius of the living child to set up methods of investigating creative purpose in the child's play and art. The value of forms produced was secondary to the importance of the response to "aesthetic logic" in the child's gestalt-forming action patterns with the instrument of the self. Using various forms of so-called projective methods and play techniques (in particular, modified versions of the Lowenfeld World-Play Technique and the Thematic Apperception Test, accompanied by a continual reference to the Rorschach categories of Form, Color, Motion, Time and Space, Animal and Human Response), I became acutely aware that what a child wanted to do most of all was to make a world in which to find a place to discover a self. This ordering reverses the general position that self-exploration produces a knowledge of the world. Furthermore, while observing the passionate world-making behavior of the child when he is given plastic materials and working dimensions which are manageable and in proportion to his need, accompanied by a population of toys, fauna and flora, and artifacts that do duty as "figures of speech" in the rhetoric of play, I have been made keenly aware of those processes which the genius in particular in later life seeks to recall.

The tendency to play may be said to be characteristic of animals reared in a nidicolous (i.e., a specifically nestlike) domestic ecology. The important point about the child's play is that it includes the spontaneous effort to be something other than what he actually is, to "act out" [1] and to dramatize speculation, which is in effect to take play out into the four-dimensional continuum by adding motion and sequence, and therefore time, to its procedures.

When Freud defined childhood's middle age as the latency period, he referred only to latent sexual drives, which, according to psychoanalytic interpretation, become less purposive when the child's mastery of body and speech directs his energies toward other types of cognitive satisfaction. Energy remains libidinal, and creativity a substitute for sex. I suggest that this period is also a time of far more general latent awareness or "half-knowledge," (4) a period of plasticity of perceptual response and "biological memory" which when employed in original gestalt-building processes must be described as intuition (in contrast to other instinctual biological drives).[2] In infancy the impulse to love is aroused to the level of passion and yet must remain unfulfilled and unformulated in any direct sense. The passion of

[1] An important term, which now is unfortunately also the metaphor for delinquency and neurotic behavior.

[2] Intuition is not necessarily benign. It is relational and structural; its value depends upon the purposes to which it is addressed.

infancy is therefore addressed to goals and purposes unknown but not entirely "unperceived," for in ordinary experience in early childhood, the parents (more specifically the nurturing figure of the mother) are the targets of love, a fact that evokes some latent foreknowledge of sexual form and function. The "distance" between the self and the objects of desire, and the natural pressure for fulfillment, are equally real, although "out of sight." The child fills in the distance between the self and the goals of desire with imagined forms. The basic evolutionary characteristics of perceptual processes, also latent in the human nervous system, become dominant as the child emerges more consciously into a perceptual participation in external nature. The reproductive urge is undoubtedly also represented in the desire "to body forth the forms of things unknown," but the biological urge toward growth becomes the psychophysical urge toward transcendence, the urge to create higher and ever more complex gestalten in perception and cultural meaning.

Freud has made plain to us that the problem of maintaining our individual transcendence of levels above our biological heritage of animal instinct and impulse is a matter of life-long effort. It begins with the cultural demand for the discontinuity of instinct, which he has described as the Oedipal situation, a climax in nature's use of isolating mechanisms in culturally elaborated form. While the child's expression of reproductive mechanisms is biologically delayed and culturally restricted, the psychological growth mechanisms have been culturally elaborated, speeded up, and highly differentiated. The child's will and need is to use energy for purposes of growth, thus following nature's own biological pattern of alternating the use of energy between self-reproduction and self-increase. Energy in itself cannot be described as "libidinal," although the body's purpose in the use of energy may be addressed to libidinal ends. It is the process we know as metabolism, which furnishes "the energy system which is the body" (to use Sir Charles Sherrington's phrase) with what D'Arcy Thompson has called "the power to do work." . . .

The child, like the poet, is his own instrument. His whole body, erotized and highly sensitized by the necessities of nurture and touch, is the tool of his mind, and serves with a passionate enjoyment in a creative engagement with the forces of nature. Examination of the psychobiography of genius suggests that the perception of wholeness has been a characteristic of all individuals who have thought more closely with the instrument of the body. Perceptual unity with nature is, of course, not a new concept.[3] . . .

In an important study, John Oman (5) comments that in every genius whose special gift is perception, either time or space seems to be a dominant intuition in childhood. We would say here that genius consists in the continuing ability to recall and to utilize the child's primary perceptual intuition of time and space. Oman recalls that his own exodus, his first sense of discontinuity and aloneness with respect to other individuals but equally one of continuity with nature, occurred when as a child of six he stood at the age of the sea on a Sunday morning in summer. His own awakening to a sense of nature as infinity and yet as a part of himself seems to have occurred quite directly in relation to the earlier experience of a Sunday morning in church. This was not a specifically religious experience, but simply a response to an open-system attitude, a state of temporal and spatial inquiry—Where am I? Who am I?—an attitude toward nature which is frequently evoked within or as a result of religiously conditioned circumstances described in childhood recollection. . . .

It is significant that adult memories of childhood, even when nostalgic and romantic, seldom suggest the need to be a child but refer to a deep desire to renew the ability to perceive as a child and to participate with the whole bodily self in the forms, colors, and motions, the sights and sounds of the external world of nature and artifact. . . . The experiences remain largely nonverbal—although not entirely so, if we take into consideration some of the astonishing and beautiful cosmic questions of the child. But such experience is subject to recall in remarkably similar terms by gifted or creative people from the most widely differing eras and backgrounds—social, cultural, and geographical.

In his autobiography (6), Bernard Berenson gives an exceptionally full and rich description of his discovery in early childhood of the

---

[3] The false metaphors of "contest" and "conquest" of nature continue to interrupt our perceptions of nature's aesthetics.

sense of "Itness" as an integration with the ongoing process in nature. The position achieved by the child in this experience of "psychological equipoise" became a stabilizing influence, a life-long goal, and also the basis of a highly skillful method of observing and learning. His experiences continued through childhood and boyhood. In particular, one balmy summer morning he "climbed up a tree stump and felt suddenly immersed in Itness.[4] I did not call it by that name, I had no need for words. It and I were one." Of these moments of exodus into the temporal and spatial continuum, Berenson says that "in consciousness this was due not to me, but to the not-me, of which I was scarcely more than the subject in the grammatical sense." As an adult he sees himself "as an energy of a given force in radiation and of a certain power of resistance," but adds that "he seems to be the same in these respects as I remember being at the end of my sixth year," when he became latently aware that the form-creating harmony of his perceiving body and the form-creating harmony of nature were one and the same process, the process which eventually enabled him to perceive and to estimate value in art as the appearance of living motion in his perceptual "readings," even of a stone fresco. The experience at the dawn of conscious life remained the "guardian angel," returning in memory to remind him that "It was my goal, It was my real happiness," the happiness of perceptual creation upon which all other creativity depends.

Further examples are to be encountered in autobiographical recollections from Africa, Asia, Europe (North and South), and the Americas. These descriptions—some fleeting, some lengthy—of the inception of a relationship with nature express not only a deep need to make a world the way the world was made, but also the need to make a piece of the real world in which one lives with others. This is, I suggest, the only truly effective counteragent to the forces of internal conflict which until recently were considered the major subjects of study, the main background to purpose in life. Once the theme of world-making is seen as a basic human goal, the emphasis upon discontinuity and the pressure toward self-knowledge repre-

---

[4] It may be remembered that Rilke as an adult at Duino underwent a similar experience in a tree cleft.

sented by the Socratic axiom "Know thyself," so essential to the differentiation of the idea of man into the image of the unique self, seems to diminish in value, or to have reached a saturation point as a useful psychosocial concept. This is not to say that the concept of the individual or of individuality is outmoded or even fully realized in social aims, but that, as a tool for the shaping of thought about human behavior, self-exploration as an aim in itself is not merely less and less effective but is unconsciously supporting a dangerous trend toward neurotic self-interest on a world-wide scale.

This point of view calls for a redefinition of human individuality, not only in terms of human relations, but also in terms of man's total relations with "outerness," with nature itself. Such a redefinition seems feasible in terms of the developing intellectual climate. The pattern of cultural evolution that has been long in the making is one in which the concept of ecology, the study of the relations between organisms and their total environment, will play a major part.

REFERENCES

1. I am here following especially the leads of Albert M. Dalcq, "Form and Modern Embryology," and Konrad M. Lorenz, "The Role of Gestalt Perception in Animal and Human Behaviour," in L. L. Whyte, ed., *Aspects of Form* (London, Percy Lund Humphries & Co. Ltd., 1951); also of L. L. Whyte on formative processes in his many publications, particularly *The Unitary Principle in Physics and Biology* (London, Cresset Press, 1949).
2. Practice of social work in the fullest sense is in fact the only field of applied human ecology that I know of. In direct relation to the ideas presented here, I find that in 1940 Dr. Eduard C. Lindeman, Professor of Social Philosophy at the New York School of Social Work, saw "Ecology" as "an instrument for the integration of science and philosophy" in a paper of that title ("Ecology: An Instrument for the Integration of Science and Philosophy," *Ecological Monographs, 10* [July 1940] pp. 367–372), although he did not apply this directly to social work.
3. The Edith Cobb Collection, now in the possession of the New York School of Social Work, Columbia University.
4. Keats' term for intuition. His *Letters* embody a highly developed theory of cognition, resembling also Wordsworth's and Traherne's.
5. John Oman, *The Natural and the Supernatural*. New York, The Macmillan Company, and Cambridge, Cambridge University Press, 1931.
6. Bernard Berenson, *Sketch for a Self-Portrait*. New York, Pantheon Books, Inc., 1940.

12

*Psychoanalysis and Zen Buddhism**

Erich Fromm

The aim of Zen is enlightenment: the immediate, unreflected grasp of reality, without affective contamination and intellectualization, the realization of the relation of myself to the Universe. This new experience is a repetition of the pre-intellectual, immediate grasp of the child, but on a new level, that of the full development of man's reason, objectivity, individuality. While the child's experience, that of immediacy and oneness, lies *before* the experience of alienation and the subject-object split, the enlightenment experience lies after it.

The aim of psychoanalysis, as formulated by Freud, is that of making the unconscious conscious, of replacing Id by Ego. To be sure, the content of the unconscious to be discovered was limited to a small sector of the personality, to those instinctual drives which were alive in early childhood, but which were subject to amnesia. To lift these out of the state of repression was the aim of the analytic technique. Furthermore, the sector to be uncovered, quite aside from Freud's theoretical premises, was determined by the therapeutic need to cure a particular symptom. There was little interest in recovering unconsciousness outside of the sector related to the symptom formation. Slowly the introduction of the concept of the death instinct and eros and the development of the Ego aspects in recent years have brought about a certain broadening of the Freudian concepts of the contents of the unconscious. The non-Freudian schools greatly widened the sector of the unconscious to be uncovered. Most radically Jung, but also Adler, Rank, and the other more recent so-called neo-Freudian

* From pp. 134–141 in *Zen Buddhism and Psychoanalysis* by D. T. Suzuki, Erich Fromm, Copyright © 1961 by Erich Fromm. Reprinted by permission of Harper & Row, Publishers.

authors have contributed to this extension. But (with the exception of Jung), in spite of such a widening, the extent of the sector to be uncovered has remained determined by the therapeutic aim of curing this or that symptom; or this or that neurotic character trait. It has not encompassed the whole person.

However, if one follows the original aim of Freud, that of making the unconscious conscious, to its last consequences, one must free it from the limitations imposed on it by Freud's own instinctual orientation, and by the immediate task of curing symptoms. If one pursues the aim of the full recovery of the unconscious, then this task is not restricted to the instincts, nor to other limited sectors of experience, but to the total experience of the total man; then the aim becomes that of overcoming alienation, and of the subject-object split in perceiving the world; then the uncovering of the unconscious means the overcoming of affective contamination and cerebration; it means the de-repression, the abolition of the split within myself between the universal man and the social man; it means the disappearance of the polarity of conscious vs. unconscious; it means arriving at the state of the immediate grasp of reality, without distortion and without interference by intellectual reflection; it means overcoming of the craving to hold on to the ego, to worship it; it means giving up the illusion of an indestructible separate ego, which is to be enlarged, preserved and as the Egyptian pharaohs hoped to preserve themselves as mummies for eternity. To be conscious of the unconscious means to be open, responding, to *have* nothing and to *be*.

This aim of the full recovery of unconsciousness by consciousness is quite obviously much more radical than the general psychoanalytic aim. The reasons for this are easy to see. To achieve this total aim requires an effort far beyond the effort most persons in the West are willing to make. But quite aside from this question of effort, even the visualization of this aim is possible only under certain conditions. First of all, this radical aim can be envisaged only from the point of view of a certain philosophical position. There is no need to describe this position in detail. Suffice it to say that it is one in which not the negative aim of the absence of sickness, but the positive one of the presence of well-being is aimed at, and that well-being is conceived in terms of full union, the immediate and uncontaminated grasp of the world. This aim could not be better described than has been done by Suzuki in terms of "the art of living." One must keep in mind that any such concept as the art of living grows from the soil of a spiritual humanistic orientation, as it underlies the teaching of Buddha, of the prophets, of Jesus, of Meister Eckhart, or of men such as Blake, Walt Whitman, or Bucke. Unless it is seen in this context, the concept of "the art of living" loses all that is specific, and deteriorates into a concept that goes today under the name of "happiness." It must also not be forgotten that this orientation includes an ethical aim. While Zen transcends ethics, it includes the basic ethical aims of Buddhism, which are essentially the same as those of all humanistic teaching. The achievement of the aim of Zen, as Suzuki has made very clear in the lectures in this book, implies the overcoming of greed in all forms, whether it is the greed for possession, for fame, or for affection; it implies overcoming narcissistic self-glorification and the illusion of omnipotence. It implies, furthermore, the overcoming of the desire to submit to an authority who solves one's own problem of existence. The person who only wants to use the discovery of the unconscious to be cured of sickness will, of course, not even attempt to achieve the radical aim which lies in the overcoming of repressedness.

But it would be a mistake to believe that the radical aim of the de-repression has no connection with a therapeutic aim. Just as one has recognized that the cure of a symptom and the prevention of future symptom formations is not possible without the analysis and change of the character, one must also recognize that the change of this or that neurotic character trait is not possible without pursuing the more radical aim of a complete transformation of the person. It may very well be that the relatively disappointing results of character analysis (which have never been expressed more honestly than by Freud in his "Analysis, Terminable or Interminable?") are due precisely to the fact that the aims for the cure of the neurotic character were not radical enough; that well-being, freedom from anxiety and insecurity, can be achieved only if the limited aim is transcended, that is, if one realizes that the limited, therapeutic aim cannot be achieved as long as it remains limited and does not become part of a wider, humanistic frame of reference. Perhaps the limited aim can be achieved with more limited and less time-consuming methods, while the time and energy consumed in the long analytic process are used fruitfully only for the radical aim of "transformation" rather than the narrow one of "reform." This proposition might be strengthened by referring to a statement made above. Man, as long as he has not reached the creative relatedness of which *satori* is the fullest achievement, at best compensates for inherent potential depression by routine, idolatry, destructiveness, greed for property or fame, etc. When any of these compensations break down, his sanity is threatened. The cure of the potential insanity lies only in the change in attitude from split and alienation to the creative, immediate grasp of and response to the world. If psychoanalysis can help in this way, it can help to achieve true mental health; if it cannot, it will only help to improve compensatory mechanisms. To put it still differently: somebody may be "cured" of a symptom, but he can not be "cured" of a character neurosis. Man is not a thing,[1] man is not a "case," and the analyst does not cure anybody by treating him as an object. Rather, the analyst can only help a man to wake up, in a process in which the analyst is engaged with the "patient" in the process of their understanding each other, which means experiencing their oneness.

In stating all this, however, we must be prepared to be confronted with an objection. If, as I said above, the achievement of the full consciousness of the unconscious is as radical and difficult an aim as enlightenment, does it make any sense to discuss this radical aim as something which has any general application? Is it not purely speculative to raise seriously the question that only this radical aim can justify the hopes of psychoanalytic therapy?

If there were only the alternative between full enlightenment and nothing, then indeed this objection would be valid. But this is not so. In Zen there are many stages of enlightenment, of which *satori* is the ultimate and decisive step. But, as far as I understand, value is set on experiences which are steps in the direction of *satori,* although *satori* may never be reached. Dr. Suzuki once illustrated this point in the

---

[1] Cf. my paper: "The Limitations and Dangers of Psychology," in *Religion and Culture,* ed. by W. Leibrecht. (New York, Harper & Brothers, 1959), pp. 31 ff.

following way: If one candle is brought into an absolutely dark room, the darkness disappears, and there is light. But if ten or a hundred or a thousand candles are added, the room will become brighter and brighter. Yet the decisive change was brought about by the first candle which penetrated the darkness.[2]

What happens in the analytic process? A person senses for the first time that he is vain, that he is frightened, that he hates, while consciously he had believed himself to be modest, brave, and loving. The new insight may hurt him, but it opens a door; it permits him to stop projecting on others what he represses in himself. He proceeds; he experiences the infant, the child, the adolescent, the criminal, the insane, the saint, the artist, the male, *and* the female within himself; he gets more deeply in touch with humanity, with the universal man; he represses less, is freer, has less need to project, to cerebrate; then he may experience for the first time how he sees colors, how he sees a ball roll, how his ears are suddenly fully opened to music, when up to now he only listened *to* it; in sensing his oneness with others, he may have a first glimpse of the illusion that his separate individual ego is some-*thing* to hold onto, to cultivate, to save; he will experience the futility of seeking the answer to life by *having* himself, rather than by being and becoming himself. All these are sudden, unexpected experiences with no intellectual content; yet afterwards the person feels freer, stronger, less anxious than he ever felt before.

So far we have spoken about *aims,* and I have proposed that if one carries Freud's principle of the transformation of unconsciousness into consciousness to its ultimate consequences, one approaches the concept of enlightenment. But as to *methods* of achieving this aim, psychoanalysis and Zen are, indeed, entirely different. The method of Zen is, one might say, that of a frontal attack on the alienated way of perception by means of the "sitting," the koan, and the authority of the master. Of course, all this is not a "technique" which can be isolated from the premise of Buddhist thinking, of the behavior and ethical values which are embodied in the master and in the atmosphere of the monastery. It must also be remembered that it is not a "five hour a week" concern, and that by the very fact of coming for instruction in

[2] In a personal communication, as I remember.

Zen the student has made a most important decision, a decision which is an important part of what goes on afterwards.

The psychoanalytic method is entirely different from the Zen method. It trains consciousness to get hold of the unconscious in a different way. It directs attention to that perception which is distorted; it leads to a recognition of the fiction within oneself; it widens the range of human experience by lifting repressedness. The analytic method is psychological-empirical. It examines the psychic development of a person from childhood on and tries to recover earlier experiences in order to assist the person in experiencing of what is now repressed. It proceeds by uncovering illusions within oneself about the world, step by step, so that parataxic distortions and alienated intellectualizations diminish. By becoming less of a stranger to himself, the person who goes through this process becomes less estranged to the world; because he has opened up communication with the universe within himself, he has opened up communication with the universe outside. False consciousness disappears, and with it the polarity conscious-unconscious. A new realism dawns in which "the mountains are mountains again." The psychoanalytic method is of course only a method, a preparation; but so is the Zen method. By the very fact that it is a method it never guarantees the achievement of the goal. The factors which permit this achievement are deeply rooted in the individual personality, and for all practical purposes we know little of them.

I have suggested that the method of uncovering the unconscious, if carried to its ultimate consequences, may be a step toward enlightenment, provided it is taken within the philosophical context which is most radically and realistically expressed in Zen. But only a great deal of further experience in applying this method will show how far it can lead. The view expressed here implies only a possibility and thus has the character of a hypothesis which is to be tested.

But what can be said with more certainty is that the knowledge of Zen, and a concern with it, can have a most fertile and clarifying influence on the theory and technique of psychoanalysis. Zen, different as it is in its method from psychoanalysis, can sharpen the focus, throw new light on the nature of insight, and heighten the sense of what it is to see, what it is to be creative, what it is to overcome the affective contaminations and false intellectualizations which are the necessary results of experience based on the subject-object split.

In its very radicalism with respect to intellectualization, authority, and the delusion of the ego, in its emphasis on the aim of well-being, Zen thought will deepen and widen the horizon of the psychoanalyst and help him to arrive at a more radical concept of the grasp of reality as the ultimate aim of full, conscious awareness.

REFERENCES

References on psychoanalysis are too numerous to mention here, but the reader might find the following list of writings on Zen useful.

a. *General:*

AMES, VAN METER. *Zen and American Thought.* University of Hawaii Press, 1962.

HERRIGEL, EUGEN. *Zen in the Art of Archery.* Pantheon, 1953.

ROSS, NANCY WILSON. *The World of Zen.* Random House, 1960.

SUZUKI, D. T. *An Introduction to Zen Buddhism* (with foreword by C. G. Jung). Grove, Evergreen Black Cat Book, 1964.

WATTS, ALAN. *This Is It.* Pantheon, 1960.

b. *Papers with research implications:*

MAUPIN, W. EDWARD. Zen Buddhism: A Psychological Review, *Journal of Consulting Psychology,* 1962, *26,* 362–378.

MAUPIN, W. EDWARD. Individual Differences in Response to a Zen Meditation Exercise, *Journal of Consulting Psychology,* 1965, *29,* 139–145.

VAN DUSEN, WILSON. LSD and Enlightenment of Zen, *Psychologia,* 1961, *4,* 11–16.

13

The Forgotten Man of Education*

LAWRENCE S. KUBIE

Every discipline has its tools, and each such tool has its own inherent errors. The finest microscope produces an image not of facts alone but of facts embedded in a setting of obscuring artifacts which the microscope itself creates. The first thing that the young microscopist is taught is how to distinguish the one from the other. A discipline comes of age and a student of that discipline reaches maturity when it becomes possible to recognize, estimate, and allow for the errors of their tools. This is true for physics, chemistry, physiology, the social sciences, the humanities, history, literature, and the arts. Within its own field each of these disciplines is meticulously self-critical about the sources of error which reside in its special instruments.

Yet there is one instrument which every discipline uses without checking its errors, tacitly assuming that the instrument is error-free. This, of course, is the human psychological apparatus. As a result of the failure to consider the sources of error in the human being himself, when our academic disciplines assemble together in our great educational institutions they reenforce the tacit, fallacious assumption that man can understand the world that lies outside of himself without concurrently understanding himself. Actually, each man is his own microscope with his own idiosyncrasies, to which he alone can penetrate. Therefore we cannot perceive the outside world without distorting our very perceptions unless we search out individually the sources of error which lie hidden within. This is precisely what every mature discipline does in its own field: yet it is what no discipline does for the broad concept of education as a whole.

* *Harvard Alumni Bulletin*, LVI (1954), 349–353.

As we view the world around us, and as we look and listen and think and feel and interact with our fellow man and his works and his history, we view all such external realities through a cloud of distorting projections of our own unconscious problems. It is a scene observed as through the wavering convection currents over a hot fire. This is why it is impossible to reduce scholars who in the true sense of the word are wise men, if they know nothing about themselves. Without self-knowledge in depth, the master of any field will be a child in human wisdom and human culture. Even the seemingly objective data of his own field at the same time represent projections of his own unresolved problems in dreamlike symbolic disguises: and as long as he knows nothing of his own inner nature, his apparent knowledge merely disguises his spiritual confusion.

What I am saying is nothing that has not been said many times since Socrates: namely, that man must know himself. When modern psychiatry adds to this ancient adage is that self-knowledge if it is to be useful and effective must comprise more than superficial self-description. It must include an understanding of unconscious as well as conscious levels of psychological processes. Yet such self-knowledge, which requires the mastery of intricate new tools of psychological exploration, is wholly overlooked throughout the entire scheme of "modern" education, from the kindergarten to the highest levels of academic training.

This deepening of our self-knowledge is in turn intimately dependent on the nature of symbolic thinking. Learning depends upon a progressive mastery of the many processes of symbolic thought. Symbols, however, are not all alike. They fall into three groups. There is the realistic form of symbolic thinking in which we are fully aware of the relationship of the symbols of language to that which they represent. Here the function of the symbol is to communicate the hard core, the bare bones, of thoughts and purposes. Secondly there is the symbol whose relationship to its root is figurative and allegorical. The purpose of this second form of symbolic thinking is to communicate by inference all of the nuances of thought and feeling, all of the collateral references which cluster around the central core of meaning. This is the symbolic language of creative thinking whether in art or science.

In technical jargon, the first is called *conscious,* and the second *pre-conscious.* Third, there is the symbolic process in which the relationship between the symbol and what it represents has been buried or distorted, so that the symbol becomes a disguised and disguising representative of unconscious levels of psychological processes. Here the function of the symbolic process is not to communicate but to hide. This is the unconscious symbolic process of the dream and of psychological illness.

Yet all three already operate together, with the consequence that every single thing we ever do or say or think or feel is a composite product of them all. Consequently when a scientist is studying atomic energy or a biological process or the chemical properties of some isotope, when a sociologist studies the structure of government and society, when a historian studies the development of events, or an economist the play of economic forces, when a classicist studies an ancient tongue, or a musicologist the intricacies of musical composition, when a theologian studies theology, each deals with his subject on all three of these levels at once. On the *conscious* level the deals with them as realities. On the *preconscious* level he deals with their allegorical and emotional import, direct and indirect. On the *unconscious* level, without realizing it, he uses his special competence and knowledge as an opportunity to express the unconscious, conflict-laden, and confused levels of his own spirit, using the language of his specialty as a vehicle for the projection outward of his internal struggles. Since this happens without his knowledge, it is a process which can take over his creative thinking in his own field, distorting and perverting it to save his unconscious needs and purposes.

The result is a structure of unconscious compromises which may render great intellectual brilliance as futile and as impotent as are any other symptomatic products of the neurotic process. It is for this reason that we can no longer tolerate with complacency the fact that art and science and every other cultural activity are hybrids, born of an unhealthy fusion of that which is finest and that which is sickest in human nature. It is a further consequence that the greater the role played by the unconscious components of symbolic thought, the wider must become the gap between erudition and wisdom. A scholar may be erudite on conscious and preconscious levels, yet so obtuse about the play of unconscious forces in his own life, that he cannot tell when he is using realistically and creatively the subject of which he is a master, or when he is using it like the inkblot on a Rorschach card. Education for wisdom must close this gap, by providing insight which penetrates into those areas of human life in which unconscious forces have always hitherto played the preponderant role.

This is the challenge which psychoanalytic psychiatry brings to the goals and techniques of education. At first thought the suggestion seems simple, a mere extension of the ancient Socratic admonition to "Know Thyself," making it read "Know Thyself in Depth." Yet these two added words, "in depth," will demand one of the most difficult cultural steps which civilized man has ever taken: a step which is essential if the man of the future is to be saved from man's present fate. And what has been that fate? It has been that in spite of a growing knowledge of the world around him he has repeated like an automaton the errors of his past; and that furthermore he has repeated these old errors in forms which become increasingly destructive and catastrophic as he becomes more educated. Whether his erudition has been in history, art, literature, the sciences, religion, or the total paraphernalia of modern culture, this has been the limiting factor in our Culture of Doom.

This automaticity of conduct which is governed predominantly by our unconscious psychological mechanisms is dependent directly upon their remaining inaccessible. Therefore, if "self-knowledge in depth" ever becomes the goal of a new concept of education, and if it becomes a part of the equipment which education brings to the cultured man, it will make it possible for man to attain freedom from his ancient slavery to those repetitive psychological processes over which at present he has no control. In his *Personal Record* Joseph Conrad describes himself as a knight in shining armor, mounted on a magnificent horse. The picture was quite flattering until on looking more closely, he noticed that little knaves were running by the head of the horse and holding onto the bridle. Thereupon he realized that he did not know who was guiding that horse; the knight on the horse's back, or the knaves running by its head. This is the image of the educated man of today. He is a noble figure on a noble charger, magnificently armed. But the knaves who trot unheeded by the horse's head, with their hands on the reins, are guiding that horse far more than is the pretentious figure of culture astride the horse's back.

Like infinity, self-knowledge is an ideal which can be approached but never reached. Therefore like education it is a process which is never finished, a point on a continuous and never-ending journey. It is relative and not absolute. Consequently, the achievement of self-knowledge is a process which goes on throughout life, demanding constant vigilance; and because it requires a continuous struggle, true self-knowledge never becomes an occasion for smug complacency.

The man who knows himself in depth does not look down his nose at the rest of the world from a perch on Mt. Olympus. Rather will he acknowledge with proper humility the impossibility of knowing himself fully, and the importance of struggling constantly against the lure of insidious, seductive illusions about himself. Nor on the other hand will he be incessantly preoccupied with his own conscious and unconscious motivations. Instead the more fully he approaches self-awareness, the more coherent and integrated become the various levels of his personality.

As a result, self-knowledge brings with it the right to trust his impulses and his intuitions. He may continue to watch himself out of the corner of his eye with vigilant self-scepticism, but he will give the center of his attention to his job and to the world around him. Thus, self-knowledge brings freedom and spontaneity to the most creative alliance of the human spirit, the alliance between conscious and preconscious processes: and it brings this spiritual liberation by freeing us from the internal blocking and distortion which occur when conscious and preconscious processes are opposed by an irreconcilable unconscious. Thus my vision of the educated man of the future is not an unreal fantasy of an individual out of whom all of the salty seasoning of preconscious and unconscious processes will have been dissolved, like a smoked ham which has soaked too long. It is rather of a man whose creative processes are relatively freed of the burden of unconscious internal conflicts.

In turn, however, this does not mean that to become educated a man must be psychoanalyzed. It means rather that new procedures must be introduced into the pattern of education which will make therapeutic analyses necessary only for those in whom the educational process has failed. The positive goal of this vital aspect of education is to shrink the dark empire in which unconscious forces have in the past played the preponderant role, and to broaden those areas of life in which conscious and preconscious processes will play the dominant role.

It is one thing, however, to describe self-knowledge in depth as the ultimate goal for culture and education. To achieve it is another. I will not presume here to write out a prescription on how this can be done. In dealing with any individual patient we know that without too much difficulty the psychiatrist can trace the interweaving patterns of complex, conscious, preconscious, and unconscious forces which have shaped an entire life. Yet many weeks, months, and even years of additional work may be required to communicate the analyst's insight to the patient himself. If the communication of insight to a single individual presents such formidable problems, we should not be surprised that the communication of insight to successive generations will require the development of basically new techniques of education, techniques which will have to start in the nursery and continue into old age, techniques which will have to circumvent adroitly the unconscious opposition of the oldsters among us who lack these insights and who feel personally threatened by them. Thus a new and critical version of the ancient battle between the generations is surely in the making.

Yet I believe that the whole future of human culture depends upon our solving this problem of how to introduce into education processes which will in essence be both preventive and curative. They will be preventive in the sense that they will limit and guide the fateful dichotomy which occurs early in life between conscious and preconscious processes on the one hand, and the inaccessible unconscious on the other. It will have to be curative as well, because we cannot expect prevention ever to work perfectly. Consequently we shall always have to build into the concepts and techniques of education certain types of therapeutic experiences, both for groups and for individuals, which will be designed to reintegrate unconscious with conscious and preconscious processes. Even to attempt this will require that we overcome not only the individual resistances and prejudices to which I have just referred, but also the entrenched opposition of many existing social, cultural, religious, and educational institutions. This is no small order: and I would hesitate to offer the challenge, if I did not have so deep a conviction that all of our vaunted culture and education, as we have known them in the past, have failed mankind completely.

Some may feel these views to be unduly pessimistic. Yet I believe that these criticisms of our educational processes are rooted in optimism, and pursue an optimistic ideal. It is not pessimism to face the fact of past failure, if our purpose in studying our failures is to learn how not to fail in the future. It was neither pessimism nor a morbid fascination with death which led medicine to the autopsy table, but rather courage, optimism, spiritual humility, and a determination to avoid the endless repetition of past error. Mankind's reward is scientific medicine; and we must now face the failure of education with the same combination of humility and determination. Because education has failed mankind in the past, it does not follow that it must necessarily continue to fail, unless we cling obstinately and defensively to methods which have already been tried without success.

Yet the tendency to prescribe more of the old medicines is deep in us. For instance, when I read that a new college president declares that what we need in education is a greater emphasis on religion, I confess that my heart sinks. This is not because he singled out religion. I have the same sinking feeling when someone says that what we need is more of the humanities, or when Hutchins and Adler call for more of the "great" books by "great" thinkers out of the past, or when a classicist calls for more of the classics, or a mathematician for more mathematics, or a chemist for more chemistry.

It is not a pretty spectacle, nor a reassuring measure of the maturity of educators, when in the face of our general cultural failure each cultural specialist cries out for larger doses of his own specific remedy. Such spiritual arrogance and obstinacy, whether from the pulpit or from the laboratory, should have no place in the deliberations of educated men. Indeed, it is a symptom of the very illness I am stressing, namely, that our educational system produces men of erudition with little wisdom or maturity; with the consequence that every cultural discipline is led by human beings who spend their time defending their vested interests in their own special fields. In this respect, the great washed have little on the great unwashed.

It is important to understand that scientists, including psychiatrists, are not immune to these frailties; and that they are equally true for all of those who carry the banners of culture. It is an old story of youthful idealism, of young confidence that *the* way to the good life is in their hands, then of a gradual disillusionment which usually is masked by a paradoxical defensiveness and a refusal to face the limitations of existing methods, turning instead in anger against anyone who is honest and sceptical enough to challenge his particular road to salvation.

All of us want to go on educating as we have in the past, making at the most only trivial curricular changes. But what mankind actually needs is a cultural stride of far grander dimensions. A little more or less of science, or of history, or of sociology, or of the classics, or of languages whether ancient or modern (for man can be as foolish in five languages as in one), or of philosophy or theology, or in the history of any of these: None of these gives to man the power to change and grow. Having devoted a lifetime to mastering some erudite discipline, and having thereby become a pew-holder in a towering cathedral with a limited seating capacity (to plagiarize Robert Nathan and *The Bishop's Wife*), it is indeed difficult for any of us to say, "This technique of mine which I have mastered at such great cost is just not enough." Instead we say, "Give the patient more of my medicine. More of the same is what he needs. Pour it down his throat. It may not have worked in the past: but more of it will surely cure him in the future."

These words are an expression of the human frailties which the artist, writer, historian, scientist, and theologian share equally with the least "cultured" man in the community. Every one of us is guilty of this—the scientists, the technologists, the classicists, the romanticists, the humanists, the musicians, the writers, the sculptors, and the dramatists. And especially is it true of the theologians of every sect and variety, because they give to this arrogance a divine sanction, in which I am sure that the Divinity would have no part. All say "Believe in me," "Believe in my way," "Believe in my special field." Few among us have the courage to say: "Do not *believe* at all. What I advocate is at best a working hypothesis to be rigorously and sceptically tested, but never believed. I ask for no credulity or faith. My challenge is to the courage and dignity of doubting, and to the duty of testing and experimenting. Man is Man not by virtue of believing, but by virtue of challenging belief. Let believing be the starting point for an investigation, but never its end." Just once in my life have I been privileged to hear a great religious teacher say from his pulpit, "It is the search for truth which is religion: and as soon as any religion believes that it has found the truth, it ceases to be religious."

Those who represent the world of the mind and of the spirit must acquire the humility which led medicine to study its defeats at the autopsy table. This was a unique moment in human culture. We need now to apply the same self-scrutiny to all of culture. And as we do this, let us stop to remind ourselves that when a patient dies, the doctor does not blame the patient: he blames himself. But when humanity fails, the artists and the writers scold, and the theologian thunders angry denunciations of human deficiencies, when they should be turning a pitiless scrutiny on themselves, their beliefs, and their techniques.

What then must education achieve? It must make it possible for human beings themselves to change. That is the next necessary goal of education. We would find it hard to prove that even the greatest works of art, of literature, of music, of philosophy, of religion have freed the hearts of men. Yet until we have found out how to make it possible for man himself to change, we have no right to revere our culture as though it were a creative and moving force in the Divine Comedy. Until what we call culture, whether with a small "c" or a capital "K," can free man from the domination of his own unconscious, it is no culture. An education which gives man only sophistication, taste, historical perspective, manners, erudite parlor conversation, and knowledge of how to use and control the forces of nature is a fraud on the human spirit, no matter what inflated pretensions and claims it makes.

It is we, the educated and the educators, who have failed mankind, not mankind which has failed us. Science and art and philosophy and religion and learning have failed; just as it is medicine which has failed when a patient dies, not the corpse. This charge is not made lightly; nor is it to be brushed aside in facile self-defense. The next goal of education is nothing less than a progressive freeing of man— not merely from external tyrannies of nature and of other men, but from internal enslavement by his own unconscious automatic mechanisms. Therefore, all of education and all of art and culture must contribute to this. It has long been recognized that in spite of technological progress, and in spite of art, literature, religion, and scholarly learning, the heart of man has not changed. This is both a challenge and a rebuke to our complacent acceptance of this bitter and devastating commentary on culture. My answer is based on the conviction that it is possible to break through the sonic barrier between conscious and unconscious processes, and thereby to bring to man for the first time in human history the opportunity to evolve beyond his enslaved past. That is why this thesis can claim for itself a realistic spiritual optimism.

Toward this goal a first step will be a deeper study of those early crisis in human development, when the symbolic process begins to splinter into conscious, preconscious, and unconscious systems. The purpose of such a study of infancy would be to illuminate the origins of the repressive processes which produce these cleavages, since it is these which must be guided and controlled. As its second goal such a study would aim at the reintegration of unconscious with preconscious and conscious processes: something which has to be done not merely once, but repeatedly throughout the entire process of growth, from infancy through childhood, puberty, adolescence, and on into adult years. Just as the battle for political freedom must be won over and over again, so too in every life the battle for internal psychological freedom must be fought and won again and again, if men are to achieve and retain freedom from the tyranny of their own unconscious processes, the freedom to understand the forces which determine their thoughts, feelings, purposes, goals, and behavior. This freedom is the fifth and ultimate human freedom; and like every other freedom, it demands eternal vigilance.

At present, except in a few experiments (like those which are made in a few pioneering institutions, such as Goddard College) education is making no effort to meet this challenge. At present a farmer is given more training for raising stock than all of our institutions of lower or higher learning offer to men and women for raising the children whose lives they will make and break.

I would not give the impression that I believe that this is all there is to education. But what I do believe is that without this at its heart education, culture, literature, art, science, and religion are all hollow frauds. Without this, education has sold humanity down the river—back into slavery. And I believe that this will continue to be true until we rescue from his present oblivion this forgotten man of education.

I want to repeat that self-knowledge in depth is not all there is to wisdom, but that it makes maturity and wisdom possible; and what is even more important, it frees us from the tyranny of those rigid compulsive mechanisms which have made impossible our psychological evolution. Without self-knowledge in depth, we can have dreams but not art, we can have the neurotic raw material of literature, but not mature literature. Without it we have no adults, but only aging children armed with words, paints, clay, and atomic weapons, none of which they understand. It is this which makes a mockery of the pretentious claims of education, of religion, of the arts, and of science. Self-knowledge is the Forgotten Man of our entire educational system and indeed of human culture in general. Without self-knowledge it is possible to be erudite, but never wise. My challenge to all of us is to have the humility to face this failure, and the determination to do something effective about it before it is too late.

14

Perception as Creative Experience: Critique of the Concept of Regression in the Service of the Ego*

Ernest G. Schachtel

The phylogenesis of perception is characterized by the increasing amount, variety, and enrichment of sensory experience. It culminates in man's allocentric mode of perception, in which independently existing objects are perceived (objectification). Because of man's openness toward the world the number of possible objects of human perception and the variety of their aspects are infinite and inexhaustible. To what extent man realizes his potentiality of allocentric perception depends on the stage he reaches in his ontogenetic development. During this development he explores, in the playful encounters of childhood, an expanding environment and an increasing variety of object aspects in exercising his growing sensory-motor capacities. While part of this exploration takes place in the spontaneous and immediate encounter with the objects, an important part consists in the increasing acquaintance with their meaning in the culture. Such learning on the one hand enriches the object world of the growing child to a degree which could never be reached by an isolated individual. On the other hand, it also increasingly supplants the child's original approach to the objects and, especially in our time, entails the danger of *closing* his openness toward the world and of reducing all experience to the perception of such preformed clichés and "angles" as make up the world of "reality" seen by the family, peer group, and society in which he grows up. The perspective from which objects are perceived may narrow to "what they are there for" and "how one deals with them."

* Chapter 10 of *Metamorphosis* by Ernest G. Schachtel, © 1959 by Basic Books, Inc., Publishers, New York.

Nature may no longer be seen as the mother of all living creatures including man, but may become an enemy to be conquered or a mere object to be exploited and used. Other people, too, may be seen from a similar viewpoint, the viewpoint of secondary autocentricity.

Where the perspective of secondary autocentricity becomes the only one and dominates all perception, allocentric as well as primary autocentric perception tend to stagnate and atrophy. In our time this stagnation tends to take the form of an alienation of man from the objects and from his own sensory capacities. The danger of this alienation is that man's dulled senses may no longer encounter the objects themselves but only what he expects and already knows about them, the labels formed by his society. The closed world of this perspective ceases to hold any wonder. Everything has its label, and if one does not know it the experts will tell him.

Another facet of such closure of the world appears in the often observed fact that older people frequently tend to feel that only the "good old times" offered any worth-while experience, that, for example, only the authors, actors, or singers they admired in their youth or young adulthood were great, only the sights seen in their youth were wonderful and exciting in a way to which the contemporary world offers no parallel. This complaint probably is as old as the human world. Its cause is not that the world has become duller, but that the capacity for allocentric interest has shriveled with the decreasing openness toward the world and the extended confinement in the familiar world of secondary autocentricity.

The world of secondary, socially shared autocentricity bears a certain resemblance, on the higher level of objectification, to the closed worlds of the animals predetermined by their relatively few needs and their innate organization, which serves the satisfaction of these needs as does their learned behavior. This resemblance is highlighted, perhaps inadvertently, by a remark in the account of an interesting recent experiment with dogs. The results of this experiment indicate that in normally raised adult dogs the curiosity with which they explore something new wears off very quickly—they become bored and lie down or turn their back on it. This is not true of puppies in the stage of playful exploration, nor is it true, as these experiments showed, of dogs raised in an environment with very restricted sensory stimulation, for these animals persist much longer in lively exploration than do the normally raised dogs. The experimenters, although emphasizing that their research does not have any bearing on humans, nevertheless comment that the normally raised dog acts more intelligently because he can satisfy his curiosity more quickly and that while "there may be something delightful about a child who can spend an hour completely absorbed in a clothespin . . . this is not intelligent, adult behavior."[1] However, the parallel drawn in this remark between dog and man obscures a crucial difference. *Only* the adult who is able to be completely absorbed, again and again, often for many hours and days, in an object that arouses his interest will be the one who enlarges his, and sometimes man's, scope of perception and of experience. A painter may spend many days, weeks or months, or even years, in looking at the same mountain, as Cézanne did, or at blades of grass or bamboo leaves or branches of a tree, as many of the Chinese and Japanese masters did, without tiring of it and without ceasing to discover something new in it. The same is true of the poet's or writer's devoted love for his object, of which Rilke speaks, of the true naturalist's perception of the plant or animal with which he has to live for long periods of time in order to acquire that intimate knowledge from which eventually new meaning and understanding will be born. This applies to all men who want to learn to know something or somebody truly and deeply. Of course, the length of time spent in such repeated encounters will bear fruit only if it does not become a blind routine in which the perceiver closes himself off from, rather than opens himself toward, that which is before him so that he merely sees the same aspect over and over again and becomes increasingly blind to the nature of the object. In the latter case he will be bored, like those who quickly turn their back on anything new. Like the experienced and mature dog, he will remain within a limited world and quickly close it again in the unlikely event that he should catch a glimpse of the vastnesses and depths un-

[1] William R. Thompson and Ronald Melzak, "Early Environment," *Scientific American,* 1956, 194:38–42. Hebb comments that "the restricted dogs . . . haven't the brains to be bored." D. O. Hebb, "The Mammal and His Environment," *American Journal of Psychiatry,* 1955, 111:826–831.

known to him. Only if the concept of intelligence is restricted to mean adaptation to the status quo is it more intelligent to be done quickly with anything new. But if man's highest capacity is that of allocentric interest to which the world never becomes a closed book, then the greater intelligence may be that which does not quickly dispose of or deal with an object but wonders at it and does not tire easily of contemplating and exploring it even if to others it may be the most familiar thing imaginable.

In such perception the glance dwells on the frontiers of human experience and becomes creative, revealing hitherto unknown vistas. It has been compared with the child's glance when it is said that the artist[2] and the wise man resemble a child. The resemblance consists in the freshness, spontaneity, interest, and openness with which the object is approached and reacted to. Just as these qualities and attitudes in the child are the prerequisite of expansion and progress in the encounter with the world, so they are in the adult. They make the encounter creative, be it in the sense of growth and enlargement of personal experience, or in the sense of enabling the artist or the scientist to add to the scope of human experience. Such openness toward and interest in the object is part of the phenomenon of creative experience which takes place in the whole human being with all his capacities and reactions even though one or the other may play a more dominant role in any particular act of creative experience. Thus, what we have seen in studying the ontogenetic development and the nature of allocentric perception can be of help in clarifying the nature of creative experience.

The problem of *creative experience* is essentially the same for all the human capacities such as perception, thought, feeling, and motor activity, comprising, in the widest sense, not only the hand that moves the brush in painting or manipulates the object to be explored or to be fashioned, but also the eye, the head, the body that approach the object from different angles, etc. It is the problem of the open encounter of the total person with the world, that is, with some part of the world. Of

[2] The word "artist," here and on the following pages, always refers not only to the artist but to the poet or writer or composer as well. Furthermore, I am considering mainly modern art and literature, from the Renaissance to the present day.

the different aspects of allocentric perception the *openness in turning toward* the object is the most basic and important one; the fullest interest in an object is possible only if the person opens himself fully toward as many object aspects as possible, that is, optimally toward the totality of the object.

The openness toward the object in creative experience is apparent both in the motivation for the encounter and in the way in which the encounter takes place. The main *motivation* at the root of creative experience is man's need to relate to the world around him, a need which, as we have seen, becomes particularly strong and striking when urgent physical needs such as for food and rest have been stilled. This need is apparent in the young child's interest in all the objects around him, in his ever renewed exploration of and play with them. It is equally apparent in the artist's lifelong effort to grasp and render something which he has envisaged in his encounter with the world, in the scientist's wonder about the nature of the object with which he is concerned, and in the interest in the objects around him of every person who has not succumbed to stagnation in a closed autocentric or sociocentric world. They all have in common the fact that they do not remain in a closed, familiar, labeled world but they want to go beyond embeddedness in the familiar and in the routine, and to relate to another object, or to the same one more fully, or from another angle, anew, afresh. In such acts of relatedness man finds both the world and himself. This does not imply that other needs may not also play a role in and color or codetermine the creative experience. It only means that without the basic need to relate to the world, without openness toward the world, the experience will not enlarge, deepen, and make more alive the person's relation to the world, that is, will not be creative.

The *quality* of the encounter that leads to creative experience consists primarily in the openness during the encounter and in the repeated and varied approaches to the object, in the free and open play of attention, thought, feeling, perception, etc. In this free play the person experiences the object in its manifold relations to himself and also tentatively tries out, as it were, a great variety of relations between the object thus approached and other objects, ideas, experiences, feelings, objects of imagination, etc. In characterizing this activity as play I do not mean that it is playful rather than serious, but that it is not bound by rigorous rules or by conventional schemata of memory, thought, or perception. It may at times be playful, too; but that is not its main characteristic. It resembles the child's free play in his encounter with the world where playfulness, too, is not the main feature but the openness, the intensity of the interest, the repeated and varied approaches, which range all the way from the grave and serious, the absorbing and tantalizing, to the playful and the fleeting.

In the earliest stages of infancy the play of the child with the objects of the environment is at first limited to and determined by what happens to impinge on his senses. Later on it increasingly expands as the child can turn actively from one object to another. From then on it may at times range freely, at other times be focused more on a particular object, idea, feeling. In such focusing, relations may be established between the specific object and others that have been encountered in ranging more widely. In the creative process the person usually focuses more and more sharply on a particular area or object. As he approaches it from various angles in the tentative play of thought, senses, and motor behavior, he also connects it with other experiences. His relatedness to the object is intensified and he becomes more open to its different aspects and possible links.

What has been learned in such unfettered and open intercourse with the world may enlarge unnoticeably and gradually the person's experience and contribute to his growth, or it may crystallize suddenly in an insight, or in a new vision of something that seemed long familiar, or in an "inspiration." But it is truly assimilated and become consciously and freely available to the person only if it is either fashioned into an objective work, as in artistic or literary creation, or is otherwise elaborated by connecting it with, and making it part of, the conscious total life and experience of the person. This usually is a more laborious process than either the long incubation period of the many encounters between person and object or the subsequent flash of insight, vision, or inspiration. Both the period of immersion in the ever renewed encounters and the period of articulating and connecting the experiences won in the free play of the varied approaches are essential for the growth and expansion of the person's relation to the world through creative experience.

In Freud's work and in post-Freudian ego psychology, especially in the work of Kris, the view is expressed that such experience, especially as it leads to artistic creation, is always the product of a *repressed libidinal or aggressive impulse* and of a *regression* to infantile modes of thought or experience, to the primary process, albeit in the service of the ego. Freud considered it probable that the artist has a constitutionally given "looseness of repression" [3] and he ascribed certain "achievements of special perfection" to the temporary removal of the repression of an unconscious impulse which, for the particular occasion, becomes ego-syntonic and manifests "a resistance in the face of opposition similar to that of obsessional symptoms." [4]

This resistance in the face of all opposition, it seems to me, is the resistance not of an Id drive but of the conviction of the truth of artistic or scientific creation in the face of the opposition by the shared autocentricity of conventional perception and thought. Such truth is more likely to be encountered by the person who has continued and expanded the child's openness toward the world on the adult level and whose sensory and intellectual capacities have not entirely succumbed to the pressure of the accepted way in which everyone perceives the "realistic" world of the conventions of the day, the era, and the society. Just as the amnesia for early childhood is not due primarily to the repression of forbidden sexual impulses but to the transformation of the total manner of perceiving and thinking, so the unseeingness which in all of us, in varying degrees, stands in the way of a more creative vision is due more often to the encroachment of an already labeled world upon our spontaneous sensory and intellectual capacities than to the repression of a libidinal impulse.

Freud assumed that the artist suffers from too strong drives in craving honor, power, wealth, fame and to be loved by women and that, since he does not have the means of obtaining these satisfactions,

[3] *Lockerheit der Verdrängungen,* S. Freud, "Vorlesungen zur Einführung in die Psychoanalyse," *Gesammelte Werke* (Imago Publishing Co., London, 1940), Vol. XI, pp. 390–391.

[4] S. Freud, "The Unconscious," *Collected Papers* (Basic Books, New York, 1959), Vol. IV, p. 127.

he turns his back on reality and tries to obtain them in his phantasies, which, if he is worldly successful with his creations, in the end will get him what he originally wanted.[5] While these drives may play a role in an artist just as well as in a businessman or in anybody else, they are in no way specific for the artist nor are they unusually strong in all artists. However, what *is* essential for the artist is that he experiences and expresses more precisely, and without being blindfolded by the sociocentric view, what happens in his encounter with the world or some aspect of it. His need to relate to the world must not be channeled as completely by the conventional patterns and schemata of his culture as is the case for most people in our time, so that his senses, his sensibilities, and his mind can be more open, more innocent, like the child who, in Andersen's tale, saw and said that the emperor was naked and did not have the beautiful clothes that everybody else had persuaded himself to see or, at least, to profess having seen. Thus, the "looseness of repression" of which Freud speaks has to do more with the artist's vision not being fettered and molded completely by the conventional views, with his being more open toward the world and himself, than with the looseness of the repression of any particular libidinal impulse.

Kris makes the additional point that in the genesis of the work of art a *regression to primary-process thought* takes place. Unlike the regression in dreams or in pathological cases, it is controlled by, and in the service of, the ego. According to him, it is this regression which permits the discharge of the repressed impulses mentioned by Freud. The regression to primary-process thought takes place, according to Kris, both in fantastic, free-wandering thought processes and in creative processes, in the former under a condition of ego weakness, in the latter in the service of the ego.[6] But the seeming similarity emphasized by Kris is deceptive, and regression to primary-process thought is not typical of the creative process.

Primary-process thought uses freely displaceable cathexes in the un-

[5] *Gesammelte Werke,* Vol. XI, p. 390.

[6] Ernst Kris, "On Preconscious Mental Processes," in David Rapaport, *Organization and Pathology of Thought* (Columbia University Press, New York, 1951), pp. 474–493, especially 485–491.

restrained tendency toward full discharge of the tension of id drives by the path of (phantasied or hallucinated) wish fulfillment, that is, in the service of the striving to return to a tensionless state.[7] There are daydreams, reveries, and idly wandering thoughts which are correctly or approximately described by the concept of primary-process thought. What the early stages of the creative process have in common with such reveries is mainly the fact that they, too, wander freely without being bound by the rules and properties of the accepted, conventional, familiar everyday world. In this free wandering they center, however, on the object, idea, problem which is the focus of the creative endeavor. What distinguishes the creative process from regression to primary-process thought is that the freedom of the approach is due not to a drive discharge function but to the openness in the encounter with the object of the creative labor.

This openness means that the sensibilities of the person, his mind and his senses, are more freely receptive, less tied to fixed anticipations and sets, and that the object is approached in different ways, from different angles, and not with any fixed purpose to use it for the satisfaction of a particular need, or the testing of one particular expectation or possibility. It seems likely that greater mobility of cathexis is found not only in mental processes serving primarily the discharge of an id drive but also in the described free play of all one's faculties in the open encounter with the world. In the latter case the function of the mobile cathexis is not primarily the discharge of an id drive in order to abolish tension but, on the contrary, the contact with a manifold, inexhaustible reality and the steeping of the person in many different aspects of the world, which takes place by means of thoughts and phantasies as well as by the play of the senses and the motor functions. Of course, the discharge of drive tension and the striving to make contact with some aspect of reality may also occur in the same train of phantasy or freely wandering thought. There may be constant transitions from one to the other, so that at one moment one may predominate, at the next the other.

The relatively undirected, freely wandering play of perception, thought, phantasy, thus is not necessarily regressive but can be and

[7] Compare Rapaport, p. 694.

often is progressive. Developmentally, the tendency to mere drive discharge and the tendency to relate to the world in many-sided sensory-motor-affective-thinking contacts move in opposite directions: the former tends to decrease, the latter to play an increasingly important role during early childhood. The free play of senses and mind in the open encounter with the world is capable of continued development as more and more aspects of the world are assimilated, while thought serving primarily discharge of tension is indeed in the service of the regressive tendency to abolish the encounter with reality and return to a state of rest and satiation.

Perhaps the idea of a regressive tendency in the creative process not only stems from the mistaken notion that freely wandering thought in the early phases of the creative process mainly serves the purpose of the discharge of libido and aggression (primary-process thought), but has received support also, perhaps unwittingly, from the tendency to judge human activity solely on the basis of the performance principle, of a quasi-industrial standard of the "goods" that the activity delivers.[8] Compared, for example, with the strictly purposeful modern manufacturing process, which regulates uniformly every movement of machine and human hand in order to avoid any waste motion and thus produce the finished product in the shortest possible time and with the smallest expense of energy, the creative process, and especially its earlier phases, may seem like an incredible waste. The analogy is easily extended to the kind of perception and thought that are directed merely to the quick recognition of any object or to its relation to the conventional schemata of familiar reality and to its use for some definite purpose within this framework. But even if the work of art, of poetry, or creative thought is acknowledged as a worth-while end in itself, expanding as it does the range of conscious human experience, the perspective of the performance principle may lead to the view that there is something "regressive" in the period of free, mobile, and open play of the mind, the senses, the hand with the many possibilities and aspects of the

[8] The concept of "performance principle" is taken from M. Marcuse, who understands it as a principle by which the members of our contemporary civilization are stratified according to their "competitive economic performances" and which is part of modern society's reality principle. Herbert Marcuse, *Eros and Civilization* (Beacon Press, Boston, 1955), p. 44.

objects only some of which may enter ultimately into the creation. Yet, it is clear that the incubation period as well as the period of execution of the work are equally important, and that the former provides the foundations for the latter.

The notion of a regressive factor in the creative process may have still other, unacknowledged ancestors. From the standpoint of a closed system, any fresh groping which in some way runs counter to the "realistic world as we know it" may appear as childish. When, for example, the cognitive functions of the ego are considered primarily as adaptive to a world already known, to familiar concepts and percepts, then the loosening of the familiar features in an open and fresh approach may be viewed as regressive in the sense of not serving the quick adaptation to known reality for immediately useful purposes.[9] Such a definition of cognition would already imply that anything short of the immediately useful orientation in the world as already known falls short of the cognitive, adaptive function of the ego, and perhaps for that reason is apt to be labeled "regressive." In such a view not the openness of the mind toward the world, but its ready recognition and use of the familiar "handles" of "reality" would be the highest cognitive and adaptive function of the ego.

The decisive shortcoming of such a view of man's coping with reality lies in the overlooking of his openness toward the world. This oversight may be facilitated by a concept of normality, of the nature of man, which derives its normative yardstick from the greatest number, from the average rather than from the full realization of man's potentialities in the course of healthy development and maturation. One of the merits of psychoanalytic theory has been its emphasis on the developmental viewpoint. This has led to a definition of normalcy in terms

[9] This seems to be the position of Bellak, who reformulates the concept of regression in the service of the ego as "a brief oscillating reduction of *certain adaptive* functions of the ego in the service of (i.e. for the facilitation of) other, specifically the synthetic ego functions." He describes this process as a decrease of cognitive, selective, adaptive functions with a consequent weakening of the "sharply defined boundaries of figure and ground, of logical, temporal, spatial and other relations," permitting a reordering into "new configurations with new boundaries under the scrutiny of the again sharply functioning adaptive forces." Leopold Bellak, "Creativity, Some Random Notes to a Systematic Consideration," *Journal of Projective Techniques,* 1958, 22:363–380, 367. In such a view the concept of regression to primary-process thought no longer retains its original meaning of thought processes serving the discharge of repressed drive impulses.

of stage of development reached (or stage regressed to). According to this definition, normalcy is identical with maturity. This viewpoint is shared by all the different psychoanalytic schools regardless of whether they define development and maturity, as Freud does, in terms of the stage of libido development and ego development or, as Sullivan does, in terms of the development of the capacity for love and respect of self and others or, as I would, in terms of the degree and stage of emergence from total embeddedness. But once the concept of normalcy is thus defined developmentally, the analyst finds himself confronted with the odd discovery that, according to his criteria, most people never reach maturity and thus do not seem to be normal. In French's work this discovery is evident in "The Future of an Illusion." In his concept of collective neuroses he makes explicit the conflict between a norm based on the greatest number, the average man, and one based on an idea of human nature and human potentialities.[10] Sullivan doubted very much that most people reach maturity according to his criteria of the capacity to love and respect others and oneself. Fromm discusses this problem in developing his concept of the "pathology of normalcy." [11]

While man's openness toward the world is clearly apparent in the child's wonder at the many objects in his environment and in his encounters, in which he discovers ever new aspects of the world, in most people the stress of life and the patterns of their culture and social group soon stifle the eager, youthful quest and close the once open mind so that it will encounter only the same, familiar objects. To their knowledgeable "realism" the suggestion of a different approach may appear unrealistic, or a regression to childish modes of behavior, or useless for the serious business of adaptation to reality as they know it. Even if they allow for the possibility of a different view of the world such allowance may be a mere word or thought without weight and substance.

Yet, in contrast to the animals, man is capable of continued growth and development throughout his life if he succeeds in remaining open to the world and capable of allocentric interest. Such openness is the basis

[10] S. Freud, *Civilization and Its Discontents* (Hogarth Press, London, 1953).
[11] Erich Fromm, *The Sane Society* (Rinehart & Co., New York, 1955), pp. 12–21.

of progress and of creative achievement in individual life as well as in the history of mankind.

On the one hand, man lives always in the world of the objects-of-use, in the perspective of secondary autocentricity. He could not exist without this perspective. In providing for his needs the objects-of-use perspective largely replaces the instinct-organization of the animals. But if man ceases to develop the allocentric mode of perception, if he loses that openness of senses and mind which transcends the object-of-use perspective and enables him to relate to others and to the world for the sake of the relationship itself, then his development stagnates in the closed world of secondary autocentricity, and the ontogentic trend of development toward objectification and allocentric interest comes to a standstill. The basic difference between animal and human mental organization, man's openness toward the world, can be increasingly realized only if man retains and develops the allocentric mode of perception, the first appearance of which is the most important step in the development of perception in the growing child.

15

Education on the Nonverbal Level *

ALDOUS HUXLEY

Early in the mid-Victorian period the Reverend Thomas Binney, a Congregationalist divine, published a book with the alluring title, *Is It Possible to Make the Best of Both Worlds?* His conclusion was that perhaps it might be possible. In spite of its unorthodox message, or perhaps because of it, the book was a best seller, which only showed, said the more evangelical of Mr. Binney's Nonconformist colleagues and Anglican opponents, how inexpressibly wicked Victorian England really was.

What Mr. Binney's critics had done (and their mistake is repeated by all those who use the old phrase disapprovingly) was to equate "making the best of both worlds" with "serving two masters." It is most certainly very difficult, perhaps quite impossible, to serve Mammon and God simultaneously—to pursue the most sordid interests while aspiring to realize the highest ideals. This is obvious. Only a little less obvious, however, is the fact that it is very hard, perhaps quite impossible, to serve God while failing to make the best of both worlds—of *all* the worlds of which, as human beings, we are the inhabitants.

Man is a multiple amphibian and exists at one and the same time in a number of universes, dissimilar to the point, very nearly, of complete incompatibility. He is at once an animal and a rational intellect; a product of evolution closely related to the apes and a spirit capable of self-transcendence; a sentient being in contact with the brute data of his own nervous system and the physical environment and at the same time the creator of a home-made universe of words and other symbols, in which he lives and moves and has anything from thirty to eighty percent of his being. He is a self-conscious and self-centered ego who is also a member of a moderately gregarious species, an individualist compelled by the population explosion to live at ever closer quarters, and in ever tighter organizations, with millions of other egos as self-

* Reprinted with permission of *DAEDALUS, Journal of the American Academy of Arts and Sciences,* Boston, Mass. Spring 1962, "Science and Technology in Contemporary Society."

centered and as poorly socialized as himself. Neurologically, he is a lately evolved Jekyll-cortex associated with an immensely ancient brain-stem-Hyde. Physiologically, he is a creature whose endocrine system is perfectly adapted to the conditions prevailing in the lower Paleolithic, but living in a metropolis and spending eight hours a day sitting at a desk in an air-conditioned office. Psychologically, he is a highly educated product of twentieth-century civilization, chained, in a state of uneasy and hostile symbiosis, to a disturbingly dynamic unconscious, a wild phantasy and an unpredictable id—and yet capable of falling in love, writing string quartets, and having mystical experiences.

Living amphibiously in all these incommensurable worlds at once, human beings (it is hardly surprising) find themselves painfully confused, uncertain where they stand or who they really are. To provide themselves with a recognizable identity, a niche in the scheme of things that they can call "home," they will give assent to the unlikeliest dogmas, conform to the most absurd and even harmful rules of thought, feeling, and conduct, put on the most extravagant fancy dress and identify themselves with masks that bear almost no resemblance to the faces they cover. "Bovarism" (as Jules de Gaultier calls it) is the urge to pretend that one is something that in fact one is not. It is an urge that manifests itself, sometimes weakly, sometimes with overpowering strength, in all human beings, and one of the conditions of its manifestation is precisely our uncertainty about where we stand or who we are. To explore our multiple amphibiousness with a view to doing something constructive about it is a most laborious process. Our minds are congenitally lazy, and the original sin of the intellect is oversimplification. Dogmatism and boveristic identification with a stereotype are closely related manifestations of the same kind of intellectual delinquency. "Know thyself." From time immemorial this has been the advice of all the seers and philosophers. The self that they urge us to know is not, of course, the stylized persona with which, bovaristically, we try to become identified; it is the multiple amphibian, the inhabitant of all those incompatible worlds that we must somehow learn to make the best of.

A good education may be defined as one which helps the boys and girls subjected to it to make the best of all the worlds in which, as human beings, they are compelled, willy-nilly, to live. An education that prepares them to make the best of only one of their worlds, or of only a few of them, is inadequate. This is a point on which, in principle, all educators have always agreed. *Mens sana in corpore sano* is an ancient educational ideal and a very good one. Unfortunately, good ideals are never enough. Unless they are accompanied by full instructions regarding the methods by which they may be realized, they are almost useless. Hell is paved with good intentions, and whole periods of history have been made hideous or grotesque by enthusiastic idealists who failed to elaborate the means whereby their lofty aspirations might be effectively, and above all harmlessly, implemented.

Just how good is modern education? How successful is it in helping young people to make the best of all the worlds which, as multiple amphibians, they have to live in? In a center of advanced scientific and technical study this question gets asked inevitably in terms of what may be called the paradox of specialization. In science and technology specialization is unavoidable and indeed absolutely necessary. But training for this unavoidable and necessary specialization does nothing to help young amphibians to make the best of their many worlds. Indeed, it pretty obviously prevents them from doing anything of the kind. What then is to be done? At the Massachusetts Institute of Technology and in other schools where similar problems have arisen, the answer to this question has found expression in a renewed interest in the humanities. Excessive scientific specialization is tempered by courses in philosophy, history, literature, and social studies. All this is excellent so far as it goes. But does it go far enough? Do courses in the humanities provide a sufficient antidote for excessive scientific and technical specialization? Do they, in the terminology we have been using, help young multiple amphibians to make the best of a substantially greater number of their worlds?

Science is the reduction of the bewildering diversity of unique events to manageable uniformity within one of a number of symbol systems, and technology is the art of using these symbol systems so as to control and organize unique events. Scientific observation is always a viewing of things through the refracting medium of a symbol system, and technological praxis is always the handling of things in ways that some symbol system has dictated. Education in science and technology is essentially education on the symbolic level.

Turning to the humanities, what do we find? Courses in philosophy, literature, history, and social studies are exclusively verbal. Observation of and experimentation with nonverbal events have no place in these fields. Training in the sciences is largely on the symbolic level, training in the liberal arts is wholly and all the time on that level. When courses in the humanities are used as the only antidote to too much science and technology, excessive specialization in one kind of symbolic education is being tempered by excessive specialization in another kind of symbolic education. The young amphibians are taught to make the best, not of all their worlds, but only of two varieties of the same world—the world of symbols. But this world of symbols is only one of the worlds in which human beings do their living and their learning. They also inhabit the nonsymbolic world of unconceptualized or only slightly conceptualized experience. However effective it may be on the conceptual level, an education that fails to help young amphibians to make the best of the inner and outer universes on the hither side of symbols is an inadequate education. And however much we may delight in Homer or Gibbon, however illuminating in their different ways Pareto and William Law, Hui-neng and Bertrand Russell may strike us as being, the fact remains that the reading of their works will not be of much help to us in our efforts to make the best of our worlds of unconceptualized, nonverbal experience.

And here, before I embark on a discussion of these nonverbal worlds, let me add parenthetically that even on the verbal level, where they are most at home, educators have done a good deal less than they might reasonably have been expected to do in explaining to young people the nature, the limitations, the huge potentialities for evil as well as for good, of that greatest of all human inventions, language. Children should be taught that words are indispensable but also can be fatal—the only begetters of all civilization, all science, all consistency of high purpose, all angelic goodness, and the only begetters at the same time of all superstition, all collective madness and stupidity, all worse-than-bestial diabolism, all the dismal historical succession of crimes in the name of God, King, Nation, Party, Dogma. Never before, thanks to the techniques of mass communication, have so many listeners been so completely at the mercy of so few speakers. Never have misused words—those hideously efficient tools of all the tyrants, war-mongers, persecutors, and heresy-hunters—been so widely and so disastrously influential as they are today. Generals, clergymen, advertisers, and the rulers of totalitarian states—all have good reasons for disliking the idea of universal education in the rational use of language. To the military, clerical, propagandist, and authoritarian mind such training seems (and rightly seems) profoundly subversive. To those who think that liberty is a good thing, and who hope that it may some day become possible for more people to realize more of their desirable potentialities in a society fit for free, fully human individuals to live in, a thorough education in the nature of language, in its uses and abuses, seems indispensable. Whether in fact the mounting pressures of overpopulation and overorganization in a world still enthusiastically dedicated to nationalistic idolatry will permit this kind of subversive linguistic education to be adopted by even the more democratic nations remains to be seen.

And now, after this brief digression, let us return to our main theme, the education of multiple amphibians on levels other than the verbal and the symbolic. "Make the body capable of doing many things," wrote Spinoza. "This will help you to perfect the mind and come to the intellectual love of God." Substitute "psychophysical organism" for "body," and you have here the summary of a program for universal education on the nonsymbolic level, supplemented by a statement of the reasons why such an education is desirable and indeed, if the child is to grow into a fully human being, absolutely necessary. The detailed curriculum for an education in what may be called the nonverbal humanities has still to be worked out. All I can do at this time is to drop a few fragmentary hints.

Two points, to begin with, must be emphatically stressed. First, education in the nonverbal humanities is not just a matter of gymnastics and football, of lessons in singing and folk dancing. All these, of course, are good, but by themselves not good enough. Such traditional methods of training young people in nonverbal skills need to be supplemented, if they are to yield their best results, by other kinds of training, beginning with a thorough training in elementary awareness. And the second point to be remembered is that education in the nonverbal humanities is a process that should be started in the kindergarten and continued through all the years of school and college—and thereafter, as self-education, throughout the rest of life.

At the end of a delightful anthology entitled *Zen Flesh, Zen Bones,* its editor, Mr. Paul Reps, has printed an English version of an ancient Tantrik text in which Shiva, in response to Parvati's questions about the nature of enlightened consciousness, gives a list of one hundred and twelve exercises in the art of being aware of inner and outer reality on its nonsymbolic levels. *Gnosce Teipsum.* But how? From the vast majority of our pastors and masters no answer is forthcoming. Here, for a blessed change, is a philosophical treatise that speaks of means as well as of ends, of concrete experience as well as of high abstractions. The intelligent and systematic practice of any half-dozen of these hundred and twelve exercises will take one further towards the realization of the ancient ideal of self-knowledge than all the roaring or pathetic eloquence of generations of philosophers, theologians, and moralists. (Let me add, in passing, that whereas Western philosophy tends to be concerned with the manipulation of abstract symbols for the benefit of the speculative and moralizing intellect, oriental philosophy is almost always essentially operational. "Perform such and such psychophysical operations," the exponents of this philosophy say, "and you will probably find yourself in a state of mind which, like all those who have achieved it in the past, you will regard as self-evidently and supremely valuable. In the context of this state of mind, speculation about man and the universe leads us, as it led earlier thinkers, to the metaphysical doctrine of *Tat tvam asi* [thou art That], and to its ethical corollary—universal compassion. In this philosophy it is the experiential element that is important. Its speculative superstructure is a thing of words, and words, though useful and necessary, should never be taken too seriously.")

Education in elementary awareness will have to include techniques for improving awareness of internal events and techniques for improving awareness of external events as these are revealed by our organs of sense. In his introductions to several of F. M. Alexander's books, John Dewey insisted upon the importance of a properly directed training in the awareness of internal events. It was Dewey's opinion that the training methods developed by Alexander were to education what education is to life in general—an indispensable condition for any kind of improvement. Dewey had himself undergone this training and so knew what he was talking about. And yet in spite of this high praise bestowed by one of the most influential of modern philosophers and educational reformers, Alexander's methods have been ignored, and schoolchildren still receive no training in the kind of internal awareness that can lead to what Alexander described as "creative conscious control."

The educational and therapeutic values of training aimed at heightening awareness of internal events was empirically demonstrated during the first quarter of the present century by the eminently successful Swiss psychiatrist, Dr. Roger Vittoz. And in recent years methods similar to those of Vittoz and to the Tantrik exercises attributed many centuries ago to Shiva have been developed and successfully used both in the treatment of neurotics and for the enrichment of the lives of the normal by the authors of *Gestalt Therapy,* Drs. Frederick F. Perls, Ralph F. Hefferline, and Paul Goodman.

All our mental processes depend upon perception. Inadequate perceiving results in poor thinking, inappropriate feeling, diminished interest in and enjoyment of life. Systematic training of perception should be an essential element in all education.

Our amphibiousness is clearly illustrated in the two modes of our awareness of external events. There is a receptive, more or less unconceptualized, aesthetic and "spiritual" mode of perceiving; and there is also a highly conceptualized, stereotyped, utilitarian, and even scientific mode. In his *Expostulation and Reply* and *The Tables Turned,* Wordsworth has perfectly described these two modes of awareness and has assigned to each its special significance and value for the human being who aspires to make the best of both worlds and so, by teaching his psychophysical organism to "do many things," to "perfect the mind and come to the intellectual love of God."

> "Why, William, on that old grey stone,
> Thus for the length of half a day,
> Why, William, sit you thus alone,
> And dream your time away?

Where are your books?—that light bequeathed
To being else forlorn and blind?
Up! Up! and drink the spirit breathed
From dead men to their kind.

You look round on your Mother Earth,
As if she for no purpose bore you;
As if you were her first-born birth,
And none had lived before you."

One morning thus, by Esthwaite lake,
When life was sweet, I knew not why,
To me my good friend Matthew spake,
And thus I made reply.

"The eye it cannot choose but see;
We cannot bid the ear be still;
Our bodies feel, where'er they be,
Against or with our will.

Nor less I deem that there are Powers
Which of themselves our minds impress;
That we can feed this mind of ours
In a wise passiveness.

Think you, 'mid all this mighty sum
Of things for ever speaking,
That nothing of itself will come,
But we must still be seeking?

Then ask not wherefore, here, alone,
Conversing as I may,
I sit upon this old grey stone
And dream my time away."

In *The Tables Turned* it is the poet who takes the offensive against
his studious friend. "Up! up! my Friend," he calls, "and quit your
books." And then, "Books!" he continues impatiently.

"Books! 'tis a dull and endless strife;
Come, hear the woodland linnet;
How sweet his music! on my life,
There's more of wisdom in it.

And hark how blithe the throstle sings!
He too is no mean preacher.
Come forth into the light of things,
Let Nature be your teacher.

One impulse from a vernal wood
May teach you more of man,
Of moral evil and of good
Than all the sages can.

Sweet is the lore which Nature brings;
Our meddling intellect
Mis-shapes the beauteous forms of things—
We murder to dissect.

Enough of Science and of Art;
Close up those barren leaves;
Come forth and bring with you a heart
That watches and receives.

Matthew and William—two aspects of the multiple amphibian that was Wordsworth, that is each one of us. To be fully human, we must learn to make the best of William's world as well as of Matthew's. Matthew's is the world of books, of the social heredity of steadily accumulating knowledge, of science and technics and business, of words and the stock of second-hand notions which we project upon external reality as a frame of reference, in terms of which we may explain, to our own satisfaction, the enigma, moment by moment, of ongoing existence. Over against it stands William's world—the world of sheer mystery, the world as an endless succession of unique events, the world as we perceive it in a state of alert receptiveness with no thought of explaining it, using it, exploiting it for our biological or cultural purposes. As things now stand, we teach young people to make the best only of Matthew's world of familiar words, accepted notions, and useful techniques. We temper a too exclusive concentration on scientific symbols, not with a training in the art of what William calls "wise passiveness," not with lessons in watching and receiving, but with the injunction to concentrate on philosophical and sociological symbols, to read the books that are reputed to contain a high concentration of "the spirit breathed from dead men to their kind." (Alas, dead men do not always breathe a spirit; quite often they merely emit a bad smell.)

It is related in one of the Sutras that on a certain occasion the Buddha preached a wordless sermon to his disciples. Instead of saying anything, he picked a flower and held it up for them to look at. The disciples gaped uncomprehendingly. Only Mahakasyapa understood what the Tathagata was driving at, and all that he did was to smile. Gautama smiled back at him, and when the wordless sermon was over, he made a little speech for the benefit of those who had failed to comprehend his silence. "This treasure of the unquestionable teaching, this Mind of Nirvana, this true form that is without forms, this most subtle Dharma beyond words, this instruction that is to be given and received outside the pale of all doctrines—this I have now handed on to Mahakasyapa." Perceived not as a botanical specimen, not as the analyzed and labeled illustration of a pre-existent symbol system, but as a nameless, unique event, in which all the beauty and the mystery of existence are manifest, a flower can become the means to enlightenment. And what is true of a flower is true, needless to say, of any other event in the inner or outer world—from a toothache to Mount Everest, from a tapeworm to The Well-Tempered Clavichord —to which we choose to pay attention in a state of wise passiveness. And wise passiveness is the condition not only of spiritual insight. ("In prayer," wrote St. Jeanne Chantal, "I always want to *do* something, wherein I do very wrong. . . . By wishing to accomplish something myself, I spoil it all.") In another context, wise passiveness, followed in due course by wise hard work, is the condition of creativity. We do not fabricate our best ideas; they "occur to us," they "come into our heads." Colloquial speech reminds us that, unless we give our subliminal mind a chance, we shall get nowhere. And it is by allowing ourselves at frequent intervals to be wisely passive that we can most effectively help the subliminal mind to do its work. The *cogito* of Descartes should be emended, said Von Baader, to *cogitor*. In order to actualize our potentialities, in order to become fully human and completely ourselves, we must not merely think; we must also permit ourselves to be thought. In Gardner Murphy's words, "Both the historical record of creative thought and the laboratory report of its appearance today, indicate clearly that creative intelligence can spring from the mind that is not strained to its highest pitch, but is utterly at ease." Watching and receiving in a state of perfect ease or wise passiveness is an art which can be cultivated and should be taught on every educational level from the most elementary to the most advanced.

Creativity and spiritual insight—these are the highest rewards of wise passiveness. But those who know how to watch and receive are rewarded in other and hardly less important ways. Receptivity can be a source of innocent and completely harmless happiness. A man or woman who knows how to make the best of both worlds—the world revealed by wise passiveness and the world created by wise activity—tends to find life enjoyable and interesting. Ours is a civilization in which vast numbers of children and adults are so chronically bored that they have to resort during their leisure hours to a regimen of non-stop distractions. Any method which promises to make life seem enjoyable and the commonplaces of everyday experience more interesting should be welcomed as a major contribution to culture and morality.

In *Modern Painters* there is a remarkable chapter on "the Open Sky"—a chapter which even by those who find Ruskin's theology absurd and his aesthetics frequently perverse may still be read with profit and admiring pleasure. "It is a strange thing," Ruskin writes, "how little in general people know about the sky. It is the part of creation in which nature has done more for the sake of pleasing man, more for the sake and evident purpose of talking to him and teaching him, than in any of her works, and it is just the part in which we least attend to her. . . . There is not a moment in any day of our lives in which nature is not producing (in the sky) scene after scene, picture after picture, glory after glory, and working always upon such exquisite and constant principles of the most perfect beauty, that it is quite certain it is all done for us and intended for our perpetual pleasure." But, in point of fact, does the sky produce in most people the perpetual pleasure which its beauty is so eminently capable of giving? The answer, of course, is No. "We never attend to it, we never make it a subject of thought. . . . We look upon it . . . only as a succession of monotonous and meaningless accidents, too common or too vain to be worthy of a moment of watchfulness or a glance of admiration. . . . Who, among the chattering crowd, can tell me of the forms and the precipices of the chain of tall white mountains that girded the horizon at noon yesterday? Who saw the narrow sunbeam that came out of the south and smote their summits until they melted and mouldered away in a dust of blue rain? . . . . All has passed unregretted as unseen; or if the apathy be ever shaken off, if even for an instant, it is only by what is gross or what is extraordinary." A habit of wise passiveness in relation to the everyday drama of the clouds and mist and sunshine can become a source, as Ruskin insists, of endless pleasure. But most of the products of our educational system prefer Westerns and alcohol.

In the art of watching and receiving Ruskin was self-educated. But there seems to be no reason why children should not be taught that wise passiveness which gave this victim of a traumatic childhood so much pleasure and kept him, in spite of everything, reasonably sane for the greater part of a long and productive life. A training in watching and receiving will not turn every child into a great stylist but, within the limits imposed by constitution, temperament, and the circumambient culture, it will make him more sensitive, more intelligent, more capable of innocent enjoyment and, in consequence, more virtuous and more useful to society.

In the United States life, liberty, and the pursuit of happiness are constitutionally guaranteed. But if life hardly seems worth living, if liberty is used for subhuman purposes, if the pursuers of happiness know nothing about the nature of their quarry or the elementary techniques of hunting, these constitutional rights will not be very meaningful. An education in that wise passiveness recommended by the saints and the poets, by all who have lived fully and worked creatively, might help us to transform the paper promises of a democratic constitution into concrete contemporary fact.

Let us now consider very briefly two other areas in which an education in the art of making the best of all our seemingly incommensurable worlds would certainly be helpful and might also turn out to be practicable within the system now prevailing in our schools and colleges. It is a matter of observable fact that all of us inhabit a world of phantasy as well as a world of first-order experience and a world of words and concepts. In most children and in some adults this world of phantasy is astonishingly vivid. These people are the visualizers of Galton's classical dichotomy. For them the world presented to their consciousness by their story-telling, image-making phantasy is as real as, sometimes more real than, the given world of sense impressions and the projected world of words and explanatory concepts. Even in nonvisualizers the world of phantasy, though somewhat shadowy, is still real enough to be retreated into or shrunk from, tormented by or voluptuously enjoyed. The mentally ill are the victims of their phantasy, and even more or less normal people find themselves tempted into folly, or inhibited from behaving as they know they ought to behave, by what goes on in the superreal but unrealistic world of their imagination. How can we make the best of this odd, alien, almost autonomous universe that we carry about with us inside our skulls?

The question has been partially answered by the apostles of those numerous religious movements stemming from "New Thought." Using a vaguely theological language and interpreting the Bible to suit themselves, they have given a religious form to a number of useful and practical methods for harnessing imagination and its suggestive power in the service of individual well-being and social stability. For about a quarter or perhaps a third of the population their methods work remarkably well. This is an important fact, of which professional educators should take notice and from whose implications they should not be ashamed to learn. Unfortunately, men and women in high academic positions tend to be intellectually snobbish. They turn up their noses at the nonscientific, distressingly "inspirational" but still astute and experienced psychologists of the modern heretical churches. This is deplorable. Truth lives, proverbially, at the bottom of a well, and wells are often muddy. No genuinely scientific investigator has any right to be squeamish about anything.

And here is another truth-containing well abhorred by academic scientists of the stricter sort. Excellent techniques for teaching children and adults to make the best of the chaotic world of their phantasy have been worked out by the Dianeticists and their successors, the Scientologists. Their Imagination Games deserve to be incorporated into every curriculum. Boys and girls, and even grown men and women, find these games amusing and, what is more important, helpful. Made the worst of, our imagination will destroy us; made the best of, it can be used to break up long-established habits of undesirable feeling, to dissipate obsessive fears, to provide symbolic outlets for anger and fictional amends for real frustrations.

In the course of the last three thousand years how many sermons have been preached, how many homilies delivered and commands roared out, how many promises of heaven and threats of hell-fire solemnly pronounced, how many good-conduct prizes awarded and how many childish buttocks lacerated with whips and canes? And what has been the result of all this incalculable sum of moralistic words, and of the rewards and savage punishments by which the verbiage has been accompanied? The result has been history—the successive generations of human beings comporting themselves virtuously and rationally enough for the race to survive, but badly enough and madly enough for it to be unceasingly in trouble. Can we do better in the future than we are doing today, or than our fathers did in the past? Can we develop methods more effective than pious talk and Pavlovian conditioning?

For an answer to these questions—or at least for some hints as to the nature of a possible answer—we must turn to history and anthropology. Like many primitive societies today, many highly civilized societies of the past provided their members with realistically amphibious methods for dealing with negative emotions and the instinctive drives that are incompatible with communal living. In these societies morality and rational behavior were not merely preached and rewarded; they were made easier by the provision of religiously sanctioned safety valves, through which the angry, the frustrated, and the anxiously neurotic could release their aggressive or self-destructive tendencies in a satisfyingly violent and yet harmless and socially acceptable way. In Ancient Greece, for example, the orgies of Dionysus and, at a somewhat later date, the Corybantic dances, sacred to the Great Mother, were safety valves through which rage and resentment found an innocuous outlet, while the paralyzing inhibitions of anxiety were swept away in a wild rush of nervous, muscular, and hormonal activity. In this ethical and therapeutic context Dionysus was known as Lusios, the Liberator. His orgies delivered the participants from the dismal necessity of running amok, or retreating into catatonia, or stoically bottling up their feelings and so giving themselves a psychosomatic illness. Corybantic dancing was regarded as a form of medical treatment and at the same time as a religious rite, cathartic to the soul no less than to the adrenalin-charged body. Which did most for morality and rational behavior—the dialogues of Plato or the orgies of Dionysus, Aristotle's *Ethics* or the Corybantic dances? My guess is that, in this competition, Lusios and the Great Mother would be found to have won hands down.

In a society like ours it would doubtless be impracticable to revive Maenadism or the congregational antics of the Dionysian orgies. But the problem of what multiple amphibians should do about their frustrations and their tendencies to aggression remains acute and still unsolved. Sixty years ago William James wrote an essay entitled *The Moral Equivalent of War*. It is an excellent essay as far as it goes; but it does not, unfortunately, go far enough. Moral equivalents must be found not only for war but also for delinquency, family squabbles, bullying, puritanical censoriousness, and all the assorted beastliness of daily life. Preaching and conditioning will never of themselves solve these problems. It is obvious that we must take a hint from the Greeks and provide ourselves with physical safety valves for reducing the pressure of our negative emotions. No ethical system which fails to provide such physical safety valves, and which fails to teach children and their elders how to use them, is likely to be effective. It will be the business of psychologists, physiologists, and sociologists to devise acceptable safety valves, of moralists and clergymen to provide rationalizations in terms of the local value systems and theologies, and for educators to find a place in the curriculum for courses in the indispensable art of letting off steam.

And there is another art that merits the educator's closest attention—the art of controlling physical pain. Pain, as recent studies have made abundantly clear, is not simply a mechanical affair of peripheral receptors and special centers in the brain, and its intensity is not directly proportional to the extent of the injury which is its cause. Pain may be aggravated or inhibited by numerous psychological and even cultural factors. Which means, of course, that to some extent at least pain is controllable. This fact, needless to say, has been known from time immemorial, and for the last century and a half (from the days of Elliotson and Esdaile) has been systematically exploited in hypnotic anesthesia. Neurological research is now discovering the organic and functional reasons for these old observations and empirical practices; a somewhat disreputable "wild" phenomenon is in process of being turned into a domesticated scientific fact, consonant with other well-known facts and safely caged within a familiar symbol-system. Taking advantage of the new-found respectability of hypnosis and suggestion, educators should now include elementary pain control in the curriculum of physical training. Control of pain through suggestion and autosuggestion is an art which, as every good dentist knows, can be learned by most children with the greatest of ease. Along with singing and calisthenics, it should be taught to every little boy and little girl who can learn it.

Training in a closely similar art may prove to be very useful as a part of ethical education. In his book *Auto-Conditioning* Professor Hornell Hart has outlined simple and thoroughly practical methods for changing moods, intensifying motivations, and implementing good intentions. There are no educational panaceas, no techniques that work perfectly in every case. But if autoconditioning produces good results in only twenty or thirty percent of those who have been instructed in the art, it deserves to take its place in every educator's armamentarium.

That we are multiple amphibians is self-evident, and the corollary of this self-evident truth is that we must attack our problems on every front where they arise—on the mental front and on the physiological front, on the front of concepts and symbols and on the front of wordless experience, on the rational front and on the irrational front, the individual front and the social front. But what should be our strategy? How are we to learn and successfully practice the art of attacking on all the fronts simultaneously? Many valuable discoveries were made by the amphibians of earlier times and alien cultures, and many discoveries are being made within our own culture today. These empirical findings of the past and the present should be studied, tested, related to the best scientific knowledge now available, and finally adapted for practical use within our educational systems. Ten million dollars from the coffers of one of the great foundations would pay for the necessary research and large-scale experimentation. Out of such research and experimentation might come, within a few years, a radical improvement in the methods currently used to prepare young people to meet the challenges of their manifold amphibiousness and to make the best of all the strangely assorted worlds in which, as human beings, they are predestined to live.

16

Student-Centered Teaching
as Experienced by a Participant*

Carl R. Rogers and Samuel Tenenbaum

INTRODUCTION † (*by Carl R. Rogers*)

In the summer of 1958 I was invited to teach a four-week course at Brandeis University. My recollection is that the title was "The Process of Personality Change." I had no great expectations for the course. It was to be one of several courses which the students were taking, meeting for three two-hour sessions per week, rather than the concentrated workshop pattern which I prefer. I learned in advance that the group was to be unusually heterogeneous—teachers, doctoral candidates in psychology, counselors, several priests, at least one from a foreign country, psychotherapists in private practice, school psychologists. The group was, on the average, more mature and experienced than would ordinarily be found in a university course. I felt very relaxed about the whole thing. I would do what I could to help make this a meaningful experience for us all, but I doubted that it could have the impact of, for example, the workshops on counseling which I had conducted.

Perhaps it was because I had very modest expectations of the group and of myself, that it went so well. I would without doubt class it as among the most satisfying of my attempts to facilitate learning in

---

* From Carl R. Rogers, *On Becoming a Person*, Houghton Mifflin, 1961, pp. 297–313. Copyright 1961 by Carl R. Rogers.

† For Dr. Rogers' earlier and lengthy discussion on the subject, see Chapter 9, "Student-Centered Teaching" in *Client-Centered Therapy* by Carl R. Rogers. Houghton Mifflin, 1951.

courses or workshops. This should be borne in mind in reading Dr. Tenenbaum's material.

I would like to digress for a moment here to say that I feel far more assurance in confronting a new client in therapy than I do in confronting a new group. I feel I have a sufficient grasp of the conditions of therapy so that I have a reasonable confidence as to the process which will ensue. But with groups I have much less confidence. Sometimes when I have had every reason to suppose a course would go well, the vital, self-initiated, self-directed learning has simply not occurred to any great degree. At other times when I have been dubious, it has gone extremely well. To me this means that our formulation of the process of facilitating learning in education is not nearly as accurate or complete as our formulations regarding the therapeutic process.

But to return to the Brandeis summer course. It was clearly a highly significant experience for almost all of the participants, as evident in their reports on the course. I was particularly interested in the report by Dr. Tenenbaum, written as much for his colleagues as for me. Here was a mature scholar, not an impressionable young student. Here was a sophisticated educator, who already had to his credit a published biography of William H. Kilpatrick, the philosopher of education. Hence his perceptions of the experience seemed unusually valuable.

I would not want it to be understood that I shared all of Dr. Tenenbaum's perceptions. Portions of the experience I perceived quite differently, but this is what made his observations so helpful. I felt particularly concerned that it seemed to him so much a "Rogers" approach, that it was simply my person and idiosyncrasies which made the experience what it was.

For this reason I was delighted to get a long letter from him a year later, reporting his own experience in teaching. This confirmed what I have learned from a wide variety of individuals, that it is not simply the personality of a specific teacher which makes this a dynamic learning experience, but the operation of certain principles which may be utilized by any "facilitator" who holds the appropriate attitudes.

I believe the two accounts by Dr. Tenenbaum will make it clear why teachers who have experienced the kind of group learning which is described can never return to more stereotyped ways of education. In spite of frustration and occasional failure, one keeps trying to discover, with each new group, the conditions which will unleash this vital learning experience.

CARL R. ROGERS AND NON-DIRECTIVE TEACHING
(*by Samuel Tenenbaum*)

As one interested in education, I have participated in a classroom methodology that is so unique and so special that I feel impelled to share the experience. The technique, it seems to me, is so radically different from the customary and the accepted, so undermining of the old, that it should be known more widely. As good a description of the process as any—I suppose the one that Carl R. Rogers, the instructor, himself would be inclined to use—would be "non-directive" teaching.

I had some notion what that term meant, but frankly I was not prepared for anything that proved so overwhelming. It is not that I am convention-bound. My strongest educational influences stem from William Heard Kilpatrick and John Dewey, and anyone who has even the slightest acquaintance with their thinking would know that it does not smack of the narrow or the provincial. But this method which I saw Dr. Rogers carry out in a course which he gave at Brandeis University was so unusual, something I could not believe possible, unless I was part of the experience. I hope I shall manage to describe the method in a way to give you some inkling of the feelings, the emotions, the warmth and the enthusiasms that the method engendered.

The course was altogether unstructured; and it was exactly that. At no moment did anyone know, not even the instructor, what the next moment would bring forth in the classroom, what subject would come up for discussion, what questions would be raised, what personal needs, feelings and emotions aired. This atmosphere of non-structured freedom—as free as human beings could allow each other to be—was set by Dr. Rogers himself. In a friendly, relaxed way, he sat down with the students (about 25 in number) around a large table and said it would be nice if we stated our purpose and introduced ourselves. There ensued a strained silence; no one spoke up. Finally, to break it, one student timidly raised his hand and spoke his piece. Another uncomfortable silence, and then another upraised hand. Thereafter, the hands rose more rapidly. At no time did the instructor urge any student to speak.

UNSTRUCTURED APPROACH

Afterwards, he informed the class that he had brought with him quantities of materials—reprints, brochures, articles, books; he handed out a bibliography of recommended reading. At no time did he indicate that he expected students to read or do anything else. As I recall, he made only one request. Would some student volunteer to set up this material in a special room which had been reserved for students of the course? Two students promptly volunteered. He also said he had with him recorded tapes of therapeutic sessions and also reels of motion pictures. This created a flurry of excitement, and students asked whether they could be heard and seen and Dr. Rogers answered yes. The class then decided how it could be done best. Students volunteered to run tape recorders, find a movie projector; for the most part this too was student initiated and arranged.

Thereafter followed four hard, frustrating sessions. During this period, the class didn't seem to get anywhere. Students spoke at random, saying whatever came into their heads. It all seemed chaotic, aimless, a waste of time. A student would bring up some aspect of Rogers' philosophy; and the next student, completely disregarding the first, would take the group away in another direction; and a third, completely disregarding the first two, would start fresh on something else altogether. At times there were some faint efforts at a cohesive discussion, but for the most part the classroom proceedings seemed to lack continuity and direction. The instructor received every contribution with attention and regard. He did not find any student's contribution in order or out of order.

The class was not prepared for such a totally unstructured approach. They did not know how to proceed. In their perplexity and frustration, they demanded that the teacher play the role assigned to him by custom and tradition; that he set forth for us in authoritative language what was right and wrong, what was good and bad. Had they not come from far distances to learn from the oracle himself? Were they not fortunate? Were they not about to be initiated in the right rituals and practices by the great man himself, the founder of the movement that bears his name? The notebooks were poised for the climactic moment when the oracle would give forth, but mostly they remained untouched.

Queerly enough, from the outset, even in their anger, the members of the group felt joined together, and outside the classroom, there was an excitement and a ferment, for even in their frustration, they had communicated as never before in any classroom, and probably never before in quite the way they had. The class was bound together by a common, unique experience. In the Rogers class, they had spoken their minds; the words did not come from a book, nor were they the reflection of the instructor's thinking, nor that of any other authority. The ideas, emotions and feelings came from themselves; and this was the releasing and the exciting process.

In this atmosphere of freedom, something for which they had not bargained and for which they were not prepared, the students spoke up as students seldom do. During this period, the instructor took many blows; and it seemed to me that many times he appeared to be shaken; and although he was the source of our irritation, we had, strange as it may seem, a great affection for him, for it did not seem right to be angry with a man who was so sympathetic, so sensitive to the feelings and ideas of others. We all felt that what was involved was some slight misunderstanding, which once understood and remedied would make everything right again. But our instructor, gentle enough on the surface, had a "whim of steel." He didn't seem to understand; and if he did, he was obstinate and obdurate; he refused to come around. Thus did this tug-of-war continue. We all looked to Rogers and Rogers looked to us. One student, amid general approbation, observed: "We are Rogers-centered, not student-centered. We have come to learn from Rogers."

ENCOURAGING THINKING

Another student had discovered that Rogers had been influenced by Kilpatrick and Dewey, and using this idea as a springboard, he said he thought he perceived what Rogers was trying to get at. He thought Rogers wanted students to think independently, creatively; he wanted students to become deeply involved with their very persons, their very selves, hoping that this might lead to the "reconstruction" of the person—in the Dewey sense of the term—the person's outlook, attitudes, values, behavior. This would be a true reconstruction of experience; it would be learning in a real sense. Certainly, he didn't want the course to end in an examination based on textbooks and lectures, followed by the traditional end-term grade, which generally means completion and forgetting.[1] Rogers had expressed the belief almost from the outset of the course that no one can teach anyone else anything. But thinking, this student insisted, begins at the fork in the road, the famed dilemma set up by Dewey. As we reach the fork in the road, we do not know which road to take if we are to reach our destination; and then we begin to examine the situation. Thinking starts at that point.

Kilpatrick also sought original thinking from his students and also rejected a regurgitant textbook kind of learning, but he presented crucial problems for discussion, and these problems aroused a great deal of interest, and they also created vast changes in the person. Why can't committees of students or individual students get up such problems for discussion?[2] Rogers listened sympathetically and said, "I see you feel strongly about this?" That disposed of that. If I recall correctly, the next student who spoke completely disregarded what had been suggested and started afresh on another topic, quite in comformity with the custom set by the class.

[1] It should be noted that Dr. Rogers neither agreed nor disagreed. It was not his habit to respond to students' contributions unless a remark was directed specifically to him; and even then he might choose not to answer. His main object, it seemed to me, was to follow students' contributions intelligently and sympathetically.

[2] One student compiled such a list, had it mimeographed, distributed it, and for practical purposes that was the end of that.

In this connection, another illustration may be in order. At the first session, Rogers brought to class tape recordings of therapeutic sessions. He explained that he was not comfortable in a teacher's role and he came "loaded," and the recordings served as a sort of security. One student continually insisted that he play the recordings, and after considerable pressure from the class, he did so, but he complied reluctantly; and all told, despite the pressure, he did not play them for more than an hour in all the sessions. Apparently, Rogers preferred the students to make real live recordings rather than listen to those which could only interest them in an academic way.

Spasmodically, through the session, students referred favorably to the foregoing suggestions, and they began to demand more insistently that Rogers assume the traditional role of a teacher. At this point, the blows were coming Rogers' way rather frequently and strongly and I thought I saw him bend somewhat before them. (Privately, he denied he was so affected.) During one session, a student made the suggestion that he lecture one hour and that we have a class discussion the next. This one suggestion seemed to fit into his plans. He said he had with him an unpublished paper. He warned us that it was available and we could read it by ourselves. But the student said it would not be the same. The person, the author, would be out of it, the stress, the inflection, the emotion, those nuances which give value and meaning to words. Rogers then asked the students if that was what they wanted. They said yes. He read for over an hour. After the vivid and acrimonious exchanges to which we had become accustomed, this was certainly a letdown, dull and soporific to the extreme. This experience squelched all further demands for lecturing. In one of the moments when he apologized for this episode ("It's better, more excusable, when students demand it."), he said: "You asked me to lecture. It is true I am a resource, but what sense would there be in my lecturing? I have brought a great quantity of material, reprints of any number of lectures, articles, books, tape recordings, movies."

By the fifth session, something definite had happened; there was no mistaking that. Students spoke to one another; they by-passed Rogers. Students asked to be heard and wanted to be heard, and what before was a halting, stammering, self-conscious group became an interacting group, a brand new cohesive unit, carrying on in a unique way; and from them came discussion and thinking such as no other group but this could repeat or duplicate. The instructor also joined in, but his role, more important than any in the group, somehow became merged with the group; the group was important, the center, the base of operation, not the instructor.

What caused it? I can only conjecture as to the reason. I believe that what happened was this: For four sessions students refused to believe that the instructor would refuse to play the traditional role. They still believed that he would set the tasks; that he would be the center of whatever happened and that he would manipulate the group. It took the class four sessions to realize that they were wrong; that he came to them with nothing outside of himself, outside of his own person; that if they really wanted something to happen, it was they who had to provide the content—an uncomfortable, challenging situation indeed. It was they who had to speak up, with all the risks that that entailed. As part of the process, they shared, they took exception, they agreed, they disagreed. At any rate, their persons, their deepest selves were involved; and from this situation, this special, unique group, this new creation was born.

IMPORTANCE OF ACCEPTANCE

As you may know, Rogers believes that if a person is accepted, fully accepted, and in this acceptance there is no judgment, only compassion and sympathy, the individual is able to come to grips with himself, to develop the courage to give up his defenses and face his true self. I saw this process work. Amid the early efforts to communicate, to find a *modus vivendi,* there had been in the group tentative exchanges of feelings, emotions and ideas; but after the fourth session, and progressively thereafter, this group, haphazardly thrown together, became close to one another and their true selves appeared. As they interacted, there were moments of insight and revelation and understanding that were almost awesome in nature; they were what, I believe, Rogers would describe as "moments of therapy," those pregnant moments when you see a human soul revealed before you, in all its breathless wonder; and then a slience, almost like reverence, would overtake the class. And each member of the class became enveloped with a warmth and a loveliness that border on the mystic. I for one, and I am quite sure the others also, never had an experience quite like this. It was learning and therapy; and by therapy I do not mean illness, but what might be characterized by a healthy change in the person, an increase in his flexibility, his openness, his willingness to listen. In the process, we all felt elevated, freer, more accepting of ourselves and others, more open to new ideas, trying hard to understand and accept.

This is not a perfect world, and there was evidence of hostility as members differed. Somehow in this setting every blow was softened, as if the sharp edges had been removed; if undeserved, students would go off to something else; and the blow was somehow lost. In my own case, even those students who originally irritated me, with further acquaintance I began to accept and respect; and the thought occurred to me as I tried to understand what was happening: Once you come close to a person, perceive his thoughts, his emotions, his feelings, he becomes not only understandable but good and desirable. Some of the more aggressive ones spoke more than they should, more than their right share, but the group itself, by its own being, not by setting rules, eventually made its authority felt; and unless a person was very sick or insensitive, members more or less, in this respect, conformed to what was expected of them. The problem—the hostile, the dominant, the neurotic—was not too acute; and yet if measured in a formal way, with a stop watch, at no time was a session free of aimless talk and waste of time. But yet as I watched the process, the idea persisted that perhaps this waste of time may be necessary; it may very well be that that is the way man learns best; for certainly, as I look back at the whole experience, I am fairly certain that it would have been impossible to learn as much or as well or as thoroughly in the traditional classroom setting. If we accept Dewey's definition of education as the reconstruction of experience, what better way can a person learn than by becoming involved with his whole self, his very person, his root drives, emotions, attitudes and values? No series of facts or arguments, no matter how logically or brilliantly arranged, can even faintly compare with that sort of thing.

In the course of this process, I saw hard, inflexible, dogmatic persons, in the brief period of several weeks, change in front of my eyes and become sympathetic, understanding and to a marked degree nonjudgmental. I saw neurotic, compulsive persons ease up and become more accepting of themselves and others. In one instance, a student who particularly impressed me by his change, told me when I mentioned this: "It is true. I feel less rigid, more open to the world. And I like myself better for it. I don't believe I ever learned so much anywhere." I saw shy persons become less shy and aggressive persons more sensitive and moderate.

One might say that this appears to be essentially an emotional process. But that I believe would be altogether inaccurate in describing it. There was a great deal of intellectual content, but the intellectual content was meaningful and crucial to the person, in a sense that it meant a great deal to him as a person. In fact, one student brought up this very question. "Should we be concerned," he asked, "only with the emotions? Has the intellect no play?" It was my turn to ask, "Is there any student who has read as much or thought as much for any other course?"

The answer was obvious. We had spent hours and hours reading; the room reserved for us had occupants until 10 o'clock at night, and then many left only because the university guards wanted to close the building. Students listened to recordings; they saw motion pictures; but best of all, they talked and talked and talked. In the traditional course, the instructor lectures and indicates what is to be read and learned; students dutifully record all this in their notebooks, take an examination and feel good or bad, depending on the outcome; but in nearly all cases it is a complete experience, with a sense of finality; the laws of forgetting begin to operate rapidly and inexorably. In the Rogers course, students read and thought inside and outside the class; it was they who chose from this reading and thinking what was meaningful to them, not the instructor.

This non-directive kind of teaching, I should point out, was not 100 per cent successful. There were three or four students who found the whole idea distasteful. Even at the end of the course, although nearly all became enthusiastic, one student to my knowledge, was intensely negative in his feelings; another was highly critical. These wanted the instructor to provide them with a rounded-out intellectual piece of merchandise which they could commit to memory and then give back on an examination. They would then have the assurance that they had learned what they should. As one said, "If I had to make a report as to what I learned in this course, what could I say?" Admittedly, it would be much more difficult than in a traditional course, if not impossible.

The Rogers method was free and flowing and open and permissive. A student would start an interesting discussion; it would be taken up by a second; but a third student might take us away in another direction, bringing up a personal matter of no interest to the class; and we would all feel frustrated. But this was like life, flowing on like a river, seemingly futile, with never the same water there, flowing on, with no one knowing what would happen the next moment. But in this there was an expectancy, an alertness, an aliveness; it seemed to me as near a smear of life as one could get in a classroom. For the authoritarian person, who puts his faith in neatly piled up facts, this method I believe can be threatening, for here he gets no reassurance, only an openness, a flowing, no closure.

A NEW METHODOLOGY

I believe that a great deal of the stir and the ferment that characterized the class was due to this lack of closure. In the lunch room, one could recognize Rogers' students by their animated discussions, by their desire to be together; and sometimes, since there was no table large enough, they would sit two and three tiers deep; and they would eat with plates on their laps. As Rogers himself points out, there is no finality in the process. He himself never summarizes (against every conventional law of teaching). The issues are left unresolved; the problems raised in class are always in a state of flux, on-going. In their need to know, to come to some agreement, students gather together, wanting understanding, seeking closure. Even in the matter of grades, there is no closure. A grade means an end; but Dr. Rogers does not give the grade; it is the student who suggests the grade; and since he does so, even this sign of completion is left unresolved, without an end, unclosed. Also, since the course is unstructured, each has staked his person in the course; he has spoken, not with the textbook as the gauge, but with his person, and thus as a self he has communicated with others, and because of this, in contradistinction to the impersonal subject matter that comprises the normal course, there develops this closeness and warmth.

To describe the many gracious acts that occurred might convey some idea of this feeling of closeness. One student invited the class to her home for a cookout. Another student, a priest from Spain, was so taken with the group that he talked of starting a publication to keep track of what was happening to the group members after they disbanded. A group interested in student counseling met on its own. A member arranged for the class to visit a mental hospital for children and adults; also he arranged for us to see the experimental work being done with psychotic patients by Dr. Lindsley. Class members brought in tape recordings and printed matter to add to the library material set aside for our use. In every way the spirit of good-will and friendliness was manifest to an extent that happens only in rare and isolated instances. In the many, many courses I have taken I have not seen the like. In this connection, it should be pointed out that the members comprised a group that had been haphazardly thrown together; they had come from many backgrounds and they included a wide age range.

I believe that what has been described above is truly a creative addition to classroom methodology; it is radically different from the old. That it has the capacity to move people, to make them freer, more open-minded, more flexible, I have no doubt. I myself witnessed the power of this method. I believe that non-directive teaching has profound implications which even those who accept this point of view cannot at present fully fathom. Its importance, I believe, goes beyond the classroom and extends to every area where human beings communicate and try to live with one another.

More specifically, as a classroom methodology, it warrants the widest discussion, inquiry and experimentation. It has the possibility of opening up a whole new dimension of thinking, fresh and original, for in its approach, in its practice, in its philosophy it differs so fundamentally from the old. It seems to me this approach ought to be tried out in every area of learning—elementary, high school, college, wherever human beings gather to learn and improve on the old. At this stage we should not be overly concerned about its limitations and inadequacies, since the method has not been refined and we do not know as much about it as we ought. As a new technique, it starts off with a handicap. We are loath to give up the old. The old is bolstered by tradition, authority and respectability; and we ourselves are its product. If we view education, however, as the reconstruction of experience, does not this presume that the individual must do his own reconstructing? He must do it himself, through the reorganization of his deepest self, his values, his attitudes, his very person. What better method is there to engross the individual; to bring him, his ideas, his feelings into communication with others; to break down the barriers that create isolation in a world where for his own mental safety and health, man has to learn to be part of mankind?

A PERSONAL TEACHING EXPERIENCE
(by Samuel Tenenbaum)*

I feel impelled to write to you about my first experience in teaching after being exposed to your thinking and influence. You may or may not know I had a phobia about teaching. Since my work with you, I began to perceive more clearly where the difficulty lay. It was mostly in my concept of the role I had to play as a teacher—the motivator, director and the production chief of a performance. I always feared being "hung up" in the classroom—I believe it's your expression and I have come to like it—the class listless, uninterested, not responding, and my yammering and yammering, until I lost poise, the sentences not forming, coming out artificially, and the time moving slowly, slowly, ever more slowly. This was the horror I imagined. I suppose pieces of this happen to every teacher, but I would put them all together, and I would approach the class with foreboding, not at ease, not truly myself.

And now comes my experience. I was asked to give two summer courses for the Graduate School of Education of Yeshiva University, but I had a perfect alibi. I was going to Europe and I couldn't. Wouldn't I give an interim course, a concentrated course of 14 sessions during the month of June; and this would not interfere with the trip? I had no excuse and I accepted—because I no longer wanted to dodge the situation and more, also, because I was determined once and for all to face it. If I didn't like to teach (I haven't taught for nearly ten years), I would learn something. And if I did, I would also learn something. And if I had to suffer, it was best this way, since the course was concentrated and the time element was short.

* As reported to Dr. Rogers one year later.

You know that I have been strongly influenced in my thinking about education by Kilpatrick and Dewey. But now I had another powerful ingredient—you. When I first met my class, I did something I never did before. I was frank about my feelings. Instead of feeling that a teacher should know and students were there to be taught, I admitted weaknesses, doubts, dilemmas, and NOT KNOWING. Since I sort of dethroned my role as a teacher to the class and myself, my more natural self came out more freely and I found myself talking easily and even creatively. By "creatively" I mean ideas came to me as I spoke, brand new ideas which I felt were good.

Another important difference: It is true that since I was influenced by the Kilpatrick methodology I always welcomed the widest discussion, but I now know, I still wanted and expected my students to know the text and the lecture material set out for them. Even worse, I now know that although I welcomed discussion, I wanted, above all things, that, after all was said and done, the final conclusions of the class to come out according to my way of thinking. Hence none of the discussions were real discussions, in the sense that it was open and free and inquiring; none of the questions were real questions, in the sense that they sought to evoke thinking; all of them were loaded, in the sense that I had pretty definite convictions about what I thought were good answers and at times right answers. Hence, I came to the class with subject matter and my students were really instruments by which situations were manipulated to produce the inclusion of what I regarded as desirable subject matter.

In this last course, I didn't have the courage to discard all subject matter, but this time I really listened to my students; I gave them understanding and sympathy. Although I would spend hours and hours preparing for each session, I found that not once did I refer to a note from the voluminous material with which I entered the room. I allowed students free rein, not holding anyone down to any set course, and I permitted the widest diversion; and I followed wherever the students led.

I remember discussing this with a prominent educator and he said, in what I thought was a disappointed and disapproving tone: "You insist, of course, on good thinking." I quoted William James, who in effect said that man is a speck of reason in an ocean of emotion. I told him that I was more interested in what I would call a "third dimension," the feeling part of the students.

I cannot say I followed you all the way, Dr. Rogers, since I would express opinions and at times, unfortunately, lecture; and that I believe is bad, since students, once authoritative opinions are expressed, tend not to think, but to try to guess what is in the instructor's head and provide him with what he might like, so as to find favor in his eyes. If I had to do it over again, I would have less of that. But I did try and I believe I succeeded in large measure to give to each student a sense of dignity, respect and acceptance; farthest from my mind was to check on them or evaluate and mark them.

And the result—and this is why I am writing you—was for me an unparalleled experience, inexplicable in ordinary terms. I myself cannot fully account for it, except to be grateful that it happened to me. Some of the very qualities which I experienced in your course I found in this which I gave. I found myself liking these particular students as I have never liked any other group of persons, and I found—and they expressed this in their final report—that they themselves began to feel warm and kindly and accepting of one another. Orally and in their papers, they told of how moved they were, how much they learned, how well they felt. For me this was a brand new experience, and I was overwhelmed and humbled by it. I have had students who, I believe, respected and admired me, but I never had a classroom experience from which came such warmth and closeness. Incidentally, following your example, I avoided setting any fixed requirements in terms of reading or classroom preparation.

That the foregoing was not "biased perception" was evidenced from reports I got outside the classroom. The students had said such nice things about me that faculty members wanted to sit in the class. Best of all, the students at the end of the course wrote Dean Benjamin Fine a letter in which they said the nicest things about me. And the Dean in turn wrote me to the same effect.

To say that I am overwhelmed by what happened only faintly reflects my feelings. I have taught for many years but I have never experienced anything remotely resembling what occurred. I, for my part, never have found in the classroom so much of the whole person coming forth, so deeply involved, so deeply stirred. Further, I question if in the traditional set-up, with its emphasis on subject matter, examinations, grades, there is, or there can be a place for the "becoming" person, with his deep and manifold needs, as he struggles to fulfill himself. But this is going far afield. I can only report to you what happened and to say that I am grateful and that I am also humbled by the experience. I would like you to know this, for again you have added to and enriched my life and being.[3]

The sorry sequence has one further extension. The sense of relatedness with others depends in appreciable part upon the feelingfulness of awareness. Experiencing another with empathy gives the person an appreciation of the deep bond which bridges our aloneness. But the alienated person, treating himself as an object, soon is treating those about him so also. This is Buber's (1958) "It-it" relationship. Like billiard balls clicking against each other, not like human beings interpenetrating with each other, such relationships are frustrating and incomplete.

Summary

This then is alienation. It is the loss of true, feelingful awareness of the *I-process,* of one's own presence in his life. It is, it will be evident, the very opposite of emancipation, in which there is heightened feelingful awareness of being the *I*, the subject of one's living.

[3] That this was not an isolated experience for Dr. Tenenbaum is indicated by a quotation from still another personal communication, many months later. He says: "With another group I taught, following the first one, similar attitudes developed, only they were more accentuated, because, I believe, I was more comfortable with the technique and, I hope, more expert. In this second group there was the same release of the person, the same exhilaration and excitement, the same warmth, the same mystery that attaches to a person as he succeeds in shedding portions of his skin. Students from my group told me that while attending other classes, their eyes would meet, drawn to one another, as if they were unique and apart, as if they were bound together by a special experience. In this second group, also, I found that the students had developed a personal closeness, so that at the end of the semester they talked of having annual reunions. They said that somehow or other they wanted to keep this experience alive and not lose one another. They also spoke of radical and fundamental changes in their person—in outlook, in values, in feelings, in attitudes both toward themselves and toward others."

17

*Search for Authenticity: Clinical Observations**

J. F. T. BUGENTAL

Actualization is the name I am suggesting for a way of being in one's life in which there is greater realization upon the potentials of human existence than is usual, at least in our culture. Actualization, to phrase the negative side, is a way of being in the world in which the needless constraints of the personal resistances and cultural inauthenticities are eliminated or markedly reduced in their limiting effects. . . . The most thorough inquiries into this area are, of course, those of Maslow. . . . Maslow's main approach to actualization has been his study of those unusual people who showed in their lives this quality. Our own studies are coming at the matter from a somewhat different angle. I have been trying to observe in more usual people those evidences of unusual realization of their potentials that would suggest what is latent to the human condition. A rough analogy might be that Maslow has talked to explorers who have gone beyond the frontier of the known and brought back reports of what lies out there. I have questioned those who live on the frontier and make occasional trips into the unknown areas. . . .

Clinical Observations

Every patient who progresses well in his therapy is a pioneer on the frontiers of our knowledge about the human experience. Each such person with whom I have had the satisfaction of working has contributed out of his very life to my accumulating appreciation for what

* From Chapter Sixteen from *The Search for Authenticity: An Existential-Analytical Approach to Psychotherapy* by J. F. T. Bugental. Copyright © 1965 by Holt, Rinehart & Winston, Inc. Reprinted by permission of Holt, Rinehart & Winston, Inc.

fuller realization of our potential may mean. Different patients, because of various influences, portray different aspects; although there seems to be a certain underlying commonality that encourages the hope of making useful generalizations. In the following pages I will describe some of the observations that are supported by being present in several different patients and that seem to me to represent expressions of the nature of actuality.

Almost without exception, the person who moves toward greater realization of his own potential shows a succession of changes in his feelings of concern. Both the substance of what elicits concern and the form in which that concern is expressed show this evolution. Early in therapy the patient is often much involved with the question of his basic "goodness" or "badness" or with his guilt for violations of social codes or with his strivings against his feelings of impotency. These all—and the many other forms such concern may take—have to do with fear of what may be revealed to be the essential (inborn) value or quality of the self.

> Howard feared that he was basically a coward; Sally that she was "born stupid"; Greta that she was innately promiscuous; Bill that he was "just constitutionally no good." Each expended much of his life in attempts to prove that what he feared to be true was not so, in efforts to disguise or hide anything that might confirm what he feared. Each hesitated to move out into his life because only in the familiar and trite was there any hope of continuing the seeming escape from the feared disclosure. So each lived like a fugitive in an unfriendly country, never daring to be himself, to be intimate with another person, to relax and let down his guard.

When the distortions of the resistances are resolved and the person enters into more authentic being, concern is less preoccupied with *Self* and becomes an involvement with living in a broader sense. In a somewhat oversimplified fashion, we may say that the person attaining to actualization is concerned significantly with much in his life but that no concern seems crucial.

Authentic concern seems to be a matter of being willing to make commitments, to let things matter, and yet to retain sufficient perspective so that one is not catastrophically imperiled or even overcome by reverses in any one or any group of concerns. This characterization picks out another aspect of neurotic concern which may be contrasted with the authentic: the neurotic often is so threatened by his restricted, covert concern that he is unable to allow himself investment in that which is truly important to him.

Lucy's fear of how people would regard her if her house were not spic-and-span so pre-empted her emotions that she had but little left to share with her children who were hungering for her more than for a clean house.

Although Tom deeply wanted to write his novel, his constant nagging fear that it would reveal he was effeminate or neurotic kept him from bringing to bear on his writing the creative potential he had.

*   *   *

As Lucy freed herself of her neurotic concern, she began to discover a world of experience that seemed to her incredibly new. "Tim (her son) called me to come see the circus on television. He was just delighted with it. Suddenly I knew he just wanted me to be delighted too. Usually I would have explained to him why we couldn't afford to go or done something else, but this time I just could see how he imagined himself at the circus and what fun that was. He didn't really expect any more than that, and I really liked imagining it with him. I mean I really did! When I went back in the kitchen I found myself starting to cry because I never knew before that sometimes that's all he wants, just for me to be delighted with him."

Tom started to college during the second year he was in therapy. This was the fourth time he'd entered college. Each time before he'd given up because his need to do exceptionally well had foundered on his fear of really trying (for if he really tried and then failed he'd be shown up so terribly; while if he wasn't really trying then of course there was no real test). Now he could say, "It's a funny experience just to listen to a professor to hear what he's saying. It may sound crazy, but I've never really done that before. I always was listening to prove to myself I already knew what he was going to say or to find out the trick he was going to pull on the exam or with the expectation that any minute I'd discover I really didn't know what it was all about and that I had no business being there at all. Now I just listen, and, you know, it's really interesting, and I get most of it, but not all, and that's alright too."

"Now I just listen," Tom says. This is the essence of authentic being. The changed concern of authentic being is that concern is directed toward that which one is intending, not dispersed on what one may be disclosing or other irrelevant matters. . . .

18

A Life of One's Own*

MARION MILNER (JOANNA FIELD, pseud.)

The author of this article, much troubled by a constricting tendency in her personal life, courageously set herself to search for the solution. Her writings reveal a process of fascinating self-discovery, which is painful at the beginning but exhilarating at the end. The following is taken from her remarkable book, A Life of One's Own.

The Coming and Going of Delight

Having discovered that the acts of my experience were an ever-receding horizon, and that my mind had a host of thoughts I never knew about, I felt a little overwhelmed with the difficulties of my enterprise. I therefore decided that it might make the problem more manageable if I were to choose some special kind of experience and try to study that in detail. Just as in my diary I had tried to record each day's best moments, so I now set out to observe these moments more carefully, to find out what might be their cause. The first thing I noticed was that in certain moods the very simplest things, even the glint of electric light on the water in my bath, gave me the most intense delight, while in others I seemed to be blind, unresponding and shut off, so that music I had loved, a spring day or the company of my friends, gave me no contentment. I therefore decided to try to find what these moods depended upon. Could I control them myself? It did seem to me sometimes that they had been influenced by a deliberate act of mine. Particularly was I struck by the effect of writing things down. It was as if I were trying to catch something and the written word provided a net which for a moment entangled a shadowy form

* From Joanna Field (pseudonym), *A Life of One's Own*. Penguin Books, 1952.

which was other than the meaning of the words. Sometimes it seemed that the act of writing was fuel on glowing embers, making flames leap up and throw light on the surrounding gloom, giving me fitful gleams of what was before unguessed at.

Not only did I find that trying to describe my experience enhanced the quality of it, but also this effort to describe had made me more observant of the small movements of the mind. So now I began to discover that there were a multitude of ways of perceiving, ways that were controllable by what I can only describe as an internal gesture of the mind. It was as if one's self-awareness had a central point of intensest being, the very core of one's I-ness. And this core of being could, I now discovered, be moved about at will; but to explain just how it is done to someone who has never felt it for himself is like trying to explain how to move one's ears.

Usually this centre of awareness seemed to be somewhere in my head. But gradually I found that I could if I chose push it out into different parts of my body or even outside myself altogether. Once on a night journey in a train when I could not sleep for the crowd of day impressions which raced through my head, I happened to "feel myself" down into my heart and immediately my mind was so stilled that in a few moments I fell into peaceful sleep. But it surprised me to think that I had lived for twenty-five years without ever discovering that such an internal placing of awareness was possible.

The first hint that I really had the power to control the *way* I looked at things happened in connection with music. Always before, my listening had been too much bothered by the haunting idea that there was far more in it than I was hearing; but occasionally I would find that I had slipped through this barrier to a delight that was enough in itself, in which I forgot my own inadequacy. But this was rare, and most often I would listen intently for a while and then find I had become distracted and was absorbed in the chatter of my own thoughts, personal preoccupations. Impatiently I would shake myself, resolving to attend in earnest for the rest of the concert, only to find that I could not lose myself by mere resolution. Gradually I found, however, that though I could not listen by direct trying I could make some sort of internal gesture after which listening just happened. I described this

effort to myself in various ways. Sometimes I seemed to put my awareness into the soles of my feet, sometimes to send something which was
myself out into the hall, or to feel as if I were standing just beside the
orchestra. I even tried to draw a little picture to remind myself of how
it felt.

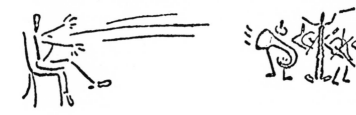

In my notes I find:

> Last Wednesday I went to the opera at Covent Garden, *Rigo-
> letto.* I was dead tired and could not listen at first (sitting on the
> miserably cramped gallery benches), but then I remembered to put
> myself out of myself, close to the music—and sometimes it closed
> over my head, and I came away rested in feeling light-limbed.

At this time also I began to surmise that there might be different
ways of looking as well as of listening.

One day I was idly watching some gulls as they soared high over-
head. I was not interested, for I recognized them as "just gulls," and
vaguely watched first one and then another. Then all at once something seemed to have opened. My idle boredom with the familiar became a deep-breathing peace and delight, and my whole attention was
gripped by the pattern and rhythm of their flight, their slow sailing
which had become a quiet dance.

In trying to observe what had happened I had the idea that my awareness had somehow widened, that I was feeling what I saw as well as
thinking what I saw. But I did not know how to make myself feel as
well as think, and it was not till three months later that it occurred to
me to apply to looking the trick I had discovered in listening. This
happened when I had been thinking of how much I longed to learn
the way to get outside my own skin in the daily affairs of life, and feel

how other people felt; but I did not know how to begin. I then remembered my trick with music and began to try "putting myself out"
into one of the chairs in the room (I was alone so thought a chair
would do to begin with). At once the chair seemed to take on a new
reality, I "felt" its proportions and could say at once whether I liked
its shape. This then, I thought, might be the secret of looking, and
could be applied to knowing what one liked. My ordinary way of
looking at things seemed to be from my head, as if it were a tower
in which I kept myself shut up, only looking out of the windows to
watch what was going on. Now I seemed to be discovering that I
could if I liked go down outside, go down and make myself part of
what was happening, and only so could I experience certain things
which could not be seen from the detached height of the tower. . . .
One might have thought that after the discovery of such a new possibility I would have been continually coming down to look at things.
Actually, however, with the press of a daily work which demanded
thought, not feeling, I seem to have forgotten the fact of this new
freedom, also I think I was afraid of it and loth to leave the security
of my tower too often.

In these ways I began to understand that my powers of perceiving
could be altered, not by directly trying to look, or trying to listen, but
by this special internal gesture.

I then began to guess that not only perceiving, but doing also
could be controlled in the same way. I find in my diary: "The secret
of playing ping-pong is to do it with a loose arm, relaxed." A similar
statement can be found, I should imagine, in almost any handbook
on any athletic sport, but to admit its truth because everyone says
so, and to prove it in one's own muscles are two very different matters. I could not believe when I first began to play that the placing
of such an exuberant ball with a tiny bat could be accomplished without effort. For I had been brought up to believe that to try was the
only way to overcome difficulty. ("Oh, Miss Smith, this sum is too
difficult."—"Well, dear, just try it.") And trying meant frowning,
tightening muscles, effort. So if ping-pong was difficult, one must
try. The result was a stiff body, full of effort, and a jerky swipe at the
ball, until someone said: "Play with a loose arm," and I tried, unbe-

lieving. At once the ball went crisply skimming the net to the far court, not once only, but again and again, as long as I could hold myself back from meddling. What surprised me was that my arm seemed to know what to do by itself, it was able to make the right judgments of strength and direction quite without my help. Here the internal gesture required seemed to be to stand aside.

My next discovery about movement was while darning stockings. I was usually clumsy-fingered, fumbling, and impatient to be finished, but slow because I did not find the task interesting enough to keep me from day-dreaming. But one day I read somewhere that one should learn to become aware of all one's bodily movements. I did not remember what else was in the book but this struck me as interesting and I decided to try. I found I could make some internal act while darning my stocking, an act of detachment by which I stood aside from my hand, did not interfere with it, but left it to put in the needle by itself. At first I found great difficulty in restraining my head from trying to do my hand's work for it, but whenever I succeeded the results startled me; for at once there came a sense of ease and I was able to work at maximum speed without any effort. I found it was not just a momentary effect, but it returned whenever I again managed to hold my interfering brain in leash. Henceforth sewing was something to look forward to, a time to enjoy the feel of movement in my hand instead of a tiresome task to be avoided as often as possible.

Although I felt that this discovery was very important to me, I did not seem able to make use of it in the way I had hoped. Although I knew what to do I hardly ever remembered to do it, like the heroes in fairy tales who used to exasperate me by forgetting to use the charm they had been expressly given. But when I did remember to do it, I was reminded of that little one-celled animal which can spread part of its own essence to flow around and envelop within itself whatever it wants for food. This spreading of some vital essence of myself was a new gesture, more diffuse than the placing of awareness beyond myself which I had tried with music; it was more like a spreading of invisible sentient feelers, as a sea anemone spreads wide its feathery fingers. Also I saw now that my usual attitude to the world was a contracted one, like the sea anemone when disturbed by a rough touch, like an amoeba shut within protective walls of its own making. I was yet to learn that state of confidence in which my feelers would always be spread whenever I wanted to perceive.

Whether it was something in the spring weather that next reminded me of this mental gesture I cannot tell. It was nearly a year later, an April heat wave in Richmond, Virginia. One evening I saw that the half-opened leaves of trees by the dusty roadside, sycamores perhaps, made a pattern against the pale sky, like tracery of old iron-work gates or the decorations on ancient manuscripts. I had an aching desire to possess the pattern, somehow to make it mine—perhaps drawing would capture it. But I was too busy to draw and did not know how to begin even had there been time. Then I remembered to spread the arms of my awareness towards the trees, letting myself flow round them and feed on the delicacy of their patterns till their intricacies became part of my being and I had no more need to capture them on paper. The quality of the delight that followed is forgotten but I find a lame attempt to make a note of it: "Gosh, I feel there's a bird singing high in the tree-tops inside me." This was the nearest memory I could find of my delight, yet it had a too familiar ring and I was uneasy lest it was not truly my own expression, vaguely suspicious that someone else had said it before me.

After this I discovered another gesture, simply to press my awareness out against the limits of my body till there was vitality in all my limbs and I felt smooth and rounded. This time I tried a more mundane description and called it simply: "That fat feeling." Later I find a note: "That fat feeling deepens one's breathing." This interested me, particularly as it was another example of a bodily effect following what I have called a purely mental gesture. Also I was not long in finding uses for the "fat feeling," for once, when returning exhausted from a day of difficult conversations, I remembered to try the pressing out gesture and after a little time found myself completely refreshed, able to respond without flagging to the demands of the evening.

A little later I found a first clue as to what was preventing me spreading my feelers whenever I needed. It was one evening when I was trying to feel out in this way while watching the players at the Chinese Theater in New York; since there were no intelligible words o engage my attention, I was finding it difficult to keep my thoughts from wandering back to the day's preoccupations which I wished to forget. I thought how much there was of entrancing interest going on before me if I only could reach it, and how petty and nagging were the anxieties of the day which continually distracted me. I had therefore tried deliberately to spread my feelers. No sooner had I made the gesture, however, than I became aware of a vague panic in the back of my mind prompting me to withdraw again into myself like a frightened spider who tucks in his legs, shamming dead.

All these experiences seemed to follow some special internal act, and my next discovery was that this act could be towards inactivity, a letting go. One day I was sitting in the sun alone on a ship's deck with the sea all about me and a gentle wind. I was restless and unhappy, worried because I seemed cut off from enjoying something which I had so often longed for in dark days of winter and cities. I knew that I ought to be happy now that I was having what I wanted, sun and leisure and sea. Suddenly I noticed that I was trying to think, and that I seemed to have taken it for granted that I would be happy if only I could think of something. Not that I had any special problem that needed solving at that particular moment, it was simply the feeling that one ought to have thoughts, ideas, something interesting to say about all one had seen and heard. But with the sun and the wind and the good food I was too turnip-headed to think, my body simply wanted to do nothing. Of course as soon as I became aware of this idea that one ought to have thoughts I realized how silly it was and I stopped trying to do anything, I simply "let go." At once the whiteness of sun-lit ropes against the sea leapt to my eyes and I was deeply content to sit and look.

I also found another example of the effects of passivity. I had always been vaguely interested in pictures, but worried because so often I could not say what I liked; I never seemed to know how to decide, except on a few occasions when a picture would seem to leap at me before I had begun to look at it, when I was still busy about something else. But one day I stopped in front of a Cézanne still-life—green apples, a white plate, and a cloth. Being tired, restless, and distracted by the stream of bored Sunday afternoon sight-seers drifting through the galleries, I simply sat and looked, too inert to remember whether I ought to like it or not. Slowly then I became aware that something was pulling me out of my vacant stare and the colors were coming alive, gripping my gaze till I was soaking myself in their vitality. Gradually a great delight filled me, dispelling all boredom and doubts about what I ought to like. . . . Yet it had all happened by just sitting still and waiting. If I had merely given a cursory glance, said: "Isn't that a nice Cézanne?" and drifted on with the crowd, always urged to the next thing, I would have missed it all. And also if I had not been too tired to think I would have said: "Here is a Cézanne, here is something one ought to like," and I would have stood there trying to like it but becoming less and less sure what I felt about it. I am reminded in writing this of another experience during fatigue, when I was too tired to think. One midsummer morning, after dancing so late that it did not seem worth while going to bed, I had walked out alone on Hampstead Heath in the bright sunlight and lain on my back amongst the bracken watching the slow march of clouds. At once I had slipped into such a happiness as I had never known till then, for this was in the days before I had begun to watch for delights and how they came.

In the next striking experience that occurred to me I perceived a new quality. We had just returned to England after two years away, and, landing at Plymouth, were meandering across Cornwall in a Sunday train which every few miles slowed up and creaked to stillness in the quiet of a village station. At first I was deep in my own thoughts, only glancing out of the window occasionally with a sense of the utter familiarity of the country and faintly disappointed that I was feeling no great emotion of home-coming, for it all seemed a little obvious and ordinary. As so often before, my emotions were failing to live up to a romantic moment. Then something happened. Perhaps I remembered to spread myself, to feel out into the landscape. I do not remember the precise gesture. But suddenly I began to notice white cottages and lanes and tidy green fields, and something, either the colors or the shapes, or the character of the land, aroused such a deep resonance in me that I sat, as if meeting a lover, aglow with an almost unbearable delight.

At this time, remembering the vague sense of panic I had observed in the Chinese Theatre, I gradually became aware of something which seemed to be preventing me making these gestures of feeling out. Certain fears began to take form, shadowy and elusive as yet, but intense as a missed heart-beat. Chiefly there seemed to be a fear of losing myself, of being overtaken by something. One day I was lying half asleep on the sands when I saw a gull alight quite close to me, with wings stretched above its back in that fashion peculiar to great winged birds when they settle on the ground. Without thinking, I felt myself into its movement with a panic ecstasy and then turned quickly round upon my fear, for the first time framing the question: "What is this ogre which tries to prevent me from feeling the reality of things?" But I was too slow, it had vanished before I could recognize its shape.

I did not find out anything more about control of mood for another year and did not progress very far in applying what I had already learnt. Then one day, when on a holiday in the Black Forest in Germany, I discovered a more vivid power of perceiving than ever before. The weather was wet and cold, my companion was nervously ill so that we were prevented from following our plan of a walking tour, and, being unable to speak German, I had little wherewith to distract either of us from depressed brooding. I was lonely and filled with a sense of inadequacy, I longed to do something, to act, as an alternative to the ceaseless chatter of worrying thoughts, I was angry with my companion for being ill and angry with myself for being so self-centered as to grumble. I felt cramped that we must stay in a town, and my only delight was when the cold night air, blowing down empty streets, brought the smell of encircling forest. I said: "If only the sun would come out then I could rest without thinking." And one morning I woke to find that the sun was out, and I went into the forest, wandering up a path to a cottage where they served drinks on little tables under apple trees, overlooking a wide valley. I sat down and remembered how I had sometimes found changes of mood follow when I tried to describe in words what I was looking at. So I said: "I see a white house with red geraniums and I hear a child crooning." And this most simple incantation seemed to open a door between me and the world. Afterwards, I tried to write down what had happened:

. . . Those flickering leaf-shadows playing over the heap of cut grass. It is fresh scythed. The shadows are blue or green, I don't know which, but I feel them in my bones. Down into the shadows of the gully, across it through glistening space, space that hangs suspended filling the gully, so that little sounds wander there, lose themselves and are drowned; beyond, there's a splash of sunlight leaping out against the darkness of forest, the gold in it flows richly in my eyes, flows through my brain in still pools of light. That pine, my eye is led up and down the straightness of its trunk, my muscles feel its roots spreading wide to hold it so upright against the hill. The air is full of sounds, sighs of wind in the trees, sighs which fade back into the overhanging silence. A bee passes, a golden ripple in the quiet air. A chicken at my feet fussily crunches a blade of grass. . . .

I sat motionless, draining sensation to its depths, wave after wave of delight flowing through every cell in my body. My attention flickered from one delight to the next like a butterfly, effortless, following its pleasure; sometimes it rested on a thought, a verbal comment, but these no longer made a chattering barrier between me and what I saw, they were woven into the texture of my seeing. I no longer strove to be doing something, I was deeply content with what was. At other times my different senses had often been in conflict, so that I could either look or listen but not both at once. Now hearing and sight and sense of space were all fused into one whole.

I do not know how long I sat there in absolute stillness, watching. Eventually, I stood up, stretched and returned along the little path down the hillside, freed from my angers and discontents and overflowing with peace. But there were many questions to be answered. Which of the things I had done had been important in the awakening of my senses? Or was it nothing I had done, but some spell from the forest and the sun? Could I repeat the experience and so have a permanent retreat for the cure of my angers and self-pity? If just looking could be so satisfying, why was I always striving to have things or to get things done? Certainly I had never suspected that the key to my private reality might lie in so apparently simple a skill as the ability to let the senses roam unfettered by purposes. I began to wonder whether eyes and ears might not have a wisdom of their own.

Discovery of the "Other"

Although relaxing and watching my thought seemed to have all these advantages, I still had not learnt how to do it continually. When considering this I ran over in my mind all the occasions on which I had managed to do it, and then I realized that it had always happened when I was alone, for when with other people I seemed to tighten up and make a protective ring between myself and the world.

I remembered how, when I had first discovered that it was possible to spread wide the invisible feelers of mind, to push myself out into the landscape or the movements of a flying bird, I had felt a panic fear. Gradually, however, as I had found that nothing terrible happened, but only great delight, I had apparently lost such feelings and in the world of nature I had begun to feel safe; but apprehension still lurked in my attempts at other kinds of perception. Sometimes in listening to music I would feel myself being carried away until neither I nor anything else existed but only sound, and in spite of the delight I would clutch wildly at some wandering thought to bring me back to the familiar world of bored selfconsciousness. Once when listening to a Brahms Quartet I suddenly wanted to gasp out: "Oh, stop, stop, he shouldn't pour out his heart like that, he'll get hurt. Those are the things one hides." And then again, in looking at architecture, I discovered fear. I had never been able to find buildings as interesting as pictures, though I felt sure they must be if only I knew how to look. I used to drift round churches with other people, famous places that everyone said ought to be seen and admired, but I always found my attention wandering, always found myself wishing they would get it over quickly and come out in the sun, for my gesture of deliberate wide perceiving never seemed to work here; or perhaps it was that I could never bring myself to try it. Then, one day after I had had some practice in learning how to relax, I was taken to see some sculpture (a form of art which I had always before found rather puzzling). But this time I discovered that by keeping very still and forgetting everything I had been told, I could slip down into a world of dark tensions, stresses and strains that forged themselves into an obscure but deep satisfaction. I felt it in my bones and in my feet and in my breathing. Soon after this I happened to be in Westminster Abbey, a place I had always found vaguely tiresome, hating the litter of monuments and chairs. I was waiting for some music to begin and looked about me, trying to break through the fog of associations and to escape from my preconceived ideas of boredom in churches. Suddenly I succeeded, suddenly I managed to strip my mind clean of all its ideas and to feel through the decoration to the bare structure of the building and the growing lines of the stone. But in an instant I found a catching in my breath, for there was here an echo of terror. Here were the same stresses and strains as in the life-size sculptures but on such a superhuman scale that they seemed to threaten my very existence. It occurred to me, after this, that perhaps in order to understand architecture one needs just as good a head for masses as a mountaineer does for heights. By keeping myself immersed in the safety of personal preoccupations and ideas about, rather than feelings of, the things I was looking at, I suppose I had managed to feel secure on all my past tours round churches; and when in the streets it was easy to be so filled with purposes as to look at buildings with a blind eye. But now that I had realized this terror of thrusting pillars and arches that loomed and brooded over me I found, as always before, the dread of annihilation merging into a deep delight.

After this I slowly came to understand more about the problem of relaxing when amongst other people. Just as I had once found that invisible feelers could be spread round things, so I now found that I could spread them round people as well. But here, more than ever, I needed to have some basis of security before I could do it, for so often I had a feeling that there was something to be guarded against, which time and again came between me and the people I wanted to know. It took me a long time to realize just what this fear was. Although I understood by now well enough that in the world of perception what I wanted was to lose myself in the thing perceived, yet it was too terrifying a thought to be fully admitted when it was a matter of another person. And since I could not recognize it for what it was, it remained at the level of blind thinking and kept me perpetually straining to guard against the very engulfment which I wanted.

In the end the knowledge of my deliverance came suddenly. Of course I had had many hints and part understandings of what I was trying to escape, but the full realization did not come until one day when I happened to have been looking back over all that I had discovered. I had just begun to ponder over the fact that all the things which I had found to be sources of happiness seemed to depend upon the capacity to relax all straining, to widen my attention beyond the circle of personal interest, and to look detachedly at my own experience. I had just realized that this relaxing and detachment must depend on a fundamental sense of security, and yet that I could apparently never feel safe enough to do it, because there was an urge in me which I had dimly perceived but had never yet been able to face. It was then that the idea occurred to me that until you have, once at least, faced everything you know—the whole universe—with utter giving in, and let all that is "not you" flow over and engulf you, there can be no lasting sense of security.

Only by being prepared to accept annihilation can one escape from that spiritual "abiding alone" which is in fact the truly death-like state.

I realized now that as long as you feel insecure you have no real capactiy to face other men and women in that skill of communication which more than any other skill requires freedom from tension. By communication I did not of course mean only intellectual conversation but the whole aesthetic of emotional relations; and just as I had, when first beginning to examine my experience, found most of my delights in natural things, I was now finding that I chiefly reckoned each day's catch of happiness in terms of my relationships with others. Of this, wordless understanding seemed to be particularly important. Before, I had been inclined to judge the value of meeting with my friends largely by what was said. Now it was the unvoiced relationship which seemed of more concern—though this was perhaps partly the result of having for eighteen months shared the life of someone who had not yet learned to talk.

Here also I began to discover a new world of direct communication, not through the symbols of words and actions and gestures, but what seemed to be an almost direct interchange of emotion which came with this spreading of invisible feelers. It was not only that my own perceptions were heightened, not only that by spreading myself out to-wards a person I could "feel the necessities of their being," it was that they also seemed to receive something, for in no other way could I explain the changes in their behavior. For instance, I was one day help-ing a very old lady from her chair to her bed. She was so old that she was past the age of reasonable understanding, and was like a child in most things, including the disinclination to go to bed. She was so heavy that I did not know how to deal with the situation at all and I felt embarrassed, tightly withdrawn, wishing it were over. Then I caught sight of her helplessly obstinate feet and something in them drew me out of myself into her problem, so that it became my problem too, and at once all her obstinacy vanished and she yielded easily to my help. Of course it was quite probable that she detected a subtle change in my clumsy efforts to help her; but there were other times when a per-son's mood would change when I had made no outward movement whatever, only spread internal feelers. So, when trying to persuade my baby to go to sleep I would often wait beside him, absolutely motionless, but my own heart filled with peace. Once I let impatience and annoyance dominate my mind he would become restless again. This may have been sheer accident, of course, but it happened so many times that in the end I found it very difficult to escape from the belief that my own state of mind did have some direct effect upon him.

Now also communication came to include the whole intricate texture of communal living. Just as I had once learnt to look at colors and shapes for their own sakes, I now began to see, as possible ends in themselves, actions like house-work which had before seemed to be nothing but tiresome routine because they were not "getting me anywhere." Now I was beginning to find that part of the day's hap-piness came while sweeping or preparing food (always before I had hated house-work because after so much time spent there was so little to show for it); I seemed to like it because it was a kind of communication, it expressed my feeling for the house I kept clean and the people who lived in it. Of course I did not always manage to achieve this disinterestedness, just as I could not always see things for their colors and shapes rather than for their use in furthering my private purposes. There were many times when I could not see my actions at all for their own sake, I must sweep from house-proudness because visitors might notice the dirt and think derogatory things, or I must cook a good dinner because that was the sort of person I liked to imagine myself. But I never found that the house-work I did for these reasons appeared in my day's list of happiness.

I now saw too how my earlier discoveries could be applied to this problem of communication. For quite early in my enterprise I had found that to want results for myself, to do things with the expectancy of happiness, was generally fatal, it made the stream of delight dry up at the source. (Of course the greater part of every day was filled with jobs which had to be done in order that something else might happen; but I am not here dealing with necessities imposed from without, only with how to manage one's actions and attitudes where there is any freedom of choice.) So now I began to find that it was no way out, as I had once hoped it would be, to want results for other people. In my exasperated self-absorption I had envied those who were always doing things for others. But as I grew more observant I began to see that this by itself was no sure way to peace, for as long as you expect results from what you do there are here even more sources of exasperation. Once you assume your right to interfere in other people's problems they become in some ways more of a worry than your own, for with your own you can at least do what you think best, but other people always show such a persistent tendency to do the wrong thing. And then it was so fatally easy to think that I knew what was good for other people; it made me feel pleasantly superior to think myself in a position to help, and also it made me feel good, feel that I was piling up some subtle advantage for myself, becoming a more admirable character. It took me a long time to learn to resist the feeling that I *ought* to interfere and try to help people for their own good. I knew others did it and so felt I ought to, although I was never too clear about what were best to be done. And then in addition to the feeling of ought, there was also the sheer pain of another person's misery, which of course grew greater, not less, as I learnt to be more perceiving. Gradually, however, I now came to understand that it was all right to do things for people as long as I did it for the sake of doing it, as a gesture of courtesy, the value being more in the act than in the result.

If I sacrificed myself for others, it must be, not because I thought they really needed what I had to give (for this might be an insult, as if I were implicitly putting myself above them), but simply as a way of expressing my feelings towards them. Here the giving was enough in itself, it was not a means to an end.

So it was that I gradually came to see what great delights were to be found in those moments of detached seeing when I could recognize another mind and yet want nothing from it. Such communication did not always require contact in time and place, for sometimes from a book or a picture I caught a human meaning to add to my stock of day's delights. I came to be not at all surprised at that tiresome attitude of superiority people seem unable to avoid when they can see meaning in a difficult work of art, although I had often been irritated by it myself, and made to feel very small by people who liked music and pictures I did not understand. For now I was myself realizing a cause for this seeming arrogance, since there were times when for me too a picture or a building or a poem would suddenly come alive. These were times when I would be left so exulting in communication, exulting in the human contact with the artist, that I really did feel in that moment of shared experience a quite new and bigger person; so it was difficult not to strut just a little, for blind thinking almost had a feeling that it had done a bit in the creating of the beautiful thing itself.

19

*I Resolve to Become a Jungle Doctor**

ALBERT SCHWEITZER

Albert Schweitzer (1875–1965) gave up his successful career in Europe and went to Africa to serve as a physician. The following, taken from his autobiography, is an interesting testimony for a theory of meta-motivation.

On October 13th, 1905, a Friday, I dropped into a letter box in the Avenue de la Grande Armée in Paris, letters to my parents and to some of my most intimate acquaintances, telling them that at the beginning of the winter term I should enter myself as a medical student, in order to go later on to Equatorial Africa as a doctor. In one of them I sent in the resignation of my post as principal of the Theological College of St. Thomas', because of the claim on my time that my intended course of study would make.

The plan which I meant now to put into execution had been in my mind for a long time, having been conceived so long ago as my student days. It struck me as incomprehensible that I should be allowed to lead such a happy life, while I saw so many people around me wrestling with care and suffering. Even at school I had felt stirred whenever I got a glimpse of the miserable home surroundings of some of my schoolfellows and compared them with the absolutely ideal conditions in which we children of the parsonage at Günsbach lived. While at the university and enjoying the happiness of being able to study and even to produce some results in science and art, I could not help thinking continually of others who were denied that happiness by their material

* From *Out of My Life and Thought* by Albert Schweitzer. Translated by C. T. Campion. Copyright 1933, 1939, © 1961 by Holt, Rinehart & Winston, Inc. Reprinted by permission of Holt, Rinehart & Winston, Inc.

circumstances or their health. Then one brilliant summer morning at Günsbach, during the Whitsuntide holidays—it was in 1896—there came to me, as I awoke, the thought that I must not accept this happiness as a matter of course, but must give something in return for it. Proceeding to think the matter out at once with calm deliberation, while the birds were singing outside, I settled with myself before I got up, that I would consider myself justified in living till I was thirty for science and art, in order to devote myself from that time forward to the direct service of humanity. Many a time already had I tried to settle what meaning lay hidden for me in the saying of Jesus! "Whosoever would save his life shall lose it, and whosoever shall lose his life for My sake and the Gospels shall save it." Now the answer was found. In addition to the outward, I now had inward happiness.

What would be the character of the activities thus planned for the future was not yet clear to me. I left it to circumstances to guide me. One thing only was certain, that it must be directly human service, however inconspicuous the sphere of it.

I naturally thought first of some activity in Europe. I formed a plan for taking charge of abandoned or neglected children and educating them, then making them pledge themselves to help later on in the same way children in similar positions. When in 1903, as warden of the theological hostel, I moved into my roomy and sunny official quarters on the second floor of the College of St. Thomas, I was in a position to begin the experiment. I offered my help now here, now there, but always unsuccessfully. The constitutions of the organizations which looked after destitute and abandoned children made no provision for the acceptance of such voluntary co-operation. For example, when the Strasbourg orphanage was burnt down, I offered to take in a few boys, for the time being, but the superintendent did not even allow me to finish what I had to say. Similar attempts which I made elsewhere were also failures.

For a time I thought I would some day devote myself to tramps and discharged prisoners. In some measure as a preparation for this I joined the Rev. Augustus Ernst at St. Thomas' in an undertaking which he had begun. He was at home from one to two P.M. and ready to speak to anyone who came to him asking for help or for a night's lodging. He did not, however, give the applicant a trifle in money, or let him wait till he could get information about his circumstances. He would offer to look him up in his lodging house that very afternoon and test the statements he had volunteered about his condition. Then, and then only, would he give him help, but as much, and for as long a time, as was necessary. What a number of bicycle rides we made with this object in the town and the suburbs, and very often with the result that the applicant was not known at the address he had given. In a great many cases, however, it provided an opportunity for giving, with knowledge of the circumstances, very seasonable help. I had some friends, too, who kindly placed a portion of their wealth at my disposal.

Already, as a student, I had been active in social service as a member of the student association known as the Diaconate of St. Thomas, which held its meetings in St. Thomas' College. Each of us had a certain number of poor families assigned to him, which he was to visit every week, taking to them the help allotted to them and making a report on their condition. The money we thus distributed we collected from members of the old Strasbourg families who supported this undertaking, begun by former generations and now carried on by us. Twice a year, if I remember right, each of us had to make his definite number of such begging appeals. To me, being shy and rather awkward in society, these visits were a torture. I believe that in these preparatory studies for the begging I have had to do in later years I sometimes showed myself extremely unskillful. However, I learned through them that begging with tact and restraint is better appreciated than any sort of stand-and-deliver approach, and also that the correct method of begging includes the good-tempered acceptance of a refusal.

In our youthful inexperience we no doubt often failed, in spite of the best intentions, to use all the money entrusted to us in the wisest way, but the intentions of the givers were nevertheless fully carried out in that it pledged young men to take an interest in the poor. For that reason I think with deep gratitude of those who met with so much understanding and liberality our efforts to be wisely helpful, and hope that many students may have the privilege of working, commissioned in this way by the charitable, as recruits in the struggle against poverty.

While I was concerned with tramps and discharged prisoners it had become clear to me that they could only be effectively helped by a number of individuals who would devote themseves to them. At the same time, however, I had realized that in many cases these could only accomplish their best work in collaboration with organizations. But what I wanted was an absolutely personal and independent activity. Although I was resolved to put my services at the disposal of some organization, if it should be really necessary, I nevertheless never gave up the hope of finding a sphere of activity to which I could devote myself as an individual and as wholly free. That this longing of mine found fulfillment I have aways regarded as a signal instance of the mercy which has again and again been vouchsafed to me.

One morning in the autumn of 1904 I found on my writing table in the college one of the green-covered magazines in which the Paris Missionary Society reported every month on its activities. A certain Miss Scherdlin used to put them there knowing that I was specially interested in this society on account of the impression made on me by the letters of one of its earliest missionaries, Casalis by name, when my father read them aloud at his missionary services during my childhood. That evening, in the very act of putting it aside that I might go on with my work, I mechanically opened this magazine, which had been laid on my table during my absence. As I did so, my eye caught the title of an article: *Les besoins de la Mission du Congo* ("The needs of the Congo Mission").[1]

It was by Alfred Boegner, the president of the Paris Missionary Society, an Alsatian, and contained a complaint that the mission had not enough workers to carry on its work in the Gaboon, the northern province of the Congo Colony. The writer expressed his hope that his appeal would bring some of those "on whom the Master's eyes already rested" to a decision to offer themselves for this urgent work. The conclusion ran: "Men and women who can reply simply to the Master's call, 'Lord, I am coming,' those are the people whom the Church needs."

[1] *Journal des Missions Evangéliques,* June, 1904, pp. 389–393.

Having finished the article, I quietly began my work. My search was over.

My thirtieth birthday, a few months later, I spent like the man in the parable who "desiring to build a tower, first counts the cost whether he have wherewith to complete it." The result was that I resolved to realized my plan of direct human service in Equatorial Africa.

With the exception of one trustworthy friend no one knew of my intention. When it became known through the letters I had sent from Paris, I had hard battles to fight with my relations and friends. Almost more than with my contemplated new start itself they reproached me with not having shown them so much confidence as to discuss it with them first. With this side issue they tormented me beyond measure during those difficult weeks. That theological friends should outdo the others in their protests struck me as all the more preposterous, because they had, no doubt, all preached a fine sermon—perhaps a very fine one —showing how St. Paul, as he has recorded in his letter to the Galatians, "conferred not with flesh and blood" beforehand about what he meant to do for Jesus.

My relatives and my friends all joined in expostulating with me on the folly of my enterprise. I was a man, they said, who was burying the talent entrusted to him and wanted to trade with false currency. Work among the savages I ought to leave to those who would not thereby be compelled to leave gifts and acquirements in science and art unused. Widor, who loved me as if I were his son, scolded me as being like a general who wanted to go into the firing line—there was no talk about trenches at that time—with a rifle. A lady who was filled with the modern spirit proved to me that I could do much more by lecturing on behalf of medical help for natives than I could by the action I contemplated. That saying from Goethe's *Faust* ("In the beginning was the Deed"), was now out of date, she said. Today propaganda was the mother of happenings.

In the many verbal duels which I had to fight, as a weary opponent, with people who passed for Christians, it moved me strangely to see them so far from perceiving that the effort to serve the love preached by Jesus may sweep a man into a new course of life, although they read in the New Testament that it can do so, and found it there quite in order. I had assumed as a matter of course that familiarity with the sayings of Jesus would produce much better appreciation of what to popular logic is nonrational, than my own case allowed me to assert. Several times, indeed, it was my experience that my appeal to the act of obedience which Jesus' command of love may under special circumstances call for, brought upon me an accusation of conceit, although I had, in fact, been obliged to do violence to my feelings to employ this argument at all. In general, how much I suffered through so many people assuming a right to tear open all the doors and shutters of my inner self!

As a rule, too, it was of no use allowing them, in spite of my repugnance, to have a glimpse of the thoughts which had given birth to my resolution. They thought there must be something behind it all, and guessed at disappointment at the slow growth of my reputation. For this there was no ground at all, seeing that I had received, even as a young man, such recognition as others usually get only after a whole life of toil and struggle. Unfortunate love experiences were also alleged as the reason for my decision.

I felt as a real kindness the action of persons who made no attempt to dig their fists into my heart, but regarded me as a precocious young man, not quite right in his head, and treated me correspondingly with affectionate mockery.

I felt it to be, in itself, quite natural that relations and friends should put before me anything that told against the reasonableness of my plan. As one who demands that idealists shall be sober in their views, I was conscious that every start upon an untrodden path is a venture which only in unusual circumstances looks sensible and likely to be successful. In my own case I held the venture to be justified, because I had considered it for a long time and from every point of view, and credited myself with the posession of health, sound nerves, energy, practical common sense, toughness, prudence, very few wants, and everything else that might be found necessary by anyone wandering along the path of the idea. I belived myself, further, to wear the protective armor of a temperament quite capable of enduring an eventual failure of my plan.

As a man of individual action, I have since that time been approached for my opinion and advice by many people who wanted to make a similar venture, but only in comparatively few cases have I taken on me the responsibility of giving them immediate encouragement. I often had to recognize that the need "to do something special" was born of a restless spirit. Such persons wanted to dedicate themselves to larger tasks because those that lay nearest did not satisfy them. Often, too, it was evident that they had been brought to their decisions by quite secondary considerations. Only a person who can find a value in every sort of activity and devote himself to each one with full consciousness of duty, has the inward right to take as his object some extraordinary activity instead of that which falls naturally to his lot. Only a person who feels his preference to be a matter of course, not something out of the ordinary, and who has no thought of heroism, but just recognizes a duty undertaken with sober enthusiasm, is capable of becoming a spiritual adventurer such as the world needs. There are no heroes of action: only heroes of renunciation and suffering. Of such there are plenty. But few of them are known, and even these not to the crowd, but to the few.

Carlyle's *Heroes and Hero Worship* is not a profound book.

Of those who feel any sort of impulse, and would prove actually fitted, to devote their lives to independent personal activity, the majority are compelled by circumstances to renounce such a course. As a rule this is because they have to provide for one or more dependents, or because they have to stick to their calling in order to earn their own living. Only one who thanks to his own ability or the devotion of friends is in worldly matters a free man, can venture nowadays to take the path of independent activity. This was not so much the case in earlier times because anyone who gave up remunerative work could still hope to get through life somehow or other, while anyone who thought of doing the same in the difficult economic conditions of today would run the risk of coming to grief not only materially but spiritually as well.

I am compelled, therefore, not only by what I have observed, but by experience also, to admit that worthy and capable persons have had to renounce a course of independent action which would have been of great value to the world, because circumstances rendered such a course impossible.

Those who are so favored as to be able to embark on a course of free personal activity must accept this good fortune in a spirit of humility. They must often think of those who, though willing and capable, were never in a position to do the same. And as a rule they must temper their own strong determination with humility. They are almost always destined to have to seek and wait till they find a road open for the activity they long for. Happy are those to whom the years of work are allotted in richer measure than those of seeking and waiting! Happy those who in the end are able to give themselves really and completely!

These favored persons must also be modest so as not to fly into a passion at the opposition they encounter; they have to meet it in the temper which says: "Ah, well, it had to be!" Anyone who proposes to do good must not expect people to roll stones out of his way, but must accept his lot calmly if they even roll a few more upon it. A strength which becomes clearer and stronger through its experience of such obstacles is the only strength that can conquer them. Resistance is only a waste of strength.

Of all the will for the ideal which exists in mankind only a small part can be manifested in action. All the rest is destined to realize itself in unseen effects, which represent, however, a value exceeding a thousandfold and more that of the activity which attracts the notice of the world. Its relation to the latter is like that of the deep sea to the waves which stir its surface. The hidden forces of goodness are embodied in those persons who carry on as a secondary pursuit the immediate personal service which they cannot make their lifework. The lot of the many is to have as a profession, for the earning of their living and the satisfaction of society's claim on them, a more or less soulless labor in which they can give out little or nothing of their human qualities, because in that labor they have to be little better than human machines. Yet no one finds himself in the position of having no possible opportunity of giving himself to others as a human being. The problem produced by the fact of labor being today so thoroughly organized, specialized, and mechanized depends only in part for its solution on society's not merely removing the conditions thus produced, but doing its very best to guard the rights of human personality. What is even more important is that sufferers shall not simply bow to their fate, but shall try with all their energy to assert their human personality amid their unfavorable conditions by spiritual activity. Anyone can rescue his human life, in spite of his professional life, who seizes every opportunity of being a man by means of personal action, however unpretending, for the good of fellow men who need the help of a fellow man. Such a man enlists in the service of the spiritual and good. No fate can prevent a man from giving to others this direct human service side by side with his lifework. If so much of such service remains unrealized, it is because the opportunities are missed.

That everyone shall exert himself in that state of life in which he is placed, to practice true humanity toward his fellow men, on that depends the future of mankind. Enormous values come to nothing every moment through the missing of opportunities, but the values which do get turned into will and deed mean wealth which must not be undervalued. Our humanity is by no means so materialistic as foolish talk is continually asserting it to be. Judging by what I have learned about men and women, I am convinced that there is far more in them of idealist will power than ever comes to the surface of the world. Just as the water of the streams we see is small in amount compared to that which flows underground, so the idealism which becomes visible is small in amount compared with what men and women bear locked in their hearts, unreleased or scarcely released. To unbind what is bound, to bring the underground waters to the surface: mankind is waiting and longing for such as can do that.

20

*Productivity and Existence** *

Martin Buber

"A remarkable and charming man, your friend," said the professor; "but what does he really *do?* I mean . . . in the intellectual sphere?"

"In the intellectual sphere . . ." I answered. "H'mm . . . in the intellectual sphere . . . he is simply there."

"How do you mean?"

"Well, his occupation is not, in fact, of a very intellectual nature, and one cannot really assert that he makes anything out of his leisure time."

"But his thoughts?"

"He contents himself for the most part with images. When they want to combine and condense into a thought, he gladly helps them and is pleased if something real comes out of them. At times, in conversation, as just now, he also shares some of these clear and fulfilled images."

"Then he does not write?"

"Oh, he once confessed to me, almost against his will, that occasionally, now and then, when his thoughts congeal, he enters a few lines in a secret book, in order, as he put it, to distinguish from then on what is actually won from what is merely *possible*."

"Then will he perhaps eventually publish something comprehensive?"

"I do not believe that he has that in mind. He has no need to enter into relation with men other than the friends life has brought him in contact with. He trusts life like a child. He said once that intensity is the only dimension that unceasingly rewards travelling."

* "Productivity and Existence" from *Pointing the Way* by Martin Buber. Translated by Maurice Friedman. Copyright © 1957 by Martin Buber.

"But why do not you, his friends, persuade him to collect his thoughts and share them with the general public? I have heard enough of them to say with certainty that they are worth while."

"We feel that his real unity lies in his personality and that only there can it exist. And we feel that we would injure his vitality, which means more to us than any book, if we induced him to store it between covers instead of pouring it into our souls, repaying living with living. He does not give away any part of himself; he only lends it, to receive it back transformed, so that all being then blooms in his presence as young faces, young gestures. That alone makes the blessing of his sharing; that calls up and enlivens ever new levels in him and renews him, indeed, time after time. In the sureness of our glance, in the buoyancy of our plan, in the sacrificial power of our undertaking, he reads the fiery writing of his transformed words. When one of our circle died, I marked that our friend went on reading him in an immortal sphere."

"But the world—you forget the world! You speak as if a book were an end in itself, whereas it is only a transmitter that bears our voices to unknown ears and hearts. I write what I am inspired to; I fling it out beyond all that is personal, into the whirl of the market, and the whirl carries it into reading-rooms and lamp-lit parlours where men whom I have never seen and never will see hear my words—and perhaps really understand. Is a book not a significant mixture of the personal and the impersonal? The book works and woos out there, and yet it is also myself. Thus separated from myself, I flow into all the world—into distant houses and perhaps into distant generations also—elevating, pleasing, angering who knows, but always in some way educating the human spirit. This thousandfold journey, this victory over all limits of individual existence, this bond with the unknown—for ever misused by vanity and yet never wholly desecrated—this is the predestined way of the thinker."

"I am familiar with this way, for at times I, too, publish a book. I know the joy of it and its terror—yes, its terror; for it is something dreadful to know that the ghost of my thought hovers in the dreams of confused and impure men, confused and impure as they. But I also know its joy—I remember how it moved me when an old beekeeper wrote me that he had read my book every day for a week on a bench in his garden in the bright hours of the afternoon, from the coming of the apple-blossoms till their withering. And, in order to be entirely fair, I shall also recall the great and creative gifts which I myself owe to books. Now I feel wholly what they are. And yet— more powerful and more holy than all writing is the presence of a man who is simply and immediately present. He need not cry through the loud-speaker of a book to that special circle of contemporary and future readers the writer calls the world. He has spoken without a medium, from mouth to ear, silently and overpoweringly, from his countenance to an eye and to an entranced soul; he has spoken in the magic fullness of togetherness to those men he calls his friends—and who are now full of the spirit because it has laid its hands upon them. Such a man will rarely produce a book. And if he does anything of this sort, the original source of the book is the life of a man who is present only in a direct way."

"Then all those who are not among the friends of such a man must remain excluded from his teaching?"

"Not at all, for those who are transformed through his teaching are forthwith, one and all, apostles—even though they do not repeat anything of it, nor even proclaim the name of the teacher; as transformed men, they are apostles through their existence, and whatever they do is done in apostleship, through the essence of his teaching which they express therein. In the life of his friends, in the life of all who meet him, and thus to distant generations, immediacy is transmitted."

"You wish, then, if I understand you rightly, to regard productivity as a lower rung of existence?"

"Rather, I regard productivity, in general, as existence only when it is rooted in the immediacy of lived life. If the man whom you call productive, the one who expresses himself in a creative work, is inferior in power, in holiness, to him who only expresses himself in his life, he is still, in so far as he is grounded in immediacy, superior to him in the noble faculty of creating form. But if you consider an individual who has shrunk to mere form the streaming, living potency, there stands before us a masquerading hobgoblin who cannot form himself but can only disguise himself in forms. No, what I said of the immediate man was not said against the productive one: I was attacking the dominant delusion of our time, that creativity is the criterion of human worth. But illegitimate creativity, creation without immediacy, is no criterion, for it is no reality. It is an illusion—and I believe in the absolute eye before which it cannot stand for a moment. Only that can be a criterion from which genuine creativity arises: that is, the immediate."

"Certainly, man can be judged only by what he is. But does not his creating, along with his acting, belong to his being?"

"Yes, when it functions as a valid organ of the living body; no, when it indicates a mere excrescence. Artifice has so much got the upper hand that the fictitious dares to usurp the place of the real. The overvaluation of productivity that is afflicting our age has so thrived and its par-technical glance has set up a senseless exclusiveness of its own that even genuinely creative men allow their organic skills to degenerate into an autonomous growth to satisfy the demand of the day. What the born deceivers never had, they give up: the ground where the roots of a genuinely lived life alone can grow. They mean, they strive for, and at last they contain nothing but creativity. Instead of bringing forth a natural creation, in a gradual selective progression from experiences to thoughts, from thoughts to words, from words to writing, and from writing to public communication, they wear themselves out turning all experience to account as public communication; they renounce true necessity and give themselves over to the arbitrary. They poison experience, for already while it is taking place they are dominated by the will to produce. Thus they prostitute their lives and are cheated of the reward for their ignominy; for how can they expect to create anything save the artificial and the transitory? They forfeit both life and art, and all that they gain is the applause of their production-mad contemporaries."

"But it appears to me that the will to create is a legitimate part of the experience of every productive man. Thus the painter is the man who paints with all his senses. His seeing is already a painting, for what he sees is not merely what his physical sight receives: it is something, two-dimensionally intensified, that vision produces. And this producing does not come later, but is present in his seeing. Even his hearing, his smelling, are already painting, for they enrich for him the graphic character of the thing; they give him not only sensations but also stimulations. In the same way the poet creates poetry with all his senses; in each of his experiences the form in which it will be phrased is immediately announced. His perceiving is already a transformation of the thing perceived into the stuff of poetry, and in its becoming each impression presents itself to him as an expression of rhythmic validity."

"That is indeed so. But this dynamic element that you find in the experience of the creative is no will to create but an ability to create. This potentiality of form also accompanies every experience that befalls the non-artistic man and is given an issue as often as he lifts an image out of the stream of perception and inserts it into his memory as something single, definite, and meaningful in itself. For the creative man this potentiality of form is a specific one, directed into the language of his particular art. If an intention is expressed in this direction, it is that of his genius, not that of a self-conscious resolution. The dynamic element of his experience does not affect its wholeness and purity. It is otherwise when in perceiving he already cherishes the deliberate intention of utilizing what he perceives. Then he disturbs the experience, stunts its growth, and taints the process of its becoming. Only the unarbitrary can grow properly and bear mature and healthy fruit. That man is legitimately creative who experiences so strongly and formatively that his experiences unite into an image that demands to be set forth, and who then works at his task with full consciousness of his art. But he who interferes with the spontaneity of perceiving, who does not allow the inner selection and formation to prevail, but instead inserts an aim from the beginning, has forfeited the meaning of this perception, the meaning that lies above all aims. And he who meets men with a double glance, an open one that invites his fellows to sincerity and the concealed one of the observer stemming from a conscious aim; he who in friendship and in love is cleft into two men, one who surrenders himself to his feelings and another who is already standing by to exploit them—this man cannot be delivered by any creative talent from the blight that he has brought upon himself and his work, for he has poisoned the springs of his life."

"You wish, then, to reintroduce into æsthetics the ethical principle that we have finally succeeded in banishing from it?"

"What was banished from æsthetics was an ideology that had degenerated into rhetoric and had thereby become false. It certainly signified a conquest of sure ground when the perspective was established that evaluated a work of art—approving or rejecting it—not by its relation to the aspirations of the artist but by its intrinsic qualities. Now for the first time we can, without promoting misunderstanding, strive towards the deeper insight: that this approval affords entrance into the outer circle only, but in the inner circle those works alone count that have given form to the meaning of being. Similarly, a gain in clarity and solidity was achieved when it was recognized that the significance of an artist does not depend upon his morals: now for the first time we can attain the deeper clarity that in inner development mastery and power accrue only to that artist who is worthy of his art."